Salty Old Editor

Salty Old Editor

An Adventure in Ink

A Memoir by
Charlotte Tillar Schexnayder

The Butler Center for Arkansas Studies
Central Arkansas Library System
BUTLER
CENTER   100 Rock Street
BOOKS   Little Rock, Arkansas 72201

First Printing, May 2012

Paperback: ISBN (13) 978-1-935106-36-4
ISBN (10) 1-935106-36-8

Copyeditor: Ali Welky
Book and cover design: H. K. Stewart
Cover photo: Gene Weser

Library of Congress Cataloging-in-Publication Data

Schexnayder, Charlotte Tillar, 1923-
 Salty Old Editor : "An Adventure in Ink" : A Memoir / by Charlotte Tillar
Schexnayder.
    pages cm
 Includes index.
 ISBN 978-1-935106-36-4 (pbk. : alk. paper)
 1. Schexnayder, Charlotte Tillar, 1923- 2. Women Legislators--Arkansas--
Biography. 3. Legislators--Arkansas--Biography. 4. Women newspaper editors--
Arkansas--Biography. 5. Newspaper editors--Arkansas--Biography. 6. Arkansas.
General Assembly. House of Representatives--Biography. 7. Arkansas--Politics and
government--1951- 8. Dumas (Ark.)--Biography. I. Title.

 F415.3.S34A3 2012
 976.7'054092--dc23
 [B]

                              2012007494

Printed in the United States of America
This book is printed on archival-quality paper that meets requirements of the
American National Standard for Information Sciences, Permanence of Paper,
Printed Library Materials, ANSI Z39.48-1984.

The publishing division of the Butler Center for Arkansas Studies
was made possible by the generosity of Dora Johnson Ragsdale and
John G. Ragsdale Jr.

To Melvin,
ever the great love
of my life

Melvin John Schexnayder Sr.
(January 20, 1920–September 12, 2007)

Table of Contents

Introduction

"**A**re you sure you want this place?" Gram (my mother) asked with obvious anxiety. My husband Melvin and I cleared a place on an inky oak desk where our five-month-old John perched. John was more interested in the colorful ball we had brought to entertain him.

We came from our home in Tillar, Arkansas, thirteen miles south on Highway 65, to Dumas, Arkansas, a town of 2,512 with the Missouri Pacific railroad tracks splitting its four-block business district. Our inspection was focused in its newspaper office where the *Dumas Clarion* was published. Located on State Highway 54 intersecting with Main Street, the office was just a block off the center of town.

As Melvin and I wondered whether we "really did want this place," we looked around, rather anxiously.

A lattice-work partition separated the front office from the "backshop," or composing room. The brick building, with plaster over lathe on the inside walls, had notable patches of plaster missing. Along the walls were wooden shelves holding an assortment of office supplies. Our inspection found these supplies to be bound double- and single-entry ledgers and cash books, loose-leaf ledger forms we knew by number, boxed envelopes and letterhead stationery, tape, paper clips, rulers, pens, paper punches, pencils, and more.

One large box held a supply of legal forms with bills of sale, quit-claim deeds, and mortgages with appropriate blanks—all selling for 10 to 25 cents to do-it-yourself lawyers. The counter, with brown wrapping paper underneath, was topped with an assortment of odds and ends—a hand paper cutter, a vase to be returned to someone who had left posies, two stained coffee cups, and a stack of the principal publication, a weekly titled the *Dumas Clarion*, waiting to be sold for five cents each.

The building, about 20 x 60 feet, was owned by E. R. Willeford. There was a concrete floor, and the building did not leak, especially in the main part, but the metal storeroom in the rear did, profusely. The rent was $40 a month, which my husband observed really was "too much, given the condition of the building."

Climate control, virtually unheard of in small newspaper plants, was relegated to window and oscillating fans for cooling and an overhead butane gas heater for heating. It was drafty in winter, we found, as we stood looking it over in late January 1954. We suspected the building could be much more uncomfortable in summer because of extra heat from the single linotype, metal-casting typesetter.

Weekly newspaper offices were notoriously messy, and this was no exception. Stacks of exchange newspapers were piled in a corner, while metal single spindles held important copy waiting to be sent to a typesetter.

What could we bring to this office? We thought, "Not much in equipment." Gram had her well-used teacher's desk which she had bought upon her retirement from the classroom when arthritis made the school's many steps unbearable. After 23 years of teaching English and serving as librarian, she could no longer climb the two steep flights at Tillar High School. "I am not going to retire," she told us, affording us added encouragement by volunteering to serve as our society editor and bookkeeper.

On the other side of the front office was a place for a worktable. "Why not use our old green kitchen table?" I thought. Melvin and Gram agreed, and she urged us to be money-wise, saying "little holes sink big ships."

We also would inherit, if we went through with the sale, a mahogany side chair with a green plastic seat, a typing stand, a small folding table, and some cane-back chairs.

I would bring my faithful "think tank"—an L. C. Smith upright typewriter with ball-bearings. I had bought it 10 years previously from Jim Carter, a soldier friend who wanted $55 for it after he knew he was headed overseas in World War II. Gram had mastered the hunt-and-peck system, delivered with much speed on her old Royal portable. Melvin eyed an upright adding machine of considerable heft and pronounced it usable.

The shop represented an even greater challenge. Its shining glory was a Model 31 linotype, but the rest of the equipment went sharply downhill. Braced wooden supports held the heavy makeup stones upon which the metal type was placed in "chases," or iron rectangular frames. Turning one over, we later discovered their age and first owner: "M. A. Bridwell 1912."

Above each of the makeup stones were elevated, slanted shelves to hold spacing material, "leads, slugs, and thins," for making up the newspaper pages and printing jobs. Assorted wooden cabinets held trays of metal type for hand-setting headlines and advertisements. Even older cabinets preserved wood type up to three and four inches in height—to be used for spectacular news or to get attention in advertisements.

The guillotine paper cutter cultivated a deep sense of fear that some employee, even ourselves, might unwittingly use it improperly and slice off a portion of a hand.

The 1890 hand-fed Babcock press in the corner was held together by baling wire, and a cotton string was attached to the electrical starter switch. A proper starting mechanism and replacement of the baling wire would become a first priority, we mused.

Standing in the corner was a hand-fed folding machine, used to fold the flat-printed sheets into sections after they were taken off the press fly. The folder did not appear dilapidated, but we knew it was old enough to be undependable.

The linotype, less aged than other equipment, cast metal lines or slugs melted from an attached pot fired by butane gas. The casting box, located just inside the storeroom, was used for recycling type no longer needed by smelting into "pigs," or two-foot bars of metal, a mixture of lead, zinc, and other alloys. The pigs were hung on a chain over the linotype pot and fed into the molten pot to provide recasting for new lines of type.

Behind the building's back wall was an entrance into the storeroom, and we hadn't the slightest idea of what was there. There seemed no order. Printing papers and sheet newsprint were stored in a dry area. So much was piled there that we never knew what we would find. Beneath all the clutter, we discovered two upright typewriters, which, we surmised, could be repaired and used. A hand-operated binding machine, which would install plastic spiral bindings, offered possibilities. We called this storeroom "the big bargain bonanza," although we really never thought we could make any extra money from it.

The building was strategically located on the block with the City Hall. Business neighbors were Dumas Electric Company, an appliance business operated by Mrs. Ellen Weeks; Moore's Drug Store, which Ike and Pearl Moore owned; Dumas Furniture Co., which genial Ralph Moore would be operating after his planned sale of the newspaper to us; Dumas Butane Co., an LP gas operation owned by Will Evans and John Harvey Leek; and a shoe repair shop operated by A. A. Fansler. These adjoined the two-story City Hall on black-top Waterman Street, also a part of State Highway 54.

The newspaper and equipment price totaled $19,500. We had $4,000 in savings, and possible stockholders were willing to finance the remainder of the purchase. We were being recruited. At a meeting of Boy Scout committeemen in the Chicot-Desha District, Jack S. Dante of Dumas asked, "Melvin, would you and Charlotte be interested in buying the *Dumas Clarion?*" And he added a real carrot, "We would help raise the money for you to buy it."

Melvin said he would confer with me. We had previously failed on negotiations for newspapers in Crossett, Arkansas, and Bastrop,

Louisiana, and we wanted to run our own weekly. The *McGehee Times*, where the two of us had been editor and advertising manager, wasn't for sale, and our choice was to remain in southeast Arkansas.

The opportunity seemed too good to pass. We could purchase half of the corporation's stock, issued in $500 certificates, and our great friend, Clarence Isch of McGehee, would buy another share. "You can pay me back whenever you can," he said, "and you just vote my share of stock as you wish." Thus, we would have major control of stock.

Jack Dante, always one of Dumas's and our greatest boosters, said he would round up the investors. He had commitments from Lee Culpepper, R. A. Adcock, Eddie Bowles, Mayor Travis Witherington, Bernard Tanenbaum, Merle F. Peterson, Sterling T. Frank, Dr. J. H. Hellums, and Dr. Guy U. Robinson.

Did we "really want this place"? We thought of the people who wanted us. Perhaps the desire for our "very own newspaper" obscured our vision of the surroundings, and we foresaw a great adventure. Melvin and I looked at one another, instead of at the plant, and affirmed, "We really do want this place."

Did I envision a secondary political career? No. Our focus was to survive and succeed at newspaper publishing. Political and public issues always were important to us, but journalism and politics were an unholy and unlikely mix in those years. Who would vote for an editor who expressed opinions in black ink, at times contrary to the public mood, scolding politicians, advocating, and chiding?

That didn't deter my strong desire for public service, imbued in me by my mother. My appointment as the first woman on the Arkansas Board of Pardons and Parole in the 1970s led me to believe I might bring energy, perseverance, and my varied experience to the political scene.

I found naysayers; I often had as a woman who broke barriers. But I reasoned that a citizen legislature, as in Arkansas, would include members with potential conflicts of interest because of primary occupations. Since legislators were part-time serving in biennial sessions, one had to depend on personal wealth or employment.

Thirty years after buying the *Clarion*, I was elected unopposed to the House of Representatives. As a newspaper editor, I was treated with obvious wariness, a bit of suspicion, and even a tinge of distrust by a few. With quiet dignity and hard work, I tried to overcome those attitudes. There was one huge advantage, however. No one dared to offer a shady deal; I owned a newspaper.

Senior House members treated me politely but with reserve. Later, veteran Rep. Bill Foster of Keo told me, "I was determined to dislike you. You were a newspaper editor. But it took me only a week to change my mind." He became a trusted advisor.

Rep. Geno Mazzanti of Lake Village approached me during the first week and counseled, "No one expects much of a freshman representative. Just sit and listen and you will be fine." My reply: "You obviously don't know me very well. I am not a sideline sitter, and I always have plans."

Once asked how I had intermingled roles over a lifetime, I replied, "I have always believed in the people of the Delta, and they have believed in me." I have drawn strength from them and my forbearers, beginning with my childhood in Tillar. Tiny towns can launch fulfilling and diverse careers such as mine. The seed for the dream was planted in my childhood.

1.
Delta Childhood

Deaths intruded upon my young life, but I learned to cope and find happiness amid family and friends. Born at 4:00 p.m. on December 25, 1923, at home in Tillar, Arkansas, I halted my family's Christmas plans, but my mother gallantly maintained that I was "her greatest blessing." The Jim Ballard family, however, never quite forgave my arrival on that holiday, as their mother, "Miss Sadie," left them to help my mother throughout the day.

My father was Jewell Stephen Tillar, son of Dr. Stephen Olin Tillar and Fannie Harrell Tillar, pioneer residents of southeast Arkansas, who came from Selma in Drew County to help found the town of Tillar after the St. Louis, Iron Mountain and Southern Railroad laid its track from Little Rock southward in 1870.

Dr. Stephen Olin Tillar fought as a gunnery sergeant with General Stonewall Jackson's forces, as often retold by my uncle Bob Tillar. Stephen Tillar was later captured and imprisoned with Confederate forces near Chicago. When he was released, he walked home barefooted and was so emaciated that his family did not recognize him. He studied medicine and became a practicing physician. My father was born on December 19, 1886, and was the youngest of his family, which also included John (born 1870, died while a ministerial student at Princeton); Hattie (1874–1937); Robert (Bob) Harrell (1880–1963), and Ina (1886–1892).

Daddy was young when his mother died, and his sister Hattie helped to rear him. He attended the one-room school in Tillar, later went to Hindman School (a forerunner to the University of Arkansas at Monticello), and finally studied at the Eastman College of Business in Poughkeepsie, New York. As a young man, he was playing along the rail tracks at a mill when a boxcar broke loose and rolled over his foot. He lay in agony until the next day when the northbound train took him to Little Rock for medical treatment to save his foot. He always walked with a slight limp.

My mother and the greatest influence of my early life was Bertha Terry, daughter of Dennie Pink Terry and Sarah Bancroft Terry. Dennie Terry, whose parents were Sam and Flavelia Terry, was born near Varner in Lincoln County. He was a twin, with his brother being named Denson Broad. The middle names described their looks as babies.

The Civil War was most difficult for Sam Terry's family, as two of the brothers went to war in the Confederate forces and never returned. Sam Terry farmed in an area now occupied by the Department of Correction. When the twins were very small, their mother Flavelia died. Sam Terry's widowed sister, Annie Mitchell (whose husband General Mitchell had owned lands around Stuttgart), had built a two-story log house on Oakwood Bayou, four miles east of Dumas in Desha County, in the late 1840s. She begged her widowed brother and his family to live with her there, and they moved there when my grandfather was a toddler.

My grandfather had an older brother, Bob, and the single bit of family lore surrounding Bob tells of his driving a team of mules and a wagon the four miles from Dumas to Oakwood Bayou. When a wild-cat jumped out of some trees onto the backs of the team, Bob beat the screaming cat with a whip all the way to his log home before the cat gave up and jumped off.

Sam Terry married a widow from Arkansas County. Each pre-ferred to live on his/her side of the Arkansas River, which separated Arkansas and Desha counties, and visited back and forth. She had a son, Wince Walton, when she married Sam Terry, and they later had a son, also named Sam, who became a successful merchant and farmer at St. Charles in Arkansas County.

The Terry house was built of hand-hewn 18-inch cypress logs cut from the Oakwood Bayou. Two stories with a "dog trot" down the middle, the house was often the site of social gatherings. Travelers also were welcome. One Saturday, a traveler named Mr. Frederick, a German cabinetmaker, stopped to ask for a drink of cool water from the cistern. He was invited to spend the night. As he did not believe in traveling on Sunday, he spent much of the next day in reading his Bible. By Monday, the Terry family liked him so much they asked him to live with them, and he resided there until his death 40 years later. Grandpa Frederick, as he was known, built beautiful furniture from the walnut trees abounding around the log house.

Born in 1868, Dennie Terry never intended "walking behind a plow" the rest of his life and after completing the fourth grade, he went to Red Fork where he worked in a store and lived in its attic. Reading extensively, he educated himself. He obtained a job as a bookkeeper at Dumas and later worked in the same capacity for R. A. Pickens & Son Company at Walnut Lake (now Pickens).

My maternal great-grandmother, Sarah Bancroft, was born in 1870 at DeValls Bluff, where her parents moved from Virginia. Her father, Edwin Bancroft, a native of Massachusetts, became a major in the Union army and later invaded the plantation of a young southern widow, Charlotte Carl Lee May. As he rode away with provisions for his troops, she stamped her foot at him but smiled. He couldn't forget the smile, so he returned to Virginia after the war, courted her, and married her.

They moved to Arkansas, where he became publisher of the *White River Journal* in the late 1860s. Thus, I always felt, I had ink in the bloodlines. However, I did not follow his example of staunch Republicanism.

The Bancroft daughters, Sarah (Sadie) and Blanche, were very young when their parents died. Sadie and Blanche were educated in the Female Academy of Little Rock operated by the Sisters of Mercy (now St. Mary's). Their brother Edwin lived with relatives. Sadie Bancroft came to Walnut Lake to teach in the one-room school in 1889 and married Dennie Terry on June 18, 1891. When their oldest daughter was born on May 15, 1892, he chose the name Bertha because he had been reading a novel by Bertha Clay and liked the name; my mother vehemently disliked it. Her siblings were Ruby St. Clair (1895–1900), Burton Carl Lee (1900–1967), Mildred Virginia (1902–1904), and Dennie Bancroft (1908–1969). The Terrys lived at Walnut Lake until 1900, when Dennie built a two-story frame store at Tillar and the family moved there.

Some of my mother's earliest memories were of sleeping in a trundle bed at the Oakwood Bayou log house and of being one of eight students at a one-room cotton storage building turned into a school at Walnut Lake. The Terrys provided room and board for the teacher, including Miss Sallie Proctor, who gave gold medals inscribed "proficiency" and "efficiency" to my mother upon her completion of the first and second grades. Remember, said Mother, that her teacher was their boarder.

Mother often related: "When we moved to Tillar, we lived in a frame house about a block or so from Papa's store. Mama never knew how many Papa would bring home to lunch when he closed the store at noon. She would send one of us children out to watch and tell her how many men were coming home with him to eat." Apparently, there were expandable menus of food available from their mercantile store and home garden. The two-story store sold everything from groceries to overalls, plows to harnesses, bolt sewing material to millinery.

Mother often related tales of the big one-room school at Tillar, where the entire student body took off on one snowy day to go rabbit hunting and the older boys once harassed the teacher by putting a pig in the pot-bellied stove to greet her when she came to make a wood fire one morning.

Since there was no high school at Tillar, Mother, at 13, was sent to Maddox Seminary for Girls, a preparatory school in Little Rock. Her father told the headmaster, "Let Bertha have what she needs and I will pay for it." Mother's "needs" that year included going to see Sarah Bernhardt perform in *Camille*, then considered a racy play.

Not wealthy but very comfortable, Mother's parents provided her with custom clothing sewn in Louisville, Kentucky, and her mother taught her to be a fine seamstress on her own. After a year in Maddox Seminary, Mother was ready for four years at Galloway College in Searcy, providing an education in the classics and music in which Mother excelled. Both a pianist and vocalist, Mother was also a talented violinist. One summer, she studied violin at the Cincinnati Conservatory of Music. In her senior year at Galloway, she developed "slow fever," necessitating her coming home to Tillar without getting her degree. Love intervened, and she and my father eloped on March 12, 1912. It was, as my mother always said, "a match made in heaven."

My brother, Jewlian Terry Wolfe Tillar, was born on September 27, 1915, and we called him "Sonny." He later changed the spelling of his first name to Julian. My father, Jewell Tillar, then worked at Harrell and Sons Mercantile Store, owned by his first cousins—Willie, Jeff, and Virgil Harrell—in Tillar. He continued there until 1928 when he was named manager of People's Furniture Company in McGehee.

One of my earliest memories is escaping the waters of the 1927 flood of the Mississippi and Arkansas Rivers which devastated southeast Arkansas. In wee hours of a morning, a cousin, Jenilee Harrell, came to our house, knocking on the front bedroom window and calling, "Cousin Jewell, get up and get the family out before the Bayou Bartholomew Bridge washes out!"

Fleeing with minimal clothing in our Model T Ford, we traveled the two miles to the bayou, crossing just before the bridge washed away. Sandbags marked the sides of the road then covered with water. Our Ford stalled, and the only way out was to hire a team of mules to pull the car through the waters. Mother put my 12-year-old brother, Sonny, out to run down the sandbags to get a team to help. For years, she said she had nightmares about "that foolish move because Sonny might have drowned."

Daddy finally drove our car and family to the hills, reaching Monticello, where a kind family named Gill hosted Mother, Julian, and me for two weeks until the floodwaters subsided. Every afternoon, Mrs. Gill baked teacakes for me, a lasting memory. Daddy went by boat to McGehee, where he lived on the second floor of People's Furniture Store, where he had scaffolded the stock prior to arrival of the floodwaters covering the first floor. Water rose around our house in Tillar but did not flood it.

Another early memory involved Papa, my Grandfather Terry. Since my grandparents Tillar died long before I was born and my Grandmother Terry died of a burst appendix in 1921, Papa was the only grandparent I knew. I dearly loved him. He was tall, authoritarian, and very devoted to me. He often "took his meals" with my family, and Mother helped to rear her brother Bancroft after their mother died.

Papa and Bancroft became important parts of my young life. In addition to his store, Papa had owned a 1,000-acre plantation near Tillar. I don't remember the store, as it burned in 1920, but I have never forgotten accompanying Papa to the farm. He had a Ford roadster, and in back of the driver's seat was a ledge where I rode. He called it my "crow's nest," and I related all I saw as he drove to and from the farm. From ages three to five, I was learning how to report. The "dog trot" house on the farm housed the Negro overseer and his family. When Papa and I would go there at noon, we joined them for lunch, and I delighted in helping to ring the outside bell, on a frame stand, to bring the "hands"—black tenant farmers—from the fields for lunch. I never tired of the "crow's nest," and every day that Papa would take me, I was ready to accompany him. We continued this practice, even after we moved to McGehee in 1928. Daddy rented a two-story house on Second Street there, and Papa moved in with us.

Relocating from the hamlet of Tillar to "a city" of several thousand like McGehee was quite a change. Mother had been invited to join the prestigious Garden Club and Bridge Club, and entertaining for them was an experience requiring Mother's best linens, china, crystal, and silver for whatever delicious refreshments she could prepare. She was a grand cook and enjoyed her skills. In Tillar, water was just $1 a month, but in McGehee, it was metered. We had a part-time maid, Lu, whom Mother had cautioned to be thrifty with water usage. On a bridge afternoon, when Lu was filling the water glasses, she came back into the kitchen and was shaking visibly. "Oh, lawsy, Miss Bertha," she said. "I done wasted a whole glass of water down that lady's back!"

Change was coming for the whole family. Widowed since 1921, Papa planned to re-marry, as he had been seeing Margaret, a McGehee business teacher originally from Paducah, Kentucky. They rented a house on Fourth Street. About 1929, Daddy rented a smaller white frame house on Third Street, and I had new playmates in McGehee. These included Mary Millerick and Katie Stone; two of us could play well together, but adding a third eventually ended with a squabble. I attended the kindergarten that warm and motherly Mrs. Coulter held in her home.

My father was kind and loving. I have snippets of memories about him, including the time he gave me a nickel for helping my mother cap strawberries. In the 1920s, a nickel then was "big money" to me. When he came home from work, I would raise my arms and run for him to pick me up and hug me.

I started school in McGehee at age five, since I would not be six until Christmas 1929. Daddy took me to school in the family's Model A Ford and let me ride on the riding board—only for several feet as he idled beside the sidewalk to the school. He then would give me a penny or two for candy available near the school. The white peppermint sticks I chose looked like blackboard chalk and were very sweet.

Our family, dyed-in-the wool Democrats, always stayed up all night to get election returns, which may have accounted for my interest in government. Papa Terry bought his first radio to hear presidential candidate Al Smith in 1928. Mother was a "stringer" for the *Arkansas Democrat* in my early years and reveled in writing. Her scoop was to cover a bank robbery in our area, duly reported even though a distant Tillar cousin was involved.

Miss Edna McQuistion was my first-grade teacher. I vividly recall that two little boys got into a fight over me, and I was so embarrassed I put my head on my desk and cried. My second-grade teacher was Miss Marybel McQuistion. These sister teachers were so dearly loved that I would have never disappointed them.

Despite the pinch of the Great Depression, we were happy until January 1931, when my father developed a severe case of pneumonia. There was no hospital in McGehee, and no wonder drugs existed. Third Street in front of our house was cordoned with a rope and red flag to stop traffic and maintain a quiet place for my father. Kind neighbors, Mr. and Mrs. R. B. Stone, took me to their house to stay during the ordeal, but I dreaded that red flag in the street. My father died on January 16, 1931, and I will always remember seeing him in the coffin placed in our home. I was so grief-stricken that I could not get out of our car at the cemetery. Dwelling on these memories can still bring tears.

That was not the end of our 1931 troubles. In a period of just three months, Papa Terry died of kidney disease, and because of five-cent-a-pound cotton, we lost his plantation at Tillar. During Papa Terry's final illness, I became dreadfully ill with mastoids, an ear infection. Mother shuttled between our house and Papa's while Mrs. Clarence (Iva) Isch sat by me. I was forced to lie still with my head packed in ice for several days—an effort to reduce the infection since no drugs were available. Mrs. Isch entertained me with string tricks, a kindness always remembered.

My mother was plunged into the financial chaos of the Depression. She had been ill with a heart condition for several years and often had to rest. However, the crises in our family made her stronger. She applied for a teaching position at the Tillar Public Schools and obtained a job as fifth- and sixth-grade teacher to start in the fall. Her monthly salary was $50 in warrants, paid only if the school district had enough funds.

Mother wondered whom she could get to help with the family. In the middle of the night, she awoke from a dream with the message, "Contact Mrs. Harper." That seemed totally unlikely, as Mrs. Harper, an elderly woman, operated a successful boarding house just two blocks up the McGehee street from us.

But Mother put on her best dress—with matching purse, shoes, and hat, of course—and went to see Mrs. Harper. The often-repeated conversation went something like this: "Mrs. Harper," said Mother, "I am not very well and I need someone to help with my family while I teach and give violin lessons after school. I had this dream, and I was told to come to see you. I know it sounds unlikely, and I have little money to offer, but I must ask, 'Would you be willing to live with us and help with the children?'"

Mrs. Harper replied, "I would be happy to do so."

2.
Tillar: Safe Haven

With the Citizens Bank outdoor clock stopped at 4:20 for years, one could assume time stood still. Life did, in fact, move at a measured pace. Tillar was among the rural towns mired in the Great Depression, and the greatest aspiration was to weather the economic storm.

For my family, it became a safe haven.

We owned a small frame house there, so Mother, Julian, and I returned in the summer of 1931. Auntie Harper came with us, and in her two years with us, she was a warm family member when we most needed one. I remember her happy hugs for me and a willing shoulder for Mother to cry on. Mother could have burdened us with her grief. She never did and often referred to her "marriage made in heaven." Men friends came to call, but she never remarried.

Growing up in Tillar had huge advantages. Uncle Bob Tillar, who butchered cattle and hogs for Tillar and Company, brought fresh meat, bacon, sausage, and ham in the winter. Behind our house was the vegetable garden and a chicken yard. A barn, once housing our milk cow, had been converted to a garage. We hired out the plowing, but our family worked the vegetable garden, from which Mother preserved and canned. My father's wonderful cousins—Willie Harrell, Virgil and Rena Harrell, Jeff and Ruby Harrell—were constantly attentive. Our town was like a big family.

Approaching the first Christmas after my father died, I sensed our bad situation and asked only for a set of doll dishes and a small watercolor set. Despite the tragedies earlier in the year, we still had the ritual of going west on the gravel road toward Monticello to cut a Christmas tree from the pine woods. Hardwoods mostly surrounded Tillar, and there were few posted signs. "Is it okay if we go out your way to cut a tree?" Mother asked. The answer always: "Sure, pick out what you want." Most often, it was a pine—but sometimes we found a pretty cedar to chop down along with boughs from native holly and haw (red berry) trees. It was an excursion for the family, with exploring to determine which tree we liked best. Invariably, the one we thought perfect had a weak side and was turned toward the living room wall to hide its defects.

On Christmas Eve, 1931, we came home from shopping in McGehee to find a large package, wrapped in tissue paper and tied with string. People did not lock houses unless they were going to be away for long time. We had no idea who had left the package, but my name was attached. On Christmas morning, I gleefully opened it and found a handmade quilt with a Dutch boy and girl pattern. Embroidered on each square was the name of a young person in Tillar, with squares having been made by the different families. I have kept this treasure as a reminder of the goodness of people in the worst of times.

There were numerous packages with my name. I received seven tea sets and a dozen small watercolor sets. Mother said, "Pick out the tea set and the coloring set you want to keep, and we will give the others to children who didn't get presents." And we did. The miracles of Christmas begin in the human heart. Opening my Christmas stocking, I found hard candy, apples, and oranges. Fresh fruit in winter was a treat, not readily available in country stores. Our Christmas tree then had no lights, but was festive with ornaments handed down in the family and paper chains, as well as silver "icicles" and tinsel from the dime store. Paper ornaments I made at school were always featured.

At our house, the holiday dinner included baked chicken and cornbread dressing, giblet gravy, Mother's homemade cranberry sauce, home-canned vegetables, rolls, ambrosia, and birthday cake. Sometimes, we also had ham and Mother's grand pecan pie.

Frequently, Uncle Bancroft and Aunt Mary came to spend the holidays with us, and our small house always managed to have room and welcome for relatives. Uncle Burt and family came from Little Rock during the holidays. Children did not have sleeping bags; we just rolled up in quilts with a pillow on the floor.

There was no hotel in Tillar, although one had existed in earlier years, but McGehee had its fine Greystone Hotel and Garland Hotel where many of the railroad people stayed. Hotels were for commercial travelers; visiting relatives were accommodated at home or stayed with other family and friends.

Tillar (population 267) offered an extended family. Then thriving with small businesses, the downtown included headquarters for the powerful Tillar & Company (headquarters for its farming operation of 20,000 plus acres), Dr. Charles H. Kimbro's medical office, Watson Drug Store, Harrell Cash Store, and Willie Harrell's Store on the west side of the rail tracks. On another downtown block were Prewitt Bros. and two smaller stores, sometimes occupied and sometimes not. Across the railroad tracks, as I remember, on the other side were the post office, J. H. Ballard Mercantile Store, Pete Sain Mercantile, and Citizens Bank.

On Highway 65 (the only paved street in town) was Burns Service Station, with a small lunch counter, and another station with a barbershop owned by Hutchins Landfair. These were at the intersection with the gravel road to Monticello 30 miles away. Up the highway to the north was S. D. Santine's Garage and Station and, across the highway, F. T. Grisham had a busy blacksmith shop. Wandering along the relatively little-traveled Highway 65, we children could always stop at Mr. Grisham's blacksmith shop. Open doors allowed us to peer inside to see him beating on his anvil and marvel at the way he forged horse-shoes into the right shape. In earlier years, there had been a horse and mule barn in town, but these had been relegated to farms in the 1930s.

South on the highway was Zieman's Garage, where Otto Zieman Sr. was a mechanic. He was also the town's justice of the peace—some speculated that Mr. Zieman meted out fines by looking at prices in the Sears Roebuck catalog. One declared, "I hope Mr. Zieman don't look at the cost of a new wood cook stove!"

The telephone office or "central" was in a house a block from downtown. The operator was "Aunt Anna Hayes," and the house, although small and holding the switchboard in the entry, always had room for any relatives who might need a place to live. We had wall-mounted phones, and our number was 18. I could go to the phone and say, "Mrs. Hayes, will you get me Miss Caroline's house?" Her answer might be, "Honey, she's out in her garden right now," or "She's not at home. I heard her say she was going to McGehee." Aunt Anna was a reliable purveyor of townspeople's whereabouts and could get help in any kind of trouble. (In later years when the regulator blew off our butane gas tank, threatening our house and neighborhood, a call to Aunt Anna brought the volunteer firemen.) She was trustworthy—and newsy—in every situation.

Mrs. A. L. Guntharp kept a boarding house, which always seemed full, whether with travelers or teachers.

Major to our town's economy was the king of crops—cotton. Gins were operated by Tillar and Company and Prewitt Bros. Fall terms were common, with some merchants not being paid until the crop was picked and ginned. How they managed to live by being paid only once a year remains a mystery. The chug-chug of gins brought our town economic vitality, and creaking wagons en route to the gin pro-vided youngsters a chance for a tagalong ride on the rear.

The Missouri Pacific Railroad, with the tracks splitting the town, was almost as important socially as economically. Passenger trains offered daily trips to Little Rock and New Orleans. Trains stopped at many small towns along the way, and for those who had no vehicles, they provided transportation to other areas for shopping or medical needs. In the evening, it was common to gather downtown to watch and speculate about who arrived and departed on the train. The town's children once heard that some famous movie star would be on the evening train, and we waited several hours only to be disappointed and see no one famous.

Arriving by train, the evening mail was put in post office boxes, as there was no town delivery—just dial lock boxes or general mail one called for as desired. John Hyde was our longtime postmaster, and looking over his glasses, appeared rather stern to me. Almost as important as the postmaster was the station agent operating his telegraph from the small frame depot. The first I remember was Mr. Hobbs, a genial agent who would not scold if we played on the hand-pulled freight wagon. A popular diversion was to walk along the train tracks, and sometimes a large group of youth would walk two miles south to Crawford's Crossing and return—just for recreation.

Providing local services in the mid-1930s, a three-car train called "The Doodlebug" ran north and south daily and stopped at every little community, including Tillar. A fun trip for children was to ride to Winchester or Dumas, if we had money and someone with a car to return us home. The conductors never seemed to mind chattering children.

Crooked Bayou, little more than a small ditch, meandered through the middle of town and was across the highway from our house. If it froze over, we could "skate" or really slide across it. We built bonfires on the ice to light the scene and keep warm. In the summer, we used string and a bent pin to fish for "crawdads" (crawfish or crayfish), or when rains overflowed its bounds, we could build rudimentary rafts to float a few feet. Crooked Bayou, the headwaters of the Boeuf River we're told, was never deep enough to do much harm except to those slipping and falling in its muddy tadpole waters.

Our frame, two-bedroom home with one bathroom also had a living room, dining room, and kitchen with a screened back porch. Wood heaters were in the living room and bedrooms, and we had a tall, round kerosene heater for the bathroom. The small kitchen stove, wood-burning, was lined with coils to heat the water for bathing and dishes. We took our major laundry out to women who boiled the clothes in open-air wash pots, hung them on outdoor lines to dry, and pressed them with flat irons heated on wood stoves. We washed the smaller pieces by hand. Getting the washing and ironing done cost 50 cents.

Even in the saddest of times, I remember music as a must for the evening. Mother gathered us around the upright piano and led us as we sang "Down by the Old Mill Stream," "Let Me Call You Sweetheart," "She'll Be Coming 'Round the Mountain," and other favorites. On request, she would sing "O Sole Mio," or "Ah, Sweet Mystery of Life." Sometimes she would overcome her grief enough to play a favorite violin solo, "Traumeri."

Radio provided major entertainment, including Amos 'n' Andy, Fred Allen, Lum and Abner, Jack Benny, and Fibber McGee and Molly. We particularly enjoyed *The Firestone Hour* and musical broadcasts. Always, there were board games or cards. In the 1930s, traveling thespians brought tent shows to our little town, and occasionally we had a visiting circus or minstrel show.

In the summertime, recreation included gliding in the front porch swing and chatting with whoever walked down the two-lane Highway 65. Before rice was planted, mosquitoes were not such a great problem. Neighborhood children engaged in hide-and-seek and tag by streetlight.

We played house beneath the shade trees in the backyard, and I climbed into a large maple tree to sit and daydream. Betty and Frankie Davidson and I loved making mud pies dotted with chinaberries. Paper dolls, sometimes hand-fashioned from Sears Roebuck and Montgomery Ward catalogs, and stamp collecting were hobbies.

In the fall, I joined neighborhood boys in playing football, and in the spring, I organized track meets with yard equipment like a dirt pit for broad jump, a long pole for javelin, and a cane stretched between two boards for high jump. In addition to the Davidson sisters, playmates were Ann Harrell, Lillian and Rosalie Santine, the Prewitt twins (Jesse and Henry), and the Landfair boys (James Ballard, Buddy, and Gerald). I later was babysitter for the youngest Landfair, Tommy. Life became even more interesting when Mr. and Mrs. John Haisty and their five children moved next door in 1936. They included Avanel, who was to become a dear chum, Sherwood, Marion, Paul, and Dale.

The Haistys had a barn, with a cow, horse, and pigs. I learned to milk a cow there, a chore relegated to the older Haisty children who would enlist help. It was fascinating for me to join the Haisty children and play in their barn loft. That scenario led to the only "switching" I ever received. Uncle Bancroft had brought me a beautiful baby doll for Christmas, and Mother sternly told me not to take it to the Haisty barn so that it would not be ruined. I was more interested in playing "house" there, put down the doll, and one of the hogs ate the doll's foot. I still remember the sting of the switch—enough to make me listen better.

We worked on a clubhouse, collected scrap iron (making about 30 cents for a little red wagon load), and never realized the scrap was going to Japan for war materiel later to be used against the United States.

Tillar was safe enough for a little girl to run errands to town. Early, I learned the value of money. When I was eight, I came home with an ice cream cone costing a nickel. Mother asked, "Where did you get the ice cream cone?" I replied, "I charged it at Burns Station." Indignantly, she admonished, "Don't you ever charge anything to me without my permission!" Thereafter, I never did. Five cents would buy a loaf of white bread, or more appealing to me, a quarter-pound Power House candy bar.

Unlike many families in the Great Depression, we never suffered for food, principally because we grew much of it. We planted pole beans (Kentucky Wonder, of course), wax beans, radishes, turnip and mustard greens, lettuce, butterbeans, corn, Irish and sweet potatoes, peanuts, squash, okra, and tomatoes. A very good summer meal consisted of four or five vegetables, cornbread, and iced tea. Sometimes we took the corn we had grown to S. D. Santine's service station where he used a small grist mill to grind it into coarse meal, the cost to us being just a small portion of the meal. Three large fig trees in our yard afforded breakfast goodies, from fresh figs to Mother's incomparable preserves.

During the Depression, hoboes rode the tops and sides of trains coming through Tillar. On many days, some hungry person came to our back porch and asked for food. Mother never turned anyone away—even though it might be as little as leftover cornbread and greens. We were not afraid of these strangers; their bedraggled appearance made us sad.

In around 1932–33, cattle were shipped by train from the drought-stricken Midwest to Tillar for grazing. Those were the only times I saw cattle drives. Neighbor children and I perched on our front yard wooden fence and watched the drovers round up cattle straying from the herd going to and from rail sidings. I think the cattle were taken to Tillar and Company pastures to graze until they could be sent to slaughter.

The Great Depression was a slow, unpredictable drama in which most of us were poor but proud, independent but relying on the kindness of others and never making light of any who might have less. Who knew the future—we might be in even more distress next month! Often I must remind my descendants that there was no welfare, no Social Security, no food stamps, and few, if any, pensions. I well recall some children making fun of a little girl whose only coat had been made of dyed-brown burlap feed sacks, called "tow-sacks." Some of us told our playmates to stop their derision.

As cruel as little children sometimes can be, adults set a better example. When one family's breadwinner went away for five years in search of work, the owners of several Tillar mercantile stores alternated, by weeks, in providing needed provisions for the mother and five children. Instead of government assistance, we had each other.

Thrift was necessary. We saved everything from string to used paper sacks. Every housewife had a button box and carefully cut buttons from garments no longer usable. Serviceable clothing was passed on to someone who could use it. I never heard of a rummage sale until I was grown. If we couldn't use something, someone else could. I personally loved the clothing that my cousin Ann passed down to me, because her family was financially "well off" and she had garments from big stores like Gus Blass Co. in Little Rock or even Stix, Baer and Fuller in St. Louis. Bartering also was a way of life. Once, Mother had a good laugh over how a girdle was traded for a used tire and ultimately for fence poles for our garden. There was one junk yard, holding half a dozen stripped-down cars, and it was located behind Sain Mercantile. Town children loved sitting in the wrecks and "driving" to nowhere.

We always had a car, the first I remember being a Model T four-door model. A notable trip occurred as our family was coming home from McGehee one evening and saw a cow straddled across the narrow two-lane highway. There being no time to take the roadside ditch, our high old Ford did a "leap-frog" over the cow. In the back-seat, I was unhurt, and not a single egg was broken in the grocery bag. The cow? She got up and ambled off.

Some people kept horses, although I never owned one. Once, while visiting Jane Wolfe, I asked to ride her striking new horse. As I tried to mount, it reared, kicked, and left its hoof print on my stomach. I was more frightened than seriously hurt. Upon further inquiry, Jane's father found he had bought a retired race horse and quickly sold the animal.

Sometimes, we hitched a horse to a wagon and went on a picnic. Twins Jesse and Henry Prewitt, and older brother Zach, owned such a rig. They asked several of us to go plum picking on the old Terry Place (which T. A. Prewitt Sr. had bought at foreclosure). We had empty five-pound lard tins to hold plums, and they were full. When we found blackberries, I had nothing but the crown of my straw hat, and I picked a hat full. But when I reached for a few more berries, I almost put my hand on a snake—and dropped the berries. Not to be outdone, I knelt down and picked up the berries from the dusty ground and washed them at home. They were delicious!

Life with Mother was always an adventure. She taught violin lessons in McGehee, and took me with her to play or sit quietly while she taught in homes. Clarence and Iva Isch became our lifelong friends as she taught their son, Clarence Jr., to become a fine violinist. Mrs. Isch always had a treat for me—a plate of cookies or some candy. A visionary, Mr. Isch taught me to see beyond the present and past.

Mother's spark took us far beyond the boundaries of our village. In 1933, Mother read about the World's Fair in Chicago, an observance of the city's centennial. Mother loved to play cards—bridge when she could and solitaire for solace. Remembering that her parents had taken her and Uncle Burt to the World's Fair in St. Louis in 1904, Mother said, "I am going to play solitaire, and if I can beat 'Old Sol' three times in a row, we are going to the Chicago World's Fair." She did, and we went.

We joined an Arkansas group boarding a Rock Island train at Choctaw Station in Little Rock. I have fragmentary memories of the Century of Progress. The tall buildings, including a Havoline thermometer, stand out because no structures in Tillar were higher the cotton gin and two-story school. I also was fascinated with the open-air sightseeing buses relaying the crowds, and best remember the transportation and GE buildings.

In 1933, Mother and I went to McGehee for her teaching and shopping. At the grocery, Pat Sherland (one of her violin students who worked there), told Mother, "I owe you for lessons. I only have two dollars, but I am going to give you one." She replied, "Oh, you can wait until later to pay me." He replied, "No, I must now."

We came home and stopped at Harrell's Cash Store, where our cousins were owners. Jeff Harrell said, "Bertha, do you have any money?" She replied, "I have a little, and Pat Sherland just gave me another dollar." Said Cousin Jeff: "Here, you take half of the little cash I have, as you might need it." Upon urging, she did. As we visited in the store, Cousin Virge Harrell approached Mother and said, "Bertha, I think you might need a little money, and here are a few dollars for you." She tried to decline, but he persisted.

Not until we reached home later that evening did we hear on the radio that President Roosevelt had closed all banks, and no one knew when or if they would reopen. Through this kindness, we had cash when many others did not. The president had been inaugurated on Saturday, March 4, 1933, and banks were closed on Sunday. Thankfully, the president called Congress into emergency session, and the Banking Act was proposed. The banks reopened four days later, but until then, no one knew what would happen. We never were to forget that uncertainty and resulting generosity.

In 1933, Auntie Harper became feeble and went to live with relatives in Eudora. Roseanna, a wonderful African-American lady, moved into the one-room servant's house with privy at the back. She became a precious addition to my life. She made wonderful brownies and had them for me when I walked home from school. Often she held me in her lap and sang to me.

Roseanna was there only two years, retiring to Grady to make her home, but I love her to this day. Her race was of no concern until some neighbor boys found some bloody cattle bones and put them at her door to threaten her. Indignant, Mother took Roseanna into our home to stay, and went from house to house to seek culprits. Several doors away, she found a boy who said, "Bones? Bones? I think I remember something about bones." Sternly reminded that what he had done was an unforgivable prank, he was disciplined but not jailed.

When Roseanna left to live in Grady, I learned responsibility. Since Mother was teaching music lessons, I went home after school, made a wood fire in the kitchen, and prepared supper. We had an electric stove, but in the winter and fall, we most often cooked on the small wood stove. After getting home from school, I would bring in the wood, and if necessary, use a hatchet to split the cypress kindling used to start fires. Our house was heated by wood, and in the colder months, we had fires in the kitchen and bedroom and a small round kerosene heater in the bathroom. We built a fire in the living room heater when we had company.

I still wonder how Mother managed. There was very little money, but she took us to wonderful attractions in Little Rock, including violinist Fritz Kreisler and the Cincinnati Symphony conducted by Eugene Ormandy, among others. We later heard violinist Yehudi Menuhin, and were invited backstage to meet him. He held his precious hands behind his back and bowed to greet us.

Holidays were special occasions, but Christmases most stand out in memory. Approaching age 10 in 1933, I badly wanted a bicycle. Uncle Bancroft had written that he would buy one, but Mother scratched through that sentence before I saw it and said he did not have the money. Imagine my unbounded delight on Christmas morning when I found a beautiful blue and white bike under the tree, as well as a Girl Scout uniform and a Mickey Mouse watch!

My bike took me on adventures along the highway and dirt roads of our tree-lined town and on a longer mile trip to Bayou Bartholomew and back. Biking was always my favorite sport.

To "College" Early

Mother decided she must finish her college degree, her senior studies having been interrupted by elopement. She engaged rooms at Mrs. Killian's boarding house in Monticello, where she, Sonny, and I lived during the summer session at Arkansas A&M College. I don't remember the boarding fare, except that Mrs. Killian was kind to us and baked cookies for me.

However, one incident is firmly in mind. I wanted a new pair of tennis shoes. Mother said she did not have the money but might receive a dividend from a small amount of stock left by my father. I watched the mailbox every day, and finally the check was there. When Mother returned from her studies, I dashed to meet her and yelled, "Mother, Mother, the check has CAME!" Ever the proper English teacher, Mother replied, "Has COME, has COME!"

We accompanied Mother two summers, and one of these was spent in Harris Hall on campus. At age 11, I applied for my first job— stuffing A&M brochures into envelopes for the princely sum of 15 cents an hour. I was proud of the 45 cents I earned and saved.

Mother also took correspondence courses and commuted to A&M when I was older. Once, a terrible storm was coming up, and her car stopped. Devout without being sanctimonious, she said, "Lord, there is a big storm coming and I need to get home. Help me to get this car fixed." When she lifted the car hood, she saw something she thought needed repair. She took a hairpin from her long hair wound in braids and used the hairpin to fix the problem. The car started, and she reached home before the storm.

Necessity prompts innovation. Mother was a master at it. She also was a master at encouragement, often telling me "you can be any-thing you want" in a time when teaching and nursing were often the best-paying careers to which a young girl could aspire.

Mother's wisdom was ever evolving out of necessity. Unsure how to assess personal property, she consulted a so-called friend, who urged her to assess her small diamond ring. Later she found that she had the only diamond assessed in Drew County. Self-reliance became foremost.

Carefully groomed with matching accessories, even in dark times, she was fashioned of gentle steel. When a neighbor turned his hogs loose to feed in our garden, she summoned him to the fence and declared, "Get those pigs out! If they get back in, I will shoot every one of them." And never did I hear an obscenity! In adult years when I faced threats in the newspaper business, I often thought of Mother's grit.

Mother was a fount of wisdom and culture. Dearly loving the classics, she often quoted Shakespeare, Keats, Yeats, Longfellow, and other greats. However, it is her words sometimes paraphrased from the Bible that have remained with me throughout my life. When times were tough, she would declare "the darkest of day is just before the dawn." If challenged, she'd say "where there's a will, there's a way" and would find it. If something was persisting in troubling her, she was philosophical, saying "this, too, shall pass."

The wisdom she imparted almost every day to me was, "To whom much is given, much is required"—a constant reminder that even though we were poor at the time, we had great responsibilities to others. It became the imprint for my life.

3.
Stability for Our Time

During my childhood, when great needs made wants hardly expressible, there were some edifices of stability in my mind.

Church

There were three churches—Methodist, Baptist, and Presbyterian—and only illness prevented attendance. Although I went to my own Presbyterian church, into which I was fully accepted at 12, I was ecumenical.

Tillar had a rare combination of church-going people. All three churches conducted their own Sunday Schools, in which doctrine was taught. However, church services were rotated. With the largest membership, the Methodists held morning worship the first and third Sundays, the Presbyterians on the second, and the Baptists on the fourth. We gathered to sing "In the Sweet Bye and Bye," "In the Garden," "The Old Rugged Cross," and other timeless hymns. Whoever preached the sermon was fine, if not wholly acceptable.

Each summer, the three churches held a joint revival, the only requirement for visiting preachers being that they could stir up a good crowd and bring in some of the un-churched. Also, which song leader could get everyone in the mood to sing long and loud!

Revivals presented a challenge to good cooks of the community. Who would feed the visiting clergy? The homeowner offering lodging was expected to provide breakfast. However, for dinner (which is what we called the noon meal) and supper (evening meal), cooks were rotated, and not one wished to be outdone by another.

Preparing a meal for the revivalists was no small effort. A week might go into the planning of menus—fried chicken or chicken and dressing; four or five vegetables; cornbread or homemade rolls; and chocolate cake, lemon pie, or blackberry cobbler (maybe all three!). Advanced preparation included getting out the best dishes to serve in the dining room and ironing the linen napkins. Nothing was too good for the visiting preachers, sometimes accompanied by compatriots enticed by culinary delights.

Morning and evening revival services stick in memory. A long, long evening began with a song and Bible service for children and young people, followed by the main preaching event. With no air conditioning, sweating was already under way, and there were errant flies and mosquitoes to swat. We all tried to crowd near ceiling fans but mostly the handheld fan was best to bat away insects. The generally jovial song leader began with traditional hymns and escalated from there.

We children sat at the back of the church, where the unruly could be more easily removed. However, I don't recall many unruly, as "Hellfire and damnation" were being preached. It was hot enough that the message was getting across, and in the end, when we all stood through many repeat verses of the call, we could hardly wait to see sinners come down the aisle. The sinners, I thought, were just like the rest of us.

Cousin Rena. was a fine pianist and a very good person. She was playing for a morning revival service when the evangelist called for a "Rose Service." He advised the congregation "to just pin a rose on the person you want to see saved." The most holier-than-thou woman immediately selected a rose from a bouquet and pinned it on Cousin, who was busily playing the hymn of invitation. Not to be outdone, Cousin finished the stanza, stood up and pinned a rose on the Holier One. There weren't many who avoided a giggle.

School

Another mark of permanence in the Great Depression years was our school. Its presence seemed authoritarian. In the country were some one-room schools, principally for African Americans, and there was no bus for any school. One either walked or "caught a ride." Going to school was a priority and a chance out of the economic mire. The school system was called equal for both races, but that was easily disproved by the quality of the buildings, although the black students had some of the most dedicated of teachers.

The white Tillar High School encompassed all grades in its two-story building dating to 1917, with elementary grades downstairs and upper grades on the second floor. Each classroom had a "cloak room" where we hung our coats. The principal's office was in the center of the second floor, which also housed the auditorium-library. The heating system in the basement depended upon coal.

Presiding over the school during my junior high and high school years was strict M. H. Russell, who put the fear of the Lord into us. It was the beginning of a career that took Mr. Russell to the presidency of Henderson College, and we knew him to be most intelligent. His command of the school was undoubted.

Our school day began at 8 a.m. and ended about 3:30. My grade school memories focus on fun times including sports and recess, although academically I did well enough to "skip a grade."

I well remember the high school football games, in which my brother Sonny substituted at guard. With no stands, we stood to cheer the Tillar Eagles as Mother entreated me to run up and down the sidelines and see if Sonny had emerged from the pile-up.

Playground equipment was limited to the "Giant Stride," a tall steel pole with chain swings attached, allowing us to go round and round, sometimes to lose grip and fall. Mostly, we played Red Rover and tag, running for sheer joy. In the fall, boys climbed a persimmon tree just off campus and tossed down fruit to sample…delicious if ripe, bitter as gall if green.

Our high school curriculum was basic, including English, algebra, geometry, general science, history and civics (government), French, speech, and drama. Basketball, journalism, music, and play practice were among the after-school activities that engaged us. Mother directed a school orchestra in which I was a dismal violinist.

We had regular assemblies, marathon musical recitals, and end-of-school plays. The recitals were so long that Miss Allie Bess, piano and voice teacher, and Mother, violin instructor, actually divided into shifts to supervise. The audience? No shifts, except to go outside and walk around a while before returning—making certain to be there when one's own performed.

There were no lunchrooms for any schools. Children sometimes brought a sack lunch with a cold sweet potato or biscuit, and often nothing at all. When Mother had noon duty and we didn't go home for lunch, she always packed extra food. She would invite lunch-less children to "come share our sandwiches." They readily agreed. Half a sandwich was better than none.

Mother insisted on treating everyone fairly, accounting for my later stands on racial matters. I remember waving at a young African-American, Harold, who worked as a store porter. Friends admonished me, "Don't wave at a colored person." "Why not?" I replied. "He is my friend." Although our town was segregated, I recall accompanying Mother to visit African-American friends.

Most of the time, we walked to school. In 1933, Mother bought a black Ford sedan with green spoke wheels. She thought green improper for a widow and had the dealer paint the spokes black. I don't remember its cost, but she paid $700 in trading for a new Plymouth in 1937. It was brown, sufficient years for mourning having passed.

We had no health classes, and along with influenza and measles, scourges of our existence were mosquitoes which caused dreaded chills and fever and required ear-ringing quinine as medication.

Dr. Kimbro was the sole source for our treatment in Tillar, and he was as imposing in height as he was thoughtful. I don't recall any assistant to help him. On call, night and day, seven days a week, he used a horse and buggy to cover the countryside roads, often mired in mud. It was said that when he was so tired that he fell asleep, his faithful horse took him home.

Dr. Kimbro's office, in the main block of downtown, had the basic examining chair and tables where he could mix pharmaceuticals. Occasionally, we would get a prescription that was filled at Watson Drug Store two doors away. The drug store had many "patent medicines" like 666, Carter's Little Liver Pills, castor oil, and various tonics. Also, it was a great socializing place with a soda fountain and wonderful proprietors, "Mammy" and "Pappy" Watson.

Finch P. Watson was also the town's fire chief, and the sole fire engine was locked in a metal storage building two blocks away on Highway 65. Once, upon receiving a fire call, he walked to the building to get the fire truck and couldn't find the keys. He returned home and asked his wife, "Glennie, where are the keys to the fire truck?"

"I don't know, Finch. Have you looked in your pocket?" He did, and there they were. The fire truck eventually arrived, but thankfully, the blaze was out. The town joke was that the fire department always saved the lot.

In the collage of memory, the Watsons stand out as always willing to help in need, medical, blazes, or not. We could depend on them, as we did Dr. Kimbro.

In the summer when I was 12, Mother and I were returning from Little Rock when she decided to stop at a filling station at Woodson for a snack. Her order of a chicken salad sandwich resulted in "ptomaine poisoning." She was very ill for a week, and, consulting with Dr. Kimbro by phone, I was her sole caregiver.

Most Tillar homes had electricity, running water, and indoor plumbing. Electric fans provided the only relief for blistering summers. Rural electrification had not reached the farms, where homes were still lighted by kerosene lamps and serviced by privies. Still, there was something magical about being invited to spend a night with my friend Evelyn Crain at her farm home. Her loving family provided a wonderful breakfast of the best-ever biscuits and home-cured ham.

My pets included a part-Husky, part-mutt dog named Boots and a flock of wild ducks, domesticated by Uncle Bob and tame enough to eat corn chops from my hands. Boots was our watchdog as well as my playmate. His greatest fault was chasing cars, resulting in his being hit and suffering a broken leg. Mother took him to a veterinarian, who charged $30 to set the leg, and she placed Boots on the back porch to recuperate. Fully recovered, he took up car chasing again. Another broken leg. Mother said, "I cannot afford another $30, so I will set his leg myself." She succeeded. Boots absolutely loved Mother and followed us to school. When he was nine, he crawled up beside Mother's car and died there to be as near as he could.

4.
Writing Becomes a Calling

While I enjoyed the outdoors, I really loved reading and writing. Mother made certain that I had access to the classics; my favorite authors were Louisa May Alcott and Robert Louis Stevenson.

The written word was fascinating. My seventh-grade English teacher, Mae (Mrs. Ralph) Clayton, said a good project would to be write a newspaper. I obtained a sheet of white butcher paper large enough to make a tabloid-size, four-page paper. Using a daily newspaper as a pattern, I ruled off the columns, and writing longhand, focused on local stories. For illustrations, I cut pictures from other newspapers. In that project, I was forever marked.

Despite the Great Depression, my school years were happy. I had "skipped" the fifth grade when my test scores prompted this move, but Mother said no to skipping the eighth grade as she thought 15 was too young to graduate from high school. I have always been grateful for her wisdom, as I recall the joy of being eighth-grade valedictorian and having Uncle Bancroft beam from the audience on that occasion.

A keen interest was our Girl Scout Troop led by Mrs. J. R. Prewitt, whom we called "Miss Caroline." Our hikes were real adventures, as she taught us the leaves of plants and trees, handy since I was allergic to poison ivy and oak, and how to identify birds. She frequently brewed sassafras tea for us in the winter.

I loved Scouting, including Camp Ouachita summer sessions where Margaret Ellen Kemp of Little Rock became a special friend. I learned to make a fire by striking rocks together and to cook over outdoor fires during our overnight camping with boulders for pillows. I reached first-class rank but couldn't achieve Eagle as I did not swim well enough. Later as a college student in Monticello, I served as Scoutmaster troop leader two years.

Miss Caroline was a lifelong influence. In 1936, she heard that First Lady Eleanor Roosevelt would visit Hot Springs for the Arkansas Centennial and, as national honorary chairman, would meet with Girl Scouts. "Our troop must go!" declared Miss Caroline.

Mr. and Mrs. S. D. Santine took their daughters, Lillian, Rosalie, Elizabeth, and Frances (we called them Sugar, Sister, Buck, and Tiny) and me there. Girl Scouts formed an honor guard lining steps along the Arlington Hotel's front entry. We saluted as the first lady passed, and I was thrilled that Eleanor Roosevelt smiled directly at me. Some columnists then declared her homely, but I was beguiled by her radiant personality. Later, President Roosevelt came to join her. An older son helped him from the limousine, and the president stood with great difficulty on his steel-braced legs. We all knew that the president had suffered from polio, but news reels and photos pictured him sitting buoyantly or operating his car with special hand controls. I was stunned at how disabled was the president whose golden voice on radio always entranced us.

A statewide centennial celebration was held at Quigley Stadium in Little Rock, with each town asked to participate. Our group donned long cotton dresses with pantaloons and joined in the massive square dance.

As a teenager, I went to Presbyterian camps for two summers. Mother accompanied us as a counselor one year, and one day when she joined a group going into nearby Benton, I went swimming in the Saline River. I stepped off into a deep hole and was going down for a third time when I latched on to a nearby hand. Some special angel was looking over me.

In basketball I found true fun. At 14, I was invited to a dance but didn't want to go, although the boy had access to a car. Mother bribed me, promising to buy a sweat suit for basketball practice. My date sat behind the wood stove while I danced away the evening.

Of below-average athletic ability, I was a substitute on the girls' basketball team until my senior year when I called plays at center. Going to tournaments was "big time" for us, including being overnight guests of host families when we played in Dumas, only 13 miles away. Once we stayed at a really rundown hotel in Little Rock when our team played, and lost, in the state girls' tournament.

With Mother being the English teacher and librarian, I had little choice but to excel academically. She demanded more of me than other students. She also sponsored the high school paper, the *Eagle*, where I ultimately became editor.

No driver's education class being available, Mother sought to teach me how to drive. My foot slipped off the brake, and our Ford went into our fig tree. No harm done, but Mother was finished with driver's education!

Our summers were quiet, except for several weeks in Hot Springs. Mother rented an apartment for a month since my brother Sonny was stationed at the Army and Navy Hospital. As a teenager, I could walk downtown and enjoy a soda at a drug store, and we could visit the auction houses on Central Avenue. With its nearby mountains for hiking, Hot Springs provided a contrast to the Delta's flat fields.

A casino and resort town, Hot Springs was a dramatic change from tranquil Tillar. Once, we were invited to dinner at the famed Belvedere Club. Etched in memory are elderly women, dripping in diamonds, oblivious to anything but the gaming tables. For a country innocent as was I, truly that was an eye-opener.

After Sonny left for the army, Mother took in roomers to supplement our income, her teaching salary having risen to $75 a month. Two who came to live in our home became family. Madge Moore of Dumas, speech and French instructor, and Mabel Moore of Sulphur Rock, sixth-grade teacher, were not related. They became older sisters to me. With marvelous humor, they made our suppers most enjoyable. Each embellished tales of our day's experiences, always laughable and sometimes memorable.

Once, they received a mail brochure asking, "Is nine cents too much to pay for a dress?" We all conferred, and declared, "No!" We pooled our money, and they ordered 100 dresses. The shipment came as we were getting ready for a school dance, and later returning home, we could hardly to wait to open the big box. It contained the foulest-smelling bunch of dirty clothes I had ever seen. Mabel declared it "odoriferous," and we had to leave it in the porch's open air. We couldn't give the contents away. Nine cents was too much to pay for a dress!

Mabel was teaching a class about healthy foods, stressing the importance of a good breakfast. "How many of you had an egg for breakfast today?" she asked. A young boy replied, "Lord, Miss Mabel, I ain't et a egg in God knows when." After all, it was the Great Depression, and eggs could be sold for cash. Sometimes Mother bartered violin lessons for whatever a family could afford, but often, parents of the violin students provided something to take home. After teaching a child of Mrs. Behz, Mother was given a dozen eggs. She tried to pay, but Mrs. Behz replied, "No, Mrs. Tillar, violin is violin, and eggs is eggs!"

Madge was my mentor in extemporaneous speaking, teaching me fundamentals I have used all my life. As a high school junior, I placed second in extemporaneous speaking at the district. Schools then participated in district literary and cultural meets, with tests for mathematics, history, and English, and performance competition in voice and piano, along with the usual track meets.

Life in Tillar was mostly tranquil for the young, despite the economic challenges. I could walk home in the dark, safely, after visiting the Prewitt twins Henry and Jesse at their home in the north part of town. I dated in high school, but never "went steady." We socialized as a group, dancing on the concrete slab at Burns Station where they had a juke box. There we could have a Coke for a nickel and a hamburger for a dime. Many times, we had only change for the juke box but had a fine time.

When someone had access to a car, we went to McGehee to dance at juke box joints. One I particularly remember was "Comp's," named for the Comptons who operated it. There was a small dance floor and snacks and soft drinks for refreshments. We learned the jitterbug, "trucking," and basic ballroom dancing.

Once weekly in summers, Mother invited town teens to our back porch for dancing to radio music. Board games were available for the quieter bunch, and we had a lighted badminton court for the active. Mother always managed to serve refreshments: lemonade, brownies, watermelon, or whatever might be available.

Another favorite recreation, when we had spending money, was going to the "two-fer" at Ritz Theatre in McGehee. For 25 cents, one could see two feature movies in one evening. Usually they were B-movies with first-runs featured alone and costing a quarter. Clark Gable, Myrna Loy, Bette Davis, Franchot Tone, Fred Astaire, Ginger Rogers, and Dick Powell were favorites of our early years. Serial western films featured Gene Autry, Roy Rogers, Dale Evans, and others. Mickey Rooney was the teen heartthrob in the "Andy Hardy series."

Visiting family was deemed important. After church, we "called on" family and friends to share experiences, tell town tales, and offer opinions. Sometimes, for entertainment, Mother read a student essay. The favorite was on transportation, its opening reading: "In the early years, man had only hisself. He got two chunks to float around on, but on a chunk, you can't depend on it!"

Once-weekly trips to McGehee provided items we couldn't find at the mercantile stores in Tillar. A McGehee grocery had a vat of peanut butter, and with a spatula, a clerk stirred vigorously, as it was not homogenized. Then he slapped a big slab of it in a cardboard carton. At 10 cents a pound, that peanut butter tasted better than any since. No additives—just the peanut butter, ma'am. My favorite shopping included dime stores in McGehee since Tillar had none. Also, First Street drug stores sold H. B. Fraser's Dairyland ice cream made in McGehee. Many city dime stores had soda fountains and lunch counters.

Special were shopping trips to Little Rock. Always dressed in Sunday best, our mothers had matching hats, purses, gloves, and shoes. Miss Allie Bess (Mrs. Davidson) and daughters Betty and Frankie made an annual trip with Mother and me before Christmas. When Mother bought a new 1937 Plymouth, it had a "governor" to limit the speed to 30 miles per hour, as that was believed to make a car last longer. As I remember, the car speed was thus regulated for a month or so, before the "governor" was removed. En route to Little Rock, Mother saw a man jump into her lane on Highway 65 at Varner. She realized he might be a prison inmate trying to escape so she stomped on the gas pedal and kept going. Thirty miles an hour seemed a crawl. At the last minute, the man jumped out of the way. We looked back to see guards flogging him and shoving him into a truck.

In Little Rock we shopped the major department stores, including Gus Blass Co., M. M. Cohn, and Pfeifers'—as well as Kress dime store and window shopping Stifft's Jewelry. Added pleasure included light fare in Blass's mezzanine restaurant. A first-floor treat was the candy counter operated by Louis Schneider, who handmade a wide array of delectable chocolates.

Other Little Rock visits were with Uncle Burt, Aunt Frances, and daughter Connie. Once, Jesse and Henry Prewitt, also visiting relatives there, invited me to join them at the "picture show," as we called movies. Our plan was to travel separate bus lines and meet at the theater. Everything went well until my return when I departed at the wrong bus stop—16 blocks from where Uncle Burt lived. Realizing my mistake at 11 o'clock on a dark night, I started speed walking. I had gone several blocks when a car pulled up beside me, and a man called, "You need a ride?" "No," I replied, "I live in the next house." I headed to a house unknown to me. The car waited until I went up on the porch, and finally pulled away. I double-timed safely to Uncle Burt's and didn't tell Mother what happened until the next morning. She was so relieved I had thought quickly enough to avoid being molested. Again, an angel was looking over my shoulder.

When friends came, we often played board games or cards. Chinese checkers were the rage. On the first Sunday in April 1939, Avanel Haisty and I were playing checkers when Mother came to us and said, "Get your coats on. There is going to be a bad storm." In the afternoon stillness was a midnight sky. A train-like roar followed. Our house was missed by a half mile, but that deadly tornado wreaked havoc north of Tillar and into Jefferson Community, leaving a dozen dead and others severely injured. Fearsome electrical storms followed all night after the afternoon twister. In the devastation was a broom straw driven into a tree.

No storm cellars existed, but we learned that some children had survived by lying flat in a ditch. "Head for the nearest ditch" became a storm mantra. (A similar tornado on the first Sunday in 1929 killed 11 people in Loggy Bayou Church north of Tillar. Thus, April Sundays became a cause for alarm.)

Sadness in a small town always involved the whole community. When one family mourned, so did all. Even for children, it was proper to wear our best clothes, take food for the bereaved family, and call to express condolences. Funeral services sometimes were held in the larger homes, and occasionally, the coffin would be carried by wagon and mules.

Holidays in Tillar often were town-wide. In my childhood, we had a community Christmas tree at the two-story Masonic Building. There were presents, often an orange and apple with hard candy in a stocking, for every child, and Santa always arrived. For Halloween, all the young people would gather for mischief such as hanging fence gates from utility poles and moving wood piles from one area to another, hard work for youngsters and nuisance for adults.

July Fourth called for celebration. On Jesse and Caroline Prewitt's grounds, a long barbecue pit would be dug. Barbecuing was a two-day ritual—preparing the pit, building to the just-right red hot hickory coals, and then adding the meat for overnight roasting. Picnic fare, spread on long tables of boards covering sawhorses, included barbecued goat and pork, homegrown watermelons, as well as potluck brought by families. Later, older children shot firecrackers and younger ones waved sparklers.

On "political years" and approaching major elections, rallies were held in groves of trees. Speeches were windy and fiery. Politics sometimes were a major sport in which we were bound to take sides. Selma, fewer than 100 in population, sometimes hosted several hundred coming from near and far.

In a tranquil time, we had no police department. Mr. Bennett was a night watchman. If we had a major problem, Madge's brother, Robert S. Moore, was a deputy sheriff in Desha County and could be summoned much faster than a Drew County deputy from as far as Monticello.

One year while I was in high school, we had a siege of prowlers. We could see someone coming to our back porch screen door, and once Mother yelled, "Get away from here!" She grabbed Daddy's old pistol, not fired in many years, and was so excited she fired through the porch roof. No more prowlers!

I graduated from high school in May 1940, and joined Euna Lee Bishop as co-valedictorian. Other class members were Glen Stanford, Georgia Lee McDuffie, P. L. (Bo) Morris, William Oliver, T. J. Hayes, J. M. McDonald, Avanel Haisty, Thurston Cooper, Ladelle Birch, and Billie Herrington.

Our class trip was to Baton Rouge and the Gulf Coast. A classmate had not absorbed history, and as we toured the Civil War battlefield in Mississippi, he asked, "Who fought this war?" A chaperone, who was a coach and history teacher, gruffly replied, "The NORTH and the SOUTH." "Well," continued the classmate, "who won?"

Mother had chaperoned senior trips to the Gulf Coast with the goal of enlarging students' limited vision. She taught manners in her classes. Some of the students had never ridden in an elevator, so the skyscraper Louisiana state capitol was eye-opening.

Madge and Mabel lived in our home for five and seven years, respectively. They paid a modest room rent, and each of us contributed a few dollars to the "kitchen pot" (an old sugar bowl) from which we paid for groceries. We never thought of them except as family, and they were with Mother when I enrolled at Arkansas A&M College in the fall of 1940. Later, Mrs. Mamie Hale lived with us. She was a fine first-grade teacher and the gentlest soul I have ever known.

If I could use just one word to sum up my childhood, it would be "adventure." Each day was an adventure, even if mundane, emotionally heavy, or financially challenging. Mother instilled in me, "The greatest day is yet to come." She was right.

5.
Expanding My Vistas

The Green Dog Bus Line approached, and I was ready for another afternoon of adventure in downtown Monticello.

Enrolled at 16 as a freshman at Arkansas A&M College, I had no automobile. Very few had cars. I frequently boarded the green-and-white college bus since downtown was several miles away.

Female students were sternly required to sign out if leaving campus, but I hadn't learned the rules. When Juliet White of Monticello asked if a group of girls would like to ride to nearby Star City on our first afternoon, we joyously said yes. She had a car! Returning from Star City, someone mentioned that we were expected to sign out. We all vowed never to tell, and somehow our very strict housemother, Caroline Royal, never found out. Thereafter, I signed out to leave the campus, or even after 6 p.m. as required for the library, commons, or other approved campus building.

Horsfall Hall, the freshman girls' dorm, had single or double rooms and community bathrooms down the hall. No boys were allowed in girls' rooms, only in the large reception area. We had rooms for sorority use, and I pledged Phi Sigma Chi during the first semester.

I joined the staff of the *Weevil Outlet*, the A&M newspaper, and one of my tasks was to sell advertising. Really it was my ploy to visit the Advance Printing Co., publishers of the weekly *Advance Monticellonian*. The lure of printer's ink outweighed the draw of the drug store where I would later stop for a soda or ice cream.

Frances Jaggers and her husband Shannon owned and operated the *Advance*. She always welcomed me, never saying that I might be a distraction. Sometimes bringing a story, I also visited with the printer, who could reach into a barrel where individual type letters were dumped and set up words, his fingers simply feeling the letter outlines. The *Advance* had more than a barrel of type, however; the backshop was well-equipped for "job printing" and the newspaper. Fascinated with the newspaper, I was encouraged by the Jaggerses and Clara B. Kennan, who demanded top performance in freshman English.

College was not a financial cinch. Room and board cost $25 a month, and tuition was $50 a semester. No scholarships were available. I couldn't get a job. After six weeks, I went to Ray Maxwell of McGehee, college board member, on a Saturday afternoon and said, "Mr. Maxwell, I need a job to help me get through school." On Monday morning, I had work in the college library.

Library service was only one of the jobs I had. Subsequently, I graded English and French papers, took up laundry and cleaning on a commission basis, and as an agent for a local florist, sold corsages for dances. Free-lancing or "stringing," I was paid 10 cents an inch for stories sent to the *McGehee Times*. Later, I worked part-time as a clerk in the campus post office. The next year, when the student postmaster was discharged, I was given the primary job, paying room and board. Counting sideline jobs, I paid all expenses, and ending my sophomore year, I owed the college only one cent!

I enjoyed college politics, running successfully for freshman class reporter, and later, student body secretary. However, I had a stinging defeat. By a few votes, I lost the election for the position I most wanted, editor of the *Weevil Outlet* student newspaper. (Since the college team was named for the boll weevil, scourge of the cotton south, the paper became the *Weevil Outlet*.)

That loss taught me a life lesson: never give up. I served as the paper's business manager, selling advertising and vowing to become a full-fledged journalist.

I enjoyed all of my classes except piano and came home with a first semester 5.8 average out of a possible 6. "I am not a musician," I explained, and Mother removed my piano commitment for the second semester. She rewarded my next 6.0 average with a stylish red hat!

Our social events were dorm parties and college dances, and we loved to jitterbug to swing band tunes in the college armory. Dates also were relegated to visits to the student commons or library and sometimes in the dorm reception areas under the ever-present eye of dorm monitors.

In my sophomore year came the crisis changing our lives. Returning to college after a weekend at home, I heard a radio report that Japanese forces had bombed Pearl Harbor. Stronger because of Great Depression trials, my generation faced an even greater challenge. Life was altered for all. When the campus National Guard was called to active duty, I saw its unit drilling with wood ceremonial rifles. A signal of tough days ahead.

The *Weevil Outlet* was published only twice a month, but on December 19, 1941, recorded reaction to Pearl Harbor:

> December 7, a date that was expected to be a calm restful Sunday on the campus, turned into an eventful patriotic show among A&M students. The occasion, as everyone knows, was the reception of the startling news of Japan's infamous attack on the U.S. possessions in the Pacific. The first inkling of the already expected but not realized trouble came via the radio about one o'clock Sunday afternoon. The news, spreading like the traditional wildfire, kept Aggies huddled about their radios most of the day....Enthusiasm plus patriotic devotion reached its pitch when the students met in a special assembly Monday morning at eleven o'clock to hear President Roosevelt make his war declaration over the radio.

Campus life after Pearl Harbor was a drastic change. Gathering at the student commons after meals, we maintained bravado, but our conversation was laced with apprehension. Young men were torn between enlisting immediately or finishing a semester before being drafted. Beneath the uncertainty and bleak news from the Pacific Theater, however, was a quiet determination that we were all together in the struggle.

Mother was not well, with a "pre-cancerous" condition that required radiation, so I spent many weekends at home. Going to the Monticello town square, I looked for someone from home and a ride to Tillar. Gasoline and tires were rationed. Sometimes, on Saturdays, I worked at Mr. Willie's Grocery and sold "a nickel plug of backy" (tobacco), or dime's worth of cheese and crackers. Home offered great food in contrast to college. Campus food was routinely tasteless, except for a pineapple-apple pie made by chef Cornelius von Peski, known as "Corney." He saved a slice for me when I missed dinner because of post office duty. Just off the campus was "Eddie P.'s"—a country store cafe where Eddie P. Kimbro and family prepared a good meal for 25 cents—two pieces of fried chicken, mashed potatoes, peas or green beans, and cornbread with iced tea. Sodas were 5 cents and desserts were 10 cents. Anyone having an extra quarter would head to Eddie P.'s.

The summer of 1942 brought both excitement and sadness. Mother was a woman far ahead of her time. In the spring of 1942, I came home to a startling announcement. "Sit down," said Mother. "I have something to tell you. You have graduated from high school in a small town and have gone to a small college, so you have not had any cosmopolitan experiences. The Tillar School Board has given teachers a bonus to attend summer school, and you and I are going to the University of Chicago!"

From a tiny town to a great metropolis filled with fine museums, art, and cultural facilities—I was surprised beyond speech, and delighted beyond bounds. I later learned that a classmate, Derrick Swantz of McGehee, had a summer job in Chicago steel mills. He was marking time until called into military service. Mom and I planned to attend a late-summer session in the university's wartime schedule, and I enrolled for the first summer session at A&M where Mother had a part-time job.

Our train trip from McGehee to Chicago, via Memphis, was an "all-nighter," filled with noisy servicemen and few women. A soldier, Bill Miller, asked me to join him for a ginger ale in the club car, and I learned he had been a law student at Michigan U. Arriving in Chicago, we took a cab to 56th Street, where we had rented a five-room apartment through the university. A family from Fort Smith, Arkansas, became our neighbors. Delicatessens on 55th St. were handy, and there I saw my first paper carton of milk, as we previously had bottles delivered to our house. The "L" line (elevated train) was accessible on 63rd St. where we found four theatres, confectioners, shops, and tap rooms.

Registration, I wrote in a diary, was "12 cards, 5 places, 2 hours." I was in public administration classes taught by Professor White, and Mom was in Library Science School, with Professor Hanne as the instructor. When I met my first class, I felt swamped, but I learned more than the subject because great diversity was reflected in the 50 assembled.

Many opportunities enlarged my cultural perspective. We heard Frederick Marriott in an organ and carillon recital at Rockefeller Memorial Chapel, and saw the University Players in Steinbeck's *The Moon Is Down*. We admired the International House with its beautiful halls and sitting room, and I dated a Filipino PhD. We toured the marvelous Art Institute; laughed at the hilarious stage show, *My Sister Eileen*, downtown; savored the exhibits at the Field Museum; and attended the symphony's "starlight series."

One afternoon, we went to the Chicago Theater where we heard Benny Goodman featuring Peggy Lee, the Ross Sisters, and Harry Reso. The movie was *They All Kissed the Bride*, starring Melvyn Douglas and Joan Crawford. Goodman played some of my then-favorites, such as "One

O'clock Jump" and "Somebody Else Is Taking My Place." Admission to the movie and big-band show (about 45 minutes) was 50 cents.

Derrick Swantz kindly escorted me to other movies featuring big bands in intermission shows, and we also swam in Lake Michigan. We heard the bands of Jimmy Dorsey, Tommy Dorsey, Alvino Rey, and Cab Calloway.

All was grand until late August when we were notified of a family tragedy just before we were to leave for home. Mother had a vivid dream in which my brother Julian (then 26) appeared to her. He was an army medic, serving as an operating room technician in the Pacific, and we had not heard from him in months. About noon the next day, a Western Union courier came to our apartment with a telegram from the War Department. Julian was dead. Only later did we learn that he had been killed when a Jeep overturned during maneuvers August 19, having previously survived the Philippines' fall to the Japanese by swimming to Bataan and later escaping to Australia.

I had had to grow up at eight when my father died. I took charge in Chicago and packed for the mournful train trip home.

Despite the terrible end to that summer, I treasure the experience. Returning for my junior year at A&M College, I needed to spend weekends with Mother at home. Mabel and Madge Moore, our cherished "roomers" who had become family, were of great comfort.

Student enrollment was decimated by the war, down to 200 or so at A&M. I was the only student in junior economics and a senior history course. There was no question of being prepared. I answered directly and I learned greatly from these classes taught by Dr. J. R. Hodges and Dr. Horace Adams. Ensuing semesters would boost enrollment with a navy V-12 program for potential pilots.

If I were to study journalism, I needed to transfer to Louisiana State University in Baton Rouge. LSU offered easier access, because of train service, than did the University of Arkansas in Fayetteville. Getting to Fayetteville was iffy—if and when the buses ran.

Christmas was a sad, sad 18th birthday for me. Uncle Bancroft tried to lighten our days by hosting Mother and me at the Memphis Peabody Hotel and having an orchestra play "Happy Birthday."

The following February 1, I undertook the challenge of my first solo trip to Baton Rouge. Mother took me to the 9 p.m. Missouri Pacific train in McGehee. I was fortunate to have a sleeping berth, but I would have to rise by 3:30 a.m. in order to disembark at Addis, Louisiana, 30 minutes later. I had only one piece of luggage, well worn from A&M years, and had shipped a steamer trunk with clothes and linens ahead. At Addis, I found a cab driven by Mr. Delahaye, who said he'd take me to the ferry on the Mississippi River. He was an unfailingly polite older man who called me "little lady." Once on the Baton Rouge side, I could get another cab—if lucky—to the campus. Later, when necessary, I walked with my suitcase to a bus stop, Stroube's Drug Store corner.

At LSU, I decided to major in sociology and take as many journalism courses as I could. A full journalism major would require additional study, an expense I could avoid. Register I did, but my trunk did not arrive for another week, leaving me with very limited outfits for sorority rush. Matching hats, purses, and shoes were fashionable. However, it wasn't accessories, just changes, I needed.

Highland Hall, my dorm, provided suites for coeds. My pleasant roommate was Margaret Abernathy of Texarkana, Arkansas, and our suitemates were Tillie Dasher and Rachel Parks of Valdosta, Georgia. Instead of sorority houses, we had chapter rooms in the Pan-Hellenic building, and I was delighted to receive a bid from Pi Beta Phi.

Journalism School most fascinated me because it housed the offices and printing plant for the *Reveille* student newspaper. I immediately sought to report for the *Reveille*, and like most students, watched (or dreaded) the sharp red pencil of Dr. James Price, faculty advisor who "marked up" the issues after they were published. Jimmy Price's corrections and observations could be stinging, but provided great teaching. Eddie Jackson was the affable composing room supervisor from whom I learned.

Close-knit, the *Reveille* staff worked until "the paper was put to bed" about 9 or 10 p.m. We often gathered for a late snack or occasionally for dinner at Brechtel's Restaurant on Highland Road. Gus Levy, our cartoonist, drew on the tablecloths there, and I never knew how the management responded.

One evening at Brechtel's, we were joined by a group of soldiers, former ROTC cadets at LSU called to active duty. They had been sent to Aberdeen Proving Grounds, Maryland, for basic training and returned to LSU for more study. That evening was memorable because the soldiers included my future life partner, Melvin John Schexnayder. I had previously wondered how to pronounce Schexnayder (Shex-nyder), but I was to pronounce and spell it for others for my lifetime!

Dr. Price asked me to attend summer school, making me eligible for the editorship at the *Reveille*, but I had committed to a summer position at the *McGehee Times* since I could live with my sorrowing mother.

Black Ink Was Magic

On my first fully paying job, $20 a week as assistant editor of the *McGehee Times* weekly in 1943, I was the girl in the corner much like Norman Rockwell painted in a New England country newspaper office.

A triangular "front office" was so arranged that the publisher, W. M. Jackson, and bookkeeper-society editor, Mary Elizabeth Haley, had the principal desks. Just a summer worker, I had a typing table and a small desk. "Assistant" was a better title than editor, for I wrote whatever was needed, sold advertising, waited on customers needing classified ads or office supplies, engaged in proofreading, and dabbled in making up pages of metal type.

I didn't mind inky hands or long hours. I was fully smitten with the newspaper business.

Often I left home in Tillar, five miles from McGehee, at 7:30 a.m. Having no car, I had regular rides with neighbors John Haisty, owner of a feed and seed store in McGehee, or Virgil Peacock, who managed a furniture store there. I learned from these two—Mr. Haisty assessed the farming picture, and Virgil focused on McGehee business and events. If they weren't available, L. M. Gary of Dumas, manager of the ration office in McGehee, offered transportation. I didn't get home until 6 or 6:30 in the evening. Often, I brought notes to write more stories. Gathering the news was a fascination that I never relinquished.

Years at the *McGehee Times* mostly reflected World War II. Having lost my only sibling in the Pacific, I could empathize with the gold star banners hanging in front windows of homes ... or the black ones signifying missing in action.

In a prevailing style of one-column makeup, a story I thought merited a two-column headline was "Sgt. Billie Seamans Recounts Adventures in Atlantic Area." The lead told the story: "St. Patrick's Day is really lucky for the Irish," declared Sgt. Billie Seamans, an aerial gunner whose Irish luck saved him and two Irish crew members when their A-20c Boston Bomber crashed into the Atlantic Ocean.

Front-page news often mirrored the war: classifications by the Desha County draft board, Office of Price Administration bulletins like cutting tomato juice ration point costs in half, updates on local servicemen, and even a story in which SEABEES, Navy construction unit, recruited enlistees who would be "paid $76 to $126 per month." The Red Cross chapter sought people to make knitted garments, and a local effort organized a United Service Organization to provide cookies, tea, and coffee for servicemen in the area.

On the first issue, I was a dud as a proofreader, as a story ended with "etaoin" several times. This occurred when a linotype operator ran fingers horizontally across the keys, etaoin shrudlu, to see if the machine was functioning properly and then forgot to remove the offending line.

Rationing being a subject of interest, I wrote, "One store reported Monday they had only one nine and some threes left in ladies shoe wear.... Frustrated merchants and disappointed buyers who waited until the last minute, now shake their heads over number 18 ration stamps effective until Oct. 31 and wonder what kind of shoes can be bought with them."

Just seven miles northeast was a relocation center housing Japanese Americans who had been moved from the West Coast. It might as well have been seven hundred miles away, as we had only casual contact with the detainees who came to McGehee for supplies. We did publish a story stating that a congressional committee said the Japanese should be released from relocation centers.

Relations sometimes were strained, as the *Rohwer Outpost* newspaper from the center taunted the McGehee baseball team after they fell 24-0 to Rohwer. Of the McGehee team, the newspaper wrote: "The Caucasian nine was a poor example of a baseball team, playing without suits, some players playing barefoot, smoking on the field of play, and otherwise turning the game into a farce."

That ill will factored into an incident at Howell Drug Store in which the locals and Japanese visitors tried to shove one another from stools at the soda fountain. After an editorial questioning the behavior of Japanese coming into McGehee businesses, the *Times* followed with this editorial:

> As for those really loyal Japanese-Americans and their valiant sons in the armed services, we think as do thousands of other Americans that a great mistake has been made, a colossal blunder. They should have been left in their homes to work and contribute their part toward the war effort rather than be made an additional burden of the taxpayers. There can be no doubt that the evacuation and concentration of loyal Japanese has been a

blow to their loyalty for it is entirely foreign to what they and children have been taught Democracy is. But if there are good and sufficient reasons about which we have not been informed, then why have we not also evacuated and concentrated our German and Italian minorities in vital eastern manufacturing centers and other places?

Price controls were in effect. Making certain they had fair prices, four beauty and barbershops advertised a hair cut at 50 cents and shampoo and set at $1. McGehee Bank showed $2 million in assets for the first time in history, resulting in another two-column headline. Another two-column banner was "Sgt. Jackie Morrison describes his 8,000 foot jump from a crashing B-17." Motorists were reminded they had to endorse gasoline ration stamps with vehicle license numbers. Letters from servicemen were featured in most issues, providing a personal touch not available in metropolitan media. When a column didn't quite fill allotted space, we used a line, "V—FOR VICTORY." Occasional grocery ads showed sirloin steak at 40 cents a pound, corn meal 8 cents for 24 ounces, salt jowls at 15 cents a pound, and watermelons at 69 cents each.

Three months' work at the *McGehee Times* sent me back to LSU with "real experience," enough for a position as the *Reveille*'s campus editor.

Most significantly, I was again to see my life-partner-to-be, Melvin Schexnayder. We were just "friends," sometimes double-dating others. Our warm friendship was interrupted when additional army training intervened. Scheduled for Officer Candidate School, Melvin was injured in training, suffering a shoulder separation followed by an operation and pneumonia. He spent 45 days at Harding Field Hospital in Baton Rouge, where I visited him. The injury made him late for his OCS class, and the army did not allow any recuperation time or leave at home before he had to report to Aberdeen, Maryland. I still wonder how he managed to complete officer training.

Then a full-fledged senior, I dearly enjoyed supervising the flow of *Reveille* copy, working on the final pages and corrections, and watching Eddie Jackson and his staff make up forms for printing. Those times reinforced the magic of black ink.

One learning experience was Reporting II, in which students worked at the *Baton Rouge Morning Advocate* and wrote under the tutelage of Maggie Dixon, managing editor and one of the best newspaperwomen I've known. She suggested I find my own feature stories.

One day I went to the Baton Rouge City Jail and asked to be locked in with women prisoners to write a story about their experiences. It was a true awakening, as I didn't realize how tough were the prisoners or circumstances which brought them there. Another time, I was in a group of reporters covering the visit of presidential candidate Wendell Willkie. I couldn't seem to catch up with him as he walked from the community center, so I just vaulted out of a low first-floor window to get some way to reach him. That was the only time I jumped out of a window to get a story.

Covering the "agriculture beat" the previous semester, I continued to write features, attracting the attention of Marjorie Arbough, Cooperative Extension Service editor, who offered me a position as feature writer-photographer. The salary was attractive, and I accepted when I completed my degree requirements in March 1944. I accompanied agents around Louisiana and wrote features for state and national publications including *Progressive Farmer* and *Farm Journal*. I liked the people and the job, and received additional offers, from a daily newspaper and national magazine. Oh, but I missed the lure of a newspaper office!

Publisher W. M. Jackson of the *McGehee Times* called in August 1944 to offer me $40 a week as editor—not assistant—and a month later, I headed "home" to live with my mother and commute to McGehee. I was told my salary was the best offered to journalism grads that year.

6.
Just a Girl

My return to McGehee on October 2, 1944, was hardly auspicious. In my neat jacket, pleated skirt, and saddle oxfords, I greeted a customer in the front office.

"I want to see the editor," he demanded.

"I am she."

Came his retort: "You can't possibly be. You're just a girl!"

Just a girl who had dreamed of this day most of her young life! Just a girl who found excitement in the gritty backshop with its pungent ink and her own office with its manual Underwood.

"Girl editor" might not have been possible before, but men were off to fight World War II. Because I had lost my only sibling in the war and my mother was a widow, I could not volunteer for the service. Openings for women were obvious with so many men away at war, and I didn't intend to fail as an editor. Neither did Bertha Adams of McGehee, a dedicated war worker who set a record for 1,800 rivets an hour at the Consolidated Bomber Plant in Fort Worth.

As editor, I had do-all responsibilities: write news, features, and editorials; sell advertising; and supervise makeup of pages. Also, I would take orders for job printing and sell office supplies in the front office when Mary Elizabeth Haley, bookkeeper and society editor, and the owner, W. M. Jackson, weren't there.

My first editorial called for local initiative in solving drainage woes of the flat southeast Arkansas Delta. Mr. Jackson gave me the latitude to write editorials as I saw them. Other local issues focused on the need for a garbage collection service and a municipal airport.

Country correspondents from the Dumas, Kelso-Kurdo, Gum Ridge, Halley, Tillar, Neal, Arkansas City, and Winchester areas filled much of the interior pages along with the McGehee social news or "society."

Only two weeks after I became editor, my job was to write the obituary of a close friend, Henry Prewitt of Tillar, killed in a foxhole in France. He and twin Jesse were like brothers to me. As I look back at that obituary, I dismiss the typos in it, no doubt unseen because of tears.

War news dominated the front pages of every issue: casualties, local heroes getting medals, war bonds, blood drives, military promotions, and draft board action.

War also dominated the editorial pages, attested by this personal-approach editorial to help McGehee meet its war bond quota of $350,000:

> How Can You Be Complacent When...
> Major Julius Hellums of Dumas needs medical supplies for sick and wounded soldiers at a hospital in Atlanta, Ga.?
> Cpl. Horace Peacock, overseas for more than two years and winner of the Bronze Star, has to have photographic supplies for his role as squadron photo man?
> Sgt. Ben Martin of McGehee as a supply sergeant in England needs supplies to give his group?
> Sgt. Marvin Shook of Rohwer, wounded in the first day of action on Leyte, requires medical attention at a hospital in the South Pacific?
> Lt. (j.g.) Jimmy Saine of Watson of the Merchant Marines is sailing the seas in a ship that War Bonds buy?
> Lester Warrick, Jr. is in action in the Philippines and is in need of ammunition and food?
> Veteran of Saipan and battle-hardened Marine, Pfc. Archie Vinson of Arkansas City knows how much effort is needed to finish the war in the Pacific?

So you see you can't afford to be complacent. Your duty is to buy
more and more war bonds.

I also began a collection of news briefs entitled "Talk of the Times,"
and I sought out servicemen on leave for their stories.

Every Friday night, I covered the Owls football team by running
up and down the sidelines and kneeling to see the plays unfold—much
to the jibes of men who didn't believe I knew football, although I was
familiar with the single wing and new T formations. In a great time to
write about high school sports, I could focus on a McGehee High running back, John (Kayo) Dottley, on his way to becoming All-State,
and later All-American and All-Pro. When my sports reporting made
the state newspapers, local fans stopped hooting at me.

Wartime had severely limited advertising because of shortage of
goods, but weekly newspapers then received some national advertising
and a fair amount of legal and political advertising. To supplant ads on
retail, I sometimes sold "signature ads" with area businesses dividing
the cost of patriotic advertising such as for war bonds.

Although it was a closed compound into which relatively few
local citizens ventured, and only a limited number of internees came to
McGehee, Rohwer Relocation Center continued to be a news source.
Toward the end of 1944, the government allowed the unjustly interned
Japanese Americans to begin returning to the western states. At that
time, there were 6,614 living in the hastily constructed barracks at
Rohwer, making it the largest city in the county. Some 3,421 Japanese
Americans had already begun relocating—and none were to remain in
Desha County, where memories probably were too painful.

Also at the end of 1944, I announced a forthcoming military edition, which would require three months of very long days (often 18
hours) for me to gather material and write copy.

In one editorial, I wrote that "McGehee is sleeping. It is not a
slumber from which we can't be aroused, but it is far more than a

doze." Among the suggestions I had were development of new business, diversification of agriculture (beyond the one crop of cotton), a new recreation park, new roads, and a planning commission.

The Office of Price Administration issued new food rationing, putting corn, peas, asparagus, green beans, and spinach on the ration list—not a problem for my mother and me for we always had a vegetable garden at our home in Tillar, and Mother canned.

However, there was dismay that sugar ration coupons 31, 32, 33, and 40 were voided. Said the OPA: "Sugar stocks are feeling the pinch of a long war. Supplies are abnormally low and military needs are high. Ships which otherwise might carry sugar are hauling supplies to the battlefront."

The *Times* was making progress. For my first three months as editor, my office and others were in the backshop or composing room (once the old post office there), while an adjoining building was being remodeled for office space. As foreman of the backshop, Lester Mansur had a perpetual grin and a pipe.

We reported that McGehee Bank had achieved $3,000,000 in assets, and Tillar Bank had $525,000. The American Legion sold $106,940 in war bonds in order to buy a bomber named for McGehee. A box on the front page advised: "Keep your chickens up, or you can be fined $2.50 a day," warns Mayor Faye Joyner, who said he had many complaints about wandering fowls.

News thought worth 60-point type and a banner headline declared: "Army Deserter and Draft Dodger Apprehended by Desha Officers." "Have I got a news story for you!" the big Scotsman and deputy sheriff Alan Templeton had announced as he burst into the *Times* office. Commandeering my Underwood manual, he beat out a staccato with two-finger typing on each hand. He always preferred to type "just the facts"—and then I would question. His big news focused on a deserter and draft dodger who had hidden out in the White River cutoff in Desha County for 13 months. Deputy Templeton, with a flair for the dramatic, explained the capture. "We [Templeton and Deputy Earl May] took the Delta Eagle train to Yancopin [the last stop before the Arkansas River bridge at Benzol]," he explained. "Got off there and bargained for a small boat to take us six miles to the hideout of the deserter." Templeton and May flagged down a train to bring the deserter to McGehee. The draft dodger was an easier catch. He was arrested while posing as a watch repairman in Dumas.

Several weeks later, Deputy Templeton burst into the *Times* office, saying "Step aside. I have another great story for you." He rapidly pecked out the tale of a military policeman, formerly stationed at the Jerome prisoner-of-war camp, committing 33 burglaries while being absent without leave 39 days. This story had repercussions, as the day after it was published under another banner headline, a second lieutenant arrived in the *Times* office and asked for the editor.

The lieutenant looked at me with great disdain. "I am going to sue you for libel," he declared.

"What's wrong with the story?" I asked.

"You had no right to print military news. I am going to sue you for libel," he ranted. He was not the first bully I encountered, nor the last. His "libel suit" was merely hot air, and it wasn't long before he was transferred.

Returning or visiting servicemen often alluded to the malaria prevalent in the Pacific Theater—but it was still a problem in southeast Arkansas as well. The Public Health Service announced that DDT would be used to kill the mosquitoes carrying malaria. I suffered with a bout of malaria the next summer and ringing in my head caused by quinine pills. Malaria was ultimately abated, but the public knew nothing of the adverse effects of DDT.

Civilian news was gathered, but much of the *Times*' front page was devoted to news of local people in the armed forces. We had pride in their accomplishments such as Lt. (j.g.) Roy Rushing's exploits as a naval air ace, joy at the liberation of Chief Machinist Mate John

Porter Collins in the Philippines, and sorrow at the loss of Pvt. Lawrence Shook, once missing in action, being declared dead. We also featured a military photo of Buddy Oliver, home on leave and once our star paperboy who sold 600 copies on McGehee streets.

The *Times* won the excellence division of the Arkansas Press Association contests in 1945. I went to Little Rock to receive the trophy. Hamilton Moses, revered president of Arkansas Power & Light Co., presided at the event, and after I had received the award, said to me: "Little Lady, I apologize. I thought you came along for the ride."

Women editors were a novelty. So much so that the APA leaders thought it would be great fun to provide tuxedo-clad "gigolo" escorts for Esther Bindursky of Lepanto and me. While not many women held titles as editors, there were many husband-wife teams in which the women were outstanding.

In addition to being editor, I was named to wartime committees, from war bonds to Red Cross. In the midst of regular duties, I spent every available minute to compile material for the special military edition of the *Times*. I worked every night and weekends in writing copy and devoted daytime hours to ad selling. Published March 15, 1945, the edition was a whopping success—44 pages with hundreds of military photos and stories and some large advertisements from area businesses. I was able to sell advertising in Arkansas City, Tillar, Dumas, Winchester, and Rohwer (where we also featured Japanese American servicemen).

Composition by linotype and printing by a hand-fed press made us tackle this edition by sections which could be stacked and then gathered by hand into the final product. When the final pages came off the press, I took a short nap on a stack of newsprint next to the press.

Our efforts at the *Times* were recognized in an editorial in the *Arkansas Gazette*, stating:

> In a 44-page Military Edition, The *McGehee Times* has made a valuable contribution to the record of Arkansas' part in this war. It is a document that will aid and simplify the work of future his-

torians. This special edition is designed to serve the purpose of a memorial to those who have given their lives for our country and to present a detailed account of Desha County in war. The *McGehee Times* tells, so far as it is possible, who Desha County's boys and girls in uniform are, and in many instances where they are. One section has an In Memoriam to the score of Japanese who went to war and to death from the Rohwer Relocation Center and a roster of the 866 who enlisted.

The section also drew the plaudits of the *Shreveport Times*, which commended the inclusion of Japanese Americans, saying in part: "The *McGehee Times*—in Desha County, Arkansas—recently issued a special edition on servicemen in Desha County. It devoted a full page to the Japanese blood-American citizens who once lived in Rohwer Relocation Center or whose next of kin live there." The edition's success dictated a sequel, in which we would publish photos and stories of county service men and women not included in the first publication.

Time stood still at the news that President Franklin D. Roosevelt had died at Warm Springs, Georgia, a message received via radio in April 1945. Every community held memorial services, and businesses closed the day of the president's national funeral. Services were held in churches, schools, and even in front of Gem Theatre in Dumas.

McGehee Association of Commerce was beginning to think post-war, and *Times* publisher W. M. Jackson, by then a state senator, suggested Highway 1, the loop road from McGehee to Watson to Dumas, be extended to Marianna.

Collection of clothing to aid the war-stricken countries overseas began in McGehee with admission to a movie being five pounds of clothing. The United Nations Clothing Drive gained over 2,500 pounds of clothing from McGehee.

Almost every edition of the *Times* included stories of men and women wounded, missing, or killed in action. Writing these was difficult as it involved contacting their families and sharing their sorrow.

When the war in Europe ended, I sought the largest wood type we had (3 and ½ inches high) for a double-line headline saying "Germans Surrender." Alas, there were not enough R's available in the font. I pondered and pondered, and finally found enough letters for "Germans Quit War." For several decades, I was kidded about that headline until my family saw it on another front page of a major daily at the Truman Library in Independence, Missouri.

More important, the German surrender issue included our first documentation of the Nazi extermination of the Jewish people, a story just beginning to be known to the American people. A first-hand report of seeing the horror of Buchenwald was sent by Capt. W. W. Bledsoe to a sister in McGehee and was made available to the *Times*. Later, it was incomprehensible to me that we knew so very little about the Holocaust.

In late 1944 and early 1945, I eagerly awaited letters from Europe. Melvin Schexnayder was on "limited service" because of an injury, but after completing OCS, volunteered for overseas duty and was in the European campaign. Love was blossoming long distance.

Melvin, a second lieutenant in 848 Ordnance Company, landed in France in late fall 1944. His unit joined in support of General Patton's forces in the battle for Germany. On August 16, 1945, his unit was aboard a troop ship in Marseilles, France, as it awaited deployment to the Battle of Japan. They had shipped their ordnance depot to the Far East in readiness. Then came the great news: the Japanese had surrendered and World War II was over. After three days on ship, Melvin learned his outfit would be heading home—one act of good fortune at the end of a terrible experience he would remember all his life.

7.
Wedding Bells

After landing at Newport News, Virginia, and traveling by train to New Orleans, Melvin visited his family in Weeks Island, Louisiana, and called to see if I could meet him in Baton Rouge. I definitely could. My esteemed cousin Jake Conner and wife Irene lived at the Heidelberg Hotel where Jake was manager. They would be happy to have me visit and meet "the lieutenant."

That wasn't enough of a visit. In the next few weeks, Melvin rode a train to McGehee so he could visit me in Tillar and meet my mother and friends. He passed review with ease, as they immediately enjoyed his intelligence, humor, and good manners. He was being reassigned to California, but we made serious plans for Christmas.

He returned with a diamond ring and a marriage proposal after Christmas Eve's Midnight Mass, providing a joyful 22nd birthday. For the New Year holiday, we were guests of the Conners in Baton Rouge, and Jake hosted an engagement party at the restaurant atop the Heidelberg Hotel. Another treat was attending the Sugar Bowl.

We were gloriously happy and it would have been wonderful to marry at that time. Reality and responsibility intervened. We needed to save enough in order to return to LSU where Melvin would complete his chemical engineering degree. Melvin headed for military duty in California, and we kept in close touch by phone—and saved our dollars.

After duty in the West, Melvin was sent to Hattiesburg, Mississippi, for discharge from the U.S. Army in April 1946. Mabel Moore and fiancé Horace Peacock took me for the anxiously awaited reunion at the Greenville, Mississippi, bus station. Melvin visited in Tillar before going to Weeks Island for several months with his parents and a summer laboratory job at Bay Chemical Co. In June, I met his family, whom I immediately liked. Although the Acadian culture differed from the Arkansas Delta, I was warmly welcomed by a traditional French-German family. Weeks Island sits atop a salt dome, and one of my memories is of descending 600 feet into the salt mine to observe its operations.

The sports passion of Weeks Island centered on its baseball team, on which Melvin was the agile second baseman and his brother-in-law, Gilbert Darcey, the catcher par excellence. On a Sunday afternoon, we all turned out for a game. Melvin didn't have to impress me, but in the ninth inning, he hit the game-winning double. Celebration erupted.

Melvin and I wanted a small wedding, but there were constraints. I was editor of the *McGehee Times* and knew most everyone in the surrounding area. Mother thought we should have a big wedding; she had eloped and had always regretted it. Many asked if they would be invited. How could I say no? Big wedding won.

I was a Presbyterian and Melvin was a Catholic, but we had agreed on a Catholic ceremony with Father W. J. Kordsmeier officiating.

Because of wartime paper shortages, I found only 250 invitations for printing at the *Times* plant. There was no church large enough for that kind of crowd. Mother had the grand idea of booking the Tillar High School gymnasium, which she would transform into a forest of pine and magnolia leaves, with help from faithful Mabel Moore and Mamie Hale, who resided in our Tillar home. Friends, notably Annabelle and Glenn Rice, pitched in. Melvin came to spend the week before our August 18 wedding as guest of the Rices, and he and Glenn spent much time in polishing antique candelabra we borrowed.

Then, it took our village to stage the wedding.

Mother hosted a noon luncheon at the Greystone Hotel in McGehee for the families and close friends. That violated the superstition foretelling bad luck if the groom sees the bride 24 hours before their wedding. However, on August 18, 1946, Melvin and I threw old customs away. In the afternoon before the 7 p.m. ceremony, we went to admire the transformed gym-auditorium.

Four hundred came to the wedding. I was given in marriage by my uncle, Bancroft Terry, and wore a long-sleeved bridal gown lent by my grand friend, Betty Davidson Prewitt. Attendants were cousin Connie Terry Smith and Melvin's brother-in-law, Gilbert Darcey. Robert Harrell and Jesse Prewitt were ushers. Our musicians were Cousin Rena (Mrs. Virgil Harrell), pianist, Miss Allie Bess (Mrs. M. R. Davidson), vocalist, and Frankie Davidson, violinist. With no place to put all those attending or even sugar for a wedding cake, there was no reception. Bancroft planned to serve champagne at our Tillar home, but he was mixed up in the joy of the moment and poured sparkling burgundy for us.

Our wedding trip was by train, as we had no car. Half of the Tillar population followed us to McGehee to see us off amid a rice shower on the 9 p.m. train. With us was cousin Constance Terry, who had married Homer Smith in Little Rock two days previously. While other passengers focused on us in the club car, we laughed about the newlyweds being accompanied by the matron of honor.

After our honeymoon at the Albert Pike Hotel in Little Rock and Arlington Hotel in Hot Springs, we returned to Tillar to gather our belongings and head for Baton Rouge. Melvin planned to finish his degree in a year, and he would receive $90 monthly on the GI Bill. I enrolled in graduate classes in journalism and obtained a job as secretary of the journalism school at $110 a month, $20 more than a graduate assistantship I was offered.

With so many veterans seeking to return to college, housing was very scarce. At first, we managed to rent a room with limited kitchen privileges, and we did not need major furnishings. Our fine china, silver, and crystal were left in Tillar. Mother had lent her car for us to move, and we planned to return it at Christmas.

My secretarial skills were extremely limited, except for fast typing, but I could handle paper grading with ease for Dr. Marvin Osborn, Journalism School director. I developed a lasting friendship with Roselia Callaghan, J-School librarian, and enjoyed graduate classes in journalism and history.

By the next semester, Melvin was able to use his veteran's preference in renting a house which we shared with Methodist minister Clifford Zircle and his family. We had the upstairs, they lived downstairs, and we jointly used the kitchen.

With no vehicle, we traveled on a very limited basis, by train or bus. And we walked with our groceries. We generally had no extra money, and one month, we ended with only 32 cents in the bank account. We were supremely happy. There was no stigma to being poor—other "GI couples" were just like us.

Awarded his degree in June 1947, Melvin was offered a graduate assistantship in chemical engineering and a job at the sugar factory on campus. I continued at the Journalism School as secretary/grad student.

For the summer session, Melvin managed to sub-let a professor's apartment in former barracks housing. Mother came to spend the summer there. In her car, we saw more of the area and had simple pleasures like enjoying bread fresh from the bakery and tasty seafood at Piccadilly Cafeteria. In graduate school and on staff, we had privileges at the Faculty Club, where we sometimes savored their delightful fare.

By fall, we had our own apartment. However, it was time for a major decision. I had developed food allergies and had lost much weight from my then-spare frame. Melvin found classes tiring and was ready to get in the workforce. In early 1948, he accepted a chemical engineering position (and company car) with the Texas & Pacific Railroad, and we moved to Marshall, Texas.

His job involved analyzing oil and water samples for steam engines. I always dreaded the possibility that he might dislocate his lame shoulder when he climbed the company water tanks for samples.

More often, he was in the company laboratories or on a train going as far as Pecos, Texas—800 miles away. The job demanded five to six days a week on the road, leaving us miserable with little home life.

Mother came to visit in Marshall in the summer of 1948. Melvin drove her 1937 Plymouth there, and on the back was a coop of chickens from Tillar. We had a flat tire on the way, and a man who stopped to help us was much amused. However, we thought the fried chicken was very tasty that summer.

My solution while Melvin was constantly traveling was to read and keep our domicile, all the while missing the news business. Occasionally, I traveled with him and particularly remember the dust storms in West Texas. Neither of us was content away from the other.

In late summer, we received a telegram from W. M. Jackson, owner of the *McGehee Semi-Weekly Times*. He asked if we would come to McGehee as editor and advertising manager. Melvin had never sold advertising, but had done well in business courses in graduate school. Tired of his constant traveling, we said to one another: "Let's try the newspaper business for a year."

Little did we then realize, it would last a half-century.

8.
A Return to McGehee

In a return for me and new adventure for Melvin, we became the staff at the *McGehee Semi-Weekly Times* in September 1948. Disillusioned by constant travel and repetitiveness of his chemical engineering career with the Texas Pacific Railroad, Melvin was fully open to changing direction. In LSU graduate school, he had enjoyed his business courses more than engineering and undoubtedly had a "better head for business" than I.

We called it "a year experiment" to determine whether Melvin liked the newspaper business I loved. Never was there any doubt that he could do the job.

We moved into my childhood home in Tillar—already expanded to three bedrooms, one for us, one for Mother, and one for boarder Mamie Hale. One bathroom sufficed. It was a pleasant arrangement. Mamie often joined her husband Bob, who worked elsewhere, for weekends. Melvin and I daily drove to McGehee to work. Our transportation was upgraded when Mother sold her 1937 Plymouth for $700, its cost when new 10 years earlier, in trade on a new green Kaiser.

The semi-weekly newspaper operation involved publishing Wednesdays and Saturdays, the later presenting an opportunity to cover Friday night sports in detail. Melvin sold the advertising and wrote sports. I wrote and edited other copy, except for the "society" or family news handled by Mary Elizabeth Haley, and planned makeup of pages. We crossed over duties as needed, and as necessary, I waited on customers buying office supplies.

We worked long hours, with little time off, but we were meeting the challenge. Each month enhanced our learning curve in publishing. Business was brisk as rural areas sought to catch up from shortages during World War II. McGehee depended on the Missouri Pacific Railroad for some 500 jobs, but agriculture also was a sustainer.

Melvin became active in the Lions Club and district Boy Scout leadership. I promoted many projects, including a community concert series at the local theater, where Florence Henderson was among the performers.

At home, Melvin was a master gardener and grew most of our vegetables. We also had range chickens until we decided to try the laying hen business on the side. Using an old garage on the vacant lot Mother owned, we adapted it for a hen house. Together, Melvin and I mixed and poured a concrete floor for it. Never again! Melvin wired the structure and built the nests.

We bought 150 registered Rhode Island Red pullets, but alas, when they were at full laying size, Newcastle disease invaded the flock. We had to destroy and burn those stricken birds, leaving less than half the flock. The remaining hens produced beautiful brown eggs, which we sold at premium prices, and all the while totally dismissed the idea of a poultry production career.

For spring and summer recreation, we enjoyed tennis on the grass court Melvin fashioned on our vacant lot. Despite his shoulder injury, he was an excellent player, and I was mediocre. We listened to baseball on radio, and occasionally enjoyed a trip to St. Louis to see the Cardinals play. Mother, proudly showing the batting stance of Stan Musial when asked, was almost as big a baseball fan as Melvin.

In 1949, my brother Julian's remains, interred since 1942 in Australia, were returned to the United States. This brought peace for Mother. She thought the military escort accompanying the casket was much like "Sonny," as we called Julian. I had been very ill with colitis, but the funeral procession stopped at our house and Melvin carried me to the car so that I could go to the cemetery.

A joy in our lives was "Mr. Willie" Harrell, Mother's suitor. Witty and lively, he was probably a decade older than Mother and was my father's first cousin. He always came for Sunday night supper with us and remained to visit Mother. Mr. Willie begged Mother to marry him, and she often said no. Finally, she said she might consider it. However, he died of a heart attack, robbing our lives of joy and good humor.

Our time off included Sunday afternoon (after going to morning Mass in McGehee), and frequently there were visitors. Mother's Uncle Sam Terry came from St. Charles to renew kinship. Also, we took the Kaiser on afternoon drives through the countryside.

These were busy, but never frantic years. Our happiness knew few bounds, except we desperately wanted a family. As a child eight years younger than my brother, I had thought six children of my own would be perfect. When I was finally pregnant in 1951, I had a devastating miscarriage, leaving me very ill in the Dermott hospital. Emotionally drained, Melvin and I decided to begin the adoption process, then very tedious and long.

Melvin and I were convinced we could successfully own and operate a weekly newspaper, and we began looking around the area. Where would we get the capital? Mother offered her house as collateral, but we wanted to undertake the purchase on our own. We had saved diligently over the years and also had the funds from our laying hen operation. We were frugal, but never stingy. The McGehee Times was not for sale, so we investigated other opportunities in Bastrop, Louisiana, and Crossett, Arkansas.

In early 1953, we learned I was pregnant, necessitating a reduced work load and more rest. We were cautiously elated, and despite a scare or two, everything was going well until I learned in September that the baby was in breech position. That meant seeing a specialist, Dr. Rodgers, in Little Rock. He decreed that as I neared delivery, I would have to live in Little Rock in order to get quickly to a hospital. Thus, Mother and I took a room at the Lafayette Hotel and our meals at Franke's Cafeteria for 10 days. Melvin worked at the *McGehee Times* and anxiously awaited, while Uncle Burt Terry was "driver on call" for the trip to St. Vincent's Infirmary.

Melvin John Schexnayder Jr. arrived safely on October 10, 1953. He was bruised by forceps, and I had multiple stitches, but both of us were fine.

Melvin, who had raced from Tillar in record time, and Mother were there to hold seven-pound, three-ounce John before I fully awakened. Melvin thought John was grandest baby he had ever seen. "Precious, precious," Mother kept repeating, as she thought of John all of her life.

Melvin returned to work and Mother to teaching at Tillar High while John and I remained in the hospital for a week. Upon our return home, there was little sleep. I was unable to nurse John, and none of the formulas seemed to agree with him. I took the first half of the night to rock him, and Melvin, the second half, with the 4 a.m. train often waking John when Melvin had just gotten him to sleep.

Never complaining, Melvin worked through this scenario, and to help, I wrote from home. Happy and yet stressed, we welcomed an opportunity to buy our own newspaper in early 1954.

Years at the *McGehee Times* had taught us the skills needed to publish our own newspaper. We already had the desire, perseverance, and ability to work long hours.

Truths we had learned included these:

Manage with one-boss rule, editorially. A showdown with a composing room foreman who sought to direct all operations quickly taught me that I had to control content and deadlines. I made editorial decisions and always faced the consequences.

Believe in your community, and the people will join you. Many communities depend on their newspaper publishers/owners for leadership.

Plain hard work exceeds inspiration, probably in proportion of 90/10.

Never leave to others some job you should do. A staff will seek to excel when the editor-publisher sets the standard.

Listen for the "little stories." They often are the most compelling because they touch the human heart. I once gained wisdom from interviewing a 90-year-old who said, "When ah walks, ah walks slow; when ah rocks, ah rocks easy; and when ah worries, ah goes to sleep."

Expect the broadly flung daggers. I didn't cause trouble but was blamed for reporting it. Many would rather blame the messenger than the culprit. Moreover, it seems more fun to fire at the messenger.

Remember that you are writing current history, and make every effort to get it right.

Rely on some humor during tough times. It's the best antidote.

If the job isn't fun, find another. I looked forward to every day. I was the eternal optimist; Melvin, the pragmatist. Together we knew how to set goals and reach them.

9.
We Were Recruited

After being recruited, we took over the *Dumas Clarion* on March 1, 1954, and faced a March 4 publication. We had named our company Desha County Printing Co. for the county we served.

We decided there would be a lively front page with more than one-column headlines and a feature I would write. The initial feature, with photos, focused on the new elementary school cafeteria, a first for the town. Two columns would become long-standing: "Desha Dispatch," with news bits on the front page, and "Clarion Chatter," my observations on the editorial page.

Our philosophy was stated in the opening editorial: "The new management which today takes over publication of the *Clarion* believes that a newspaper should be a service institution, dedicated to the best interests of the hometown, county, state and nation; devoted to a fair and complete presentation of the news, and engaged in presenting the best possible advertising medium."

We had expected to get the *Clarion* out in time for afternoon sales. Mother and I would split time in keeping baby John and in working at the office as soon as we moved to Dumas. In the meanwhile I would work as much as possible from our home in Tillar and get into the office sporadically.

I completed all the copy for the publication and thought Melvin and Mama would be home in time for supper. When they hadn't arrived by 7, I called.

"What's happening?" I inquired of Melvin.

"We hadn't reckoned with the machinery here," he explained, "but we ought to be home by 9 or 10."

Among the problems he had encountered was that there was no tympan paper—an oily, tough, hard paper—to pack the old Babcock press cylinder. Of inventive mind, Melvin went to Bud Adams's Mercantile and bought cotton batting to pack the press. By the next week, however, we had acquired tympan paper.

Obviously, we needed better machinery, but the income stream was hardly sufficient for immediate changes. Subscriptions were $2.00 a year and $3.00 outside a 40-mile radius of Dumas. Advertising was 25 cents a column inch, and classifieds were 3 cents a word. Single copies of the eight- to twelve-page *Clarion* were 5 cents. We soon had "newsboys" who would buy copies for 3 cents each and make 2 cents profit.

We initiated a church page with signature sponsors paying $5 a week, and the 25 we obtained brought in a then-appreciated $125. For comparison, Wolff Brothers advertised 256 spring and Easter dresses on sale at $5 each. Cokes were 5 cents each, and regular gasoline was 27 cents a gallon at Bowman Station.

Marching on with revenues we could generate, our first effort was to replace the string starter for the press with an electric switch. The newspaper press, early 1900s vintage, required two operators. The pressman hand-fed sheet newsprint from a wooden platform at the side, and a "printer's devil," often a high school part-timer, caught the papers as they sailed off the fly of the drum and kept them neatly stacked. The press capacity was four pages at a time, with the papers being flipped to print four pages on the reverse side. In addition, we had a four-page folder, as undependable as the press.

After a month's publication, we changed the *Clarion* from six-column format to seven-column in order to offer more news and advertising space. We bought new chases, or forms, in which to make up the pages of metal type.

Of the changeover, we wrote: "We are indebted to Jimmy Chambers, printing machinery and paper salesman for Western Newspaper Union (Little Rock), who spent Saturday in our shop and went over the big press inch by inch. It was necessary to make many adjustments, and there was plenty of ink on us when we got through."

Seldom was the country correspondence typed, and we edited and typed it. Sometimes, we could hardly discern a name or spelling. Always interesting, the correspondence presented the flavor of the multiple communities in our area. We had correspondents in Kelso, Neal, Winchester, Tillar, Gould, Jefferson, Cypress Creek, Arkansas City, Wells Bayou, and Webb. After a couple of issues, it became evident we couldn't print all the news we could get, thus prompting the new chases.

We experimented with hand-set type for headlines. There was Bodoni typeface, and occasionally, we went to the bold, wide Cooper. We called the latter type "fish market" because George Wong, fish market owner, always wanted it in his ads while we were in McGehee.

We had been newspaper owners for a month when Mick Westbrook came in and announced he wanted to renew his subscription, then $2 annually. When he handed Mother a $10 bill, she started to give him change. "No, I'll renew for five years," he declared. It was a huge vote of confidence.

We had one bank, Merchants & Farmers, two blocks down Waterman Street, and the Missouri Pacific depot was three blocks away. Both were important to the newspaper. We made our monthly note payments at the bank. Our photos were sent to Little Rock, and later Guthrie, Oklahoma, by the nine p.m. train in order to speed up the needed engravings.

Across the railroad track dividing downtown was the post office—equally important, as our papers were delivered by mail carriers. We were developing a "paper boy system," composed mostly of young boys, often barefoot but not by choice, who sold the papers on the street. This was a new opportunity, and soon we had dozens wanting to make spending money.

Problems inside the plant continued. As we noted, "Because our linotype, the typesetting machine, decided to take a vacation when we wanted it to work, we are having to leave out some of the community news this week and limit the *Clarion* to eight pages. Linotype willing, the news will be in next week's paper." We made up for it—the next week had 12 pages.

We found perspective, however, in how well things were going in the mid-1950s. When I interviewed Dr. C. H. Kimbro of Tillar, our former family physician who had practiced 53 years, he remembered covering a 15-mile radius in a horse and buggy and being home only one night in three months. And he never turned down a call.

Our role was much easier by comparison.

As a signal event approached, Dumas's observance of its 50th anniversary as an incorporated city, I spent every possible moment getting copy ready ahead of time. In celebrating the city's 50 years, we compiled a historical record in a 34-page edition, a record for the *Clarion*. We had a dignified correspondent in West Dumas, Mamie L. Mitchell, who often pronounced church events "a success financially, numerically and spiritually." So it was with that July 29, 1954, edition.

Melvin and I believed in participation in civic events. We borrowed a Model T Ford from Charlie Zieman in Tillar and dressed in 1904 attire. During our drive from Tillar to Dumas, we drew many stares from passing motorists, who must have observed, "There goes an old timey couple." Melvin grew a mustache for the celebration; when he shaved it, baby John didn't recognize him.

We were fortunate to have summer help. We were delighted at the enthusiasm of Edwin Maxson of Watson, our journalism intern from the University of Arkansas in Fayetteville. He wrote a feature on some old settlement remains, believed to be Napoleon, the first county seat of Desha County, which had crumbled block by block into the Mississippi River. W. J. Lempke of the university's journalism department came for a look and said he thought it was Prentiss, Mississippi, a town which had burned during the Civil War. We never resolved the issue, but Mr. Lempke was seldom wrong.

Most of our editorials focused on stimulating development of Dumas in diverse ways, from industrialization to a concert series. At least the editorial idea of an industrial commission came to fruition in several months. Haskell (Hack) Wolff, Chamber president and owner of Wolff Brothers department store, named a committee to begin raising $60,000 for industrial efforts, a significant move for our town.

In observance of National Newspaper Week, we announced an open house, and a few brave souls showed up to inspect our efforts. I wrote: "The weekly newspaper's ability to put into words that which is the heartbeat of the community makes it a vigilant force for human freedom, rights and justice." We reaffirmed our dedication to these causes. In the years to come, we would be tried often as we endeavored to carry out this belief.

I also observed that the two most important traits for a weekly newspaper editor/reporter were "humility and humor—humility at the trust the public places in a weekly newspaper and a sense of humor to offset the long hours and constant problems."

In one of the most unusual stories I covered, we used a four-column headline leading into the story of Cecil Rice, who was facing a trial for first-degree murder in the disappearance of his wife, Agnes. Rice was charged in the crime without evidence of corpus delicti. In the trial, Sheriff Robert S. Moore said that he had obtained two confessions from Rice, the first one on December 12, 1952, when he made a statement saying he had killed his wife, or at least he thought he did. "I found her on the floor, I was unable to awaken her. She was dead. I put her in the river," Rice told him. However, a number of sightings of Agnes Rice were brought by the defense. The jury found Cecil Rice not guilty. To this day, no trace has been found of Agnes Rice.

That story sold many newspapers, but it was the important times in people's lives—births, graduations, weddings, promotions, recognitions, deaths—that the weekly could cover completely and earn a real place in people's lives.

In November, I wrote about moving from Tillar to Dumas, calling it "an exceedingly difficult chore at best but worse when our *Clarion*'s linotype went on the blink." Moving day was most notable because our son John walked for the first time—from the bedroom where he had napped to our kitchen where Mother and I made sandwiches. That trimmed some of the sadness Mother felt at leaving Tillar, where she had lived 54 years.

We had found a house at 322 Court Street, on a dead-end street ending in a cow pasture. Built in 1947, the house included two bedrooms, bath, living room, dining room, kitchen, and cubicle back porch on a 100 x 260 lot. The price was $10,000, and Melvin qualified for a GI loan. Since the ranch-style wasn't large enough for all of us, Mother used her $3,000 prize in a teacher essay sponsored by Lion Company to build a sitting room, bedroom, and bath for herself on the north end. These quarters, to John, were "our room" where he and Gram retreated for her to read to him.

For Christmas, we wished for "some machinery which won't break down on press day, or the day before press day." We wished a Happy New Year to our staff including Linnie Stuart, linotype operator; Joe Fletcher and Leonard Avera Jr., printers; Freddie Williams, printer's devil; and Bertha T. Tillar, who performed a multiplicity of tasks in our office and home. Our hard year was highlighted on Christmas Eve when Mayor Travis Witherington and wife Doris brought a dozen red roses to honor our work. We couldn't have afforded a single blossom.

We could, however, afford to bring "all the little news" to the people. Witness one such report: "Biggest oddity in the news this week is a fowl story. It seems that Forrest Freeman and his father, J. E.

Freeman of Dumas, went to Snow Lake Sunday and spent some time driving around the countryside. When a chicken darted in front of the Freemans' truck, they said, 'Goodbye, chicken,' and thought no more about it. The Freemans came home Sunday, and then traveled about town and near Pendleton on Monday. A little later when Forrest Freeman stopped by E. C. Freeman's store, E. C. thought he spied a chicken head. The men crawled under the truck and there was the chicken as perky as could be."

There were times of drama as well. Dumas police called Melvin in the middle of the night to report a shooting. Melvin dressed hastily and went to the scene. The shooter was inside a house; the woman's body lay in the street. Melvin was more adventuresome than he later became because he photographed the woman lying in the street without knowing where the shooter was. Later, Melvin photographed the shooter as he lay wounded in the house.

"What would you have done if he had fired at you instead?" I worried.

"I don't know," Melvin replied, but after that, he was more judicious at crime scenes.

We were to chase police calls for years, going to fires and wrecks in the wee hours to record the news first-hand along with covering vital family news that made a weekly paper so valuable to its readers.

The year brought another crime story. A relative of the famed Barker Clan, notorious in the 1930s, had been picking cotton near Dumas when he traded a stolen car for a truck. Our town marshal, Dayton Allison, discovered that the man was a parolee from San Quentin, thus providing a headline story. But we also reported in the same issue that six of seven members of the J. M. Robertson family had mumps on the left side only. Only in a weekly!

In January 1955, I was elected president of Arkansas Press Women, a milestone for me. Then, the Press Women held meetings along with Arkansas Press Association.

Our business hours were quite different from now. Stores closed on Thursday afternoons, an opportunity for Mother to drive John and me to Tillar to visit friends and cousins. On one such trip, a low-flying crop duster went under the power lines and just cleared our Kaiser car! Saturday was the busiest day of the week, with tenant families flooding in from farms to spend the day and well into the night. Getting a parking space along Main Street allowed people to sit in cars and watch the town come to life. People visited up and down Main for hours, went to the movies at Gem Theatre, sipped sodas at Meador Pharmacy, and watched the arrival of the evening train before loading their groceries/essentials and going home about midnight. Mrs. Ida Adams lived a block from downtown, but drove there early to get a good parking spot, walking home and later returning to sit in her car to visit with the crowd.

Severe cuts in cotton acreage were forcing tenant families off farms, causing me to write in "Clarion Chatter": "We believe there are two possible courses of action to keep people from leaving our farms and our county. First, we should encourage the planting of other crops besides rice and cotton. Secondly, we should do everything in our power to get and hold industry which will provide jobs for the part-time or small acreage farmer."

That year began our drive to raise a $40,000 match toward a $100,000 speculative building for industry, and the *Clarion* was active in the campaign. We also joined in a drive to raise a $25,000 match toward a similar grant from the Robert E. Lee Wilson Foundation for an elementary school addition.

Our second year began with plenty of news: 22 front-page stories, two one-column mug shots (individual photos), "Desha Dispatch" news column, and a feature on ham radio operators Jack Frank of Dumas and Clarence Isch of McGehee. There also was adequate advertising to make the newspaper payroll and payments, and we were parsimonious at home, our family drawing $50 weekly to meet expenses and using a big garden to advantage.

Major news was arrival of the Salk vaccine to be given to all children, and later to private patients, to prevent the dreaded polio. In another lead story, town leaders begged the Highway Commission to put a hard surface on Highway 54 west of town.

I wrote a feature on the family of Marion and Theresa Kozubski, who became American citizens on April 6. In 1940, Marion had been taken by German SS troops invading Poland to become a prison farm laborer in Germany, and he "gave himself up" to Americans liberating him in 1945. The Kozubskis came to America in 1949 under the displaced persons law. (The family became important to us, as son Jerry and daughter Kristina joined our staff as teenagers and were key employees for 35 and 37 years.)

Advertising sold for 35 cents a column inch. Delta Bottling Co. advertised that a pony and attendant would be available for parties when "you furnish 24 Pop Kola crowns (tops)" and called 112 to make reservations. For $2.50 a week, one could own a Philco refrigerator. Bubble Up, bottled in Dumas, sold for 15 cents for a six-bottle carton. Ford, Plymouth, Chevrolet, and Dodge were mainstays in national advertising placed through agencies. We counted on regular advertisers Wolff Brothers, Freeman Firestone Store, Arkansas Power & Light Co., and Dante's Store.

When Bill Hadley of KATV came to town for the citizenship awards, we reported: "We held our breath until Bill Hadley and his pilot were airborne Tuesday night, but they were nonchalant about the operation. With a powerful searchlight on their four-passenger plane, they flooded unlighted airstrip south of town with light and were off in a wink. Four or five cars from Dumas drove to see them off."

Sometimes we crowed about our effectiveness. For example, "Desha Dispatch" on June 23, 1955, commented: "Never underestimate the power of the press. On the strength of a news story stating the city was going to make a drive on collection of auto license fees, 133 auto tags have been purchased in a week's time. On Friday, the day that most readers received their papers, the collector's office was rushed by 40 persons buying city auto tags, M. H. Wood reports. At $2.50 per tag, the city has collected $332.50 for the tags."

Dumas was growing. An editorial noted: "The City Council, meeting last week, took steps to enforce an ordinance that says no pigs can be raised in the city limits. The action came after a resident made a telling point of saying she saw no reason to make every resident connect to the sanitary sewer when there were filthy pigs in some parts of town....Pretty soon the only 'sooie' we'll hear here is when the Razorback games go on the air."

Editorials from my trusty L. C. Smith manual upright were seldom so trivial as the pig law, but early on, they were points for disagreement. At one of our company meetings, a stockholder questioned an editorial stance I had taken. Dr. J. H. Hellums stood and quieted the questioner when he said, "Charlotte told us that she and Melvin were in charge of editorial policy. You may as well remember that." We bought out the disagreeable stockholder within a month. I always felt that one had to be an autocrat to run a weekly newspaper's operation.

We weren't in the newspaper business for the money, but it did have some sideline benefits. I wrote: "Courtesy of the grand people of this area, we have been living off the fat of the land. Mrs. Tom Smith sent us some juicy roasting ears; L. M. Gary, some tasty cantaloupes and home-grown tomatoes, and Mrs. Ben Johnson, a pound of wonderful homemade butter. Add to that two bushels of peas which Mrs. Bob Hoover of Dark Corner gave to us, and half a bushel of pink-wrap tomatoes picked from the farm of Calvin Rowe at Watson and brought to us by Watson Supt. C. B. Harrod."

Times were changing in Dumas, if ever so slowly. Six sewing machines fashioning garments in the rear of Dante's Department Store formed the nucleus for an industry ultimately employing more than 300. Dumas Grain Dryer Association was formed to build large grain dryers for rice and soybeans. Dredging began on the Tensas-

Boeuf Drainage Project, and construction started on the garment industry building. Signal change was coming in the form of natural gas lines for Dumas. Wood fires would continue for some time, but in Dumas, natural gas soon would replace butane.

The most exciting news of 1955 was the *Clarion's* move from the cellar (no previous recognition) to the sweepstakes award for weeklies in the Arkansas Press Association contests. It was an early Christmas present for an over-worked family.

Covering the news was sometimes emotionally draining. Odell Thatch and his four children burned to death in a house fire—a tragic story of kerosene poured over a wood fire. The memory of those five coffins coming down the steps at First Baptist Church haunts me a half-century later. Our people responded with typical compassion and generosity to the surviving mother.

Caring is a keystone of Delta communities. At Neal community, where Mrs. C. B. Kidd, longtime weekly correspondent, had been ill, her son Charles had cared for her and had no time to get his corn crop into the barn. In a single day, eight farm friends with trailers harvested the corn and put it in the crib.

10.
Full Ownership

By 1956, we had scrimped, saved, and accumulated enough confidence and generous credit from Merchants & Farmers Bank to buy out initial investors. Our family was still doing the lion's share of the work and spending minimally on ourselves. Yet, it was such an energizing time as we sought to build the *Clarion*, and we had exceptional cooperation from the community. I began a series on leaders of the community, giving the editorial page a new dimension.

In a simple time, I reported in our front-page column "Desha Dispatch": "Unless someone commits a crime between now and then, there won't be a single criminal case on the docket for Circuit Court when the January term is held at Arkansas City Monday. This has not happened in at least nine years and maybe longer."

Changes were coming. The City Council called a special election on construction of natural-gas transmission and distribution lines. Previously, butane gas and wood provided heating. The city government included Mayor Travis Witherington and councilmen W. E. (Billy) Free Jr., John Puryear, Haskell Wolff, Guy U. Robinson, Forrest Freeman, and Joe Lee McKennon. Showing Dumas's progressive attitude, the vote was 397 to 11 for the gas transmission bond issue. Since legal notice for the issue ran more than 14,000 words—set and proofread in our plant—the revenue helped the bottom line.

Assets at Merchants & Farmers Bank topped $4 million, and retail sales in Desha County were reported to be more than $14.5 million. In a time of segregation, the School Board voted to propose an

$81,000 bond issue to "build six rooms at the colored school and six rooms at Dumas Elementary." Schools were segregated but hardly equal, and the board was trying to improve facilities. A 70-mill school tax was proposed, and our long editorial endorsed the issue.

Our steady advertisers were Dumas Motor Co., Merchants & Farmers Bank, Wolff Brothers, Meador Pharmacy, Gem Theatre, LaGrone's (clothing store), Gill Tire Store, Dumas Electric Co., Martin Chevrolet, Saveway Food Market, Arkansas Power & Light Co., McKennon Implement Co., S. T. Frank Insurance Agency, Freeman Firestone, Dante's, W. B. Loyd & Sons, Eugene Lee Grocery, Priddy Insurance, and McDonald Irrigation. We also could count on Alton Farmer Electric Service, John Puryear Hardware Store, Matthews Motor Co., Kroger, Delta Bottling, O. L. Puryear and Sons, Failla's of Gould, and others for periodic ads. Martin Chevrolet announced that Herman Vickers, who had been a railroad engineer in McGehee, would serve as a salesman. He was to become the Chevrolet dealer and a Dumas leader.

In two years, we managed to place the *Clarion* in contest contention, but Melvin and I were astounded to learn that our newspaper had won weekly sweepstakes in the Arkansas Press contests. Donning our best suits, we went to Little Rock to accept the award from Col. T. H. Barton, Lion Oil magnate, at the APA convention in January. I presided over the meeting of the Arkansas Press Women.

In a column on the mail receipts, I noted that much of it sought free space in our newspaper, via "matted material" which could be cast into type, fillers, and public relations handouts. And I affirmed we intended only to cover news impacting local people.

Lincoln-Desha Telephone Co., owned by Ted and Kay Adair, converted from hand-crank phones to dial on March 18, 1956, thus eliminating the friendly operators who had kept track of the community in filling the calls. Lois Grubb, who completed a 28-year career at the switchboard, said she had handled an estimated five million calls.

Dantan Inc. opened in the new industrial building, and Winthrop Rockefeller, chairman of the Arkansas Industrial Development Commission, spoke at a banquet marking the occasion. Dantan's Petti Pat sportswear (named in honor of Pat Tanenbaum, daughter-in-law of Bernard Tanenbaum who started the venture) then was sold in Pfeifers' of Little Rock and J. C. Penney. The *Clarion* published an eight-page congratulatory section for Dantan, then managed by Harold Jones and father, Mont.

Dumas growth led us to call for a City Planning Commission. More than 50 new homes had been constructed in two years. We called for an entry in the State Community Accomplishment Contest. A front-page editorial called attention to two prospective industrialists' visit and urged citizens to "Speak Out FOR Dumas." During the year, we would continually focus on the need for industrial jobs, more space for the library, and improved school facilities.

We were accustomed to people calling the *Clarion* all kinds of names, including *Clarionete, Cline, Calarion, Coronet,* and the like. Even tolerated was a reader who came in and said, "I wants a *Clown.* I loves meat and I wants to see which place is selling it the cheapest."

Newspaper production was a struggle. In April, I wrote: "If your *Clarion* is late this week, and at 11 a.m. Thursday, it looks as though it might be, it will be because the newspaper press went ker-plunk right in the middle of operations on press day." I explained that the early 1900s Babcock press was not the oldest piece of equipment we had, as we had a folder manufactured in 1885.

Reported on that issue's front page was a town tragedy, a truck demolished at a train crossing. We could have sold the picture to the Associated Press, but Melvin and I were saddened by its horrible graphics. Instead of showing the bodies of two victims, we covered that area with "cutlines" or identification in type out of respect for the family.

The *Clarion* won its first national award, "for exceptional service to safety," from the National Safety Council, and several months later, placed in the National Editorial Association feature story and agricultural news coverage contests.

Our newspaper office was a "show and tell" place. Three youngsters brought in an antique iron shoe they found in their yard and declared it was a museum piece. Adults frequently displayed huge rattlesnakes they had killed or notable produce from their gardens.

Rising in the middle of the night was nothing unusual for Melvin as he would be called to photograph wrecks. It was never easy to cover bad things happening to good people. One incident proved especially difficult. He found our former Tillar neighbors, John and Grace Haisty, badly injured in an accident north of Dumas. Melvin saw a roll of bills in Mr. Haisty's pocket and took it to the Haistys' oldest son, Sherwood Haisty. Years later, Sherwood wrote that it was all the cash the family had at the time.

In the fall of 1956, I became involved in the fight to prevent the Corps of Engineers from re-routing the Arkansas River navigation channel through Arkansas County, thus bypassing much of Desha County. I spoke against the move at a hearing in Pine Bluff and editorially called for the people of Desha County to get "steamed up." Dumas Chamber of Commerce became involved and held a meeting for opponents. The public outcry forced the Corps to change plans and cut the navigation canal between Desha and Arkansas counties below Pendleton. Ultimately, it was one of the most significant editorial stands we took.

We established a tradition of stands on general election ballot issues, and many times, citizens came to get copies of the *Clarion* to read before deciding how to vote. I also was called at home to discuss issues.

Our first color advertisement, for Dante's—utilizing red ink—was a challenge, requiring the same sheet of paper fed through the press twice in order to get separate red and black ink registers.

News stories sometimes broke nearby. Mother, John, and I were having breakfast on a November morning when we saw gasoline tanks catch fire at Matthews, an oil company a half-block away. J. M. Matthews, the firm's owner; his employees; and Dumas volunteer firemen, some of whom had trained on fire control at Pine Bluff Arsenal, saved the day by keeping other tanks cooled, thus preventing our end of town from burning.

11.
Numerous Ups and Downs

With the grand news that we were expecting our second child, again in October, I kept on working half-day at the plant and half-day at home. I wanted to appear in modest dress for the annual Chamber of Commerce banquet in May. My dress became of little concern as the featured speaker turned up intoxicated. His ramblings didn't diminish my joy upon being chosen as "Woman of the Year," while a town institution, C. W. (Rock) Meador, was named "Man of the Year."

In four or five editorials each week, I covered multiple issues, mostly local, including industrial development, Salk vaccinations for all under 40, a Dumas sign on Highway 65, city planning, and expansion of fish farming and a processing plant. Our good friend Billy Free, who was to become Dumas's progressive mayor for 27 years, used to say: "Never fight with someone who buys ink by the barrel." I found that editorials of our small newspaper were influential.

Dumas was growing along the main highway, with new service stations being erected by W. C. Carter and Minter Carter, and J. M. Matthews's multi-service business moving to a new location at the Highways 65/165 intersection. A. G. West built the first drive-in, the Delta Dip, ultimately called "Brownie's" for Warren Brown who bought and operated it. New homes were rising in former cow pastures along the highway.

From the beginning, we were involved in many of the efforts—from park development to the industrial fund. "Advocacy journalism" was not in our vocabulary, but I had always believed that we couldn't be bystanders and make change happen. Melvin and I were fully involved to the extent of our time and energy. To support the city's industrial fund drive, we borrowed $3,000 and needed three years to pay off the loan. However, we also knew a barber who gave half of the $400 he had.

The *Clarion* production was riddled with problems. Our printer-pressman Joe Fletcher was at National Guard camp when the belt broke on the ancient press on press day. (The year before, it was the rack which broke at the same time.) Break-downs meant we would work late in getting our paper to the post office in time for readers to have it the next day.

When Melvin climbed on a small stool to reach office supplies for sale, he fell and said he had sprained his ankle. An x-ray showed no break, and he walked on a badly swollen foot for six weeks before another x-ray revealed a broken bone. Then it was into a cast for 13 weeks. Our friends were marvelous—from sending cooked meals for us to offering to help. "I can't run a newspaper press," said leading merchant Haskell Wolff, "but I would be glad to sweep out!"

I had thought it modest to work at home through pregnancy, but I faced a new challenge. I went downtown to sell advertising. I hope my sales were more on the merits of the *Clarion*'s being a vigorous newspaper than on sympathy for an expectant mother.

Even though our editorial page always stirred conversation, it was the issue of September 12, 1957, that made some tempers red hot. I called for reason in the implementation of the school desegregation decision by the U.S. Supreme Court. Always a loyal Democrat, I dared to question Governor Orval Faubus's calling out the National Guard to prevent integration of Little Rock schools. I was taught at home that all people have value and rights, and I knew that integration was a reality. In fact, my mother, who had taught 23 years in Tillar, said that integration ought to begin with the first-graders since young children were not as prejudiced as those in high schools.

The editorial, mild compared to some others I had written, commented:

> Although many Dumas people are heartily applauding the action of Governor Faubus in calling out the National Guard to "preserve the peace," and halt integration plans for Little Rock schools, we can only see it as a losing effort, and one which will be costly to the state in many ways.
>
> We have never believed that tolerance could be legislated or enforced by court decision, but Arkansas is one of the 48 states and is bound by "the law of the land," until that law is changed....And it is unlikely that the 13th Amendment or the decision of the Supreme Court will be revoked...
>
> The very costly effect of calling out the National Guard in Little Rock and halting the integration plans of Little Rock school board, of which Little Rockians had known for two years, is that there is no end in sight to the controversy and violence which may result. Had the Guard been alerted rather than called out, the Little Rock police may well have handled any disturbances. Now the public will never know how things may have gone.
>
> The Little Rock controversy has been costly, too, in the kind of publicity Arkansas has gotten over the nation, in the treatment of such established newsmen as Dr. Benjamin Fine of the *New York Times*, and in the state's program to attract industry. But most costly of all is that both sides are so stirred up that mediation and reason seem impossible.

A tepid editorial, I thought, as I pondered keeping the peace. However, it led to threats and cancellations of subscriptions. A reader called to threaten Melvin, then on crutches. "I will break your other leg," he told Melvin, who answered, "Come see if you are man enough to do it." Thankfully, it turned out to be a hollow threat. I cried because he was targeted, but it only reinforced my editorial resolve.

Advertising became harder to sell. The gem through all of the desegregation controversy, though, was the sterling quality of the Dumas School Board, which strongly intended to adhere to the nation's laws.

Three weeks later on the occasion of National Newspaper Week, I wrote:

> We endeavor to interpret the news, by giving you a staff-written and local editorial page. No one pens our editorials for us, unless such editorials are identified. Each editorial represents our considered opinion of an issue, and all readers are invited to write their rebuttals to such editorials so long as they sign their names. The possibility of creating controversy will not deter us from speaking out on the issues of the day. We have always believed that an editorial page is the heart and soul of a newspaper, and as long as we publish a newspaper, we shall always feel free to express our opinions as readers are at liberty to write their comments.

The problem was that the vicious comments made to us were vocal, and no one would sign a letter except Fred Wells of Oakland, California, urging us to read *U.S. News and World Report* on the "race problem."

Entering the world at this time of controversy, our daughter Sarah was born October 6, 1957, at the Desha County Hospital. I managed to get my writing done before and after. On the week of her birth came the news that the *Dumas Clarion* had topped the weekly division of the Arkansas Press Association's contests for 1957—a grand bonus during a happy and demanding time.

With a new baby and a four-year-old who was often ill with allergies, I often wrote after 10 p.m. My children learned to go to sleep to the sound of Mama's staccato from my L. C. Smith as I pounded out editorials and news stories. Melvin and I often worked until 2 a.m. and rose at 7 a.m. Sometimes, to get more galleys out of one linotype, he later went to the office at 5 a.m. and worked until the linotype operator (Linnie Stuart) came in at 8 a.m. Then it was home for breakfast, and later back to work. At least we didn't work those hours on Sunday.

With excessive rain, the crop losses in Desha County topped more than $1.5 million in 1957, making it a woeful year for merchants. At Christmastime, Aaron Zeno, a Winchester businessman, was prompted to send a paper bag to Merle Peterson, Ford dealer, with the enclosed poem:

> I want to send nuts and candy;
> They would come in handy;
> No cotton, no corn, big rains made me sag:
> So, you're just getting an empty bag!

Christmas, however, was a bonanza for a weekly newspaper. We could always sell greeting ads, even to businesses that hadn't advertised all year.

On Christmas week, we went to Wolff Brothers to buy the family presents. Melvin loaded them in the back seat and went back in the store to speak to friends; when he returned, every present was gone. Someone must have enjoyed a good Christmas, but we had to scrap for more gifts, and never again left wrapped gifts in an unlocked car.

Our efforts to gather the news were basic. Mother called to get the "personals"—the social news of Dumas. We had built a network of country correspondents, who wrote the comings and goings of their communities, at first for 5 cents a column inch and later increased to 10 cents and 25 cents. Given a free subscription, they also received commissions ($1) on every subscription sold.

At the beginning of 1958, correspondents included C. C. Stuart for county schools; Louise Burns, Tillar; Lois Jean Williams, A. L. Reed High; Mrs. Harry Pewitt, Watson; Mrs. D. T. Clayton, Jefferson; Mrs. Mildred Roberts and Mrs. B. R. McGowan, McGehee; Mrs. E. E. Norris, Wells Bayou; Mrs. E. G. Sponenbarger, Arkansas City; Mrs. Leana Merritt, Kelso; Mrs. Mary Eldridge, Oakwood Bayou; Mrs. Cloyce Stevens, 43 Canal; Ruth Ellen White, Garrett Bridge; Gwen Standridge, Winchester; Ellen Olivia Mabry, Pea Ridge; Mrs. Mamie Mitchell, Dumas Colored People (as we then referred to African Americans); and Mrs. C. R Davis, Pendleton. Their weekly reports were conscientiously read in their communities, and errors, if irritating, still were mostly overlooked. Country correspondents gave communities a sense of pride and importance. Theirs was a time-consuming task, but they were considered key leaders in their communities.

Melvin covered the civic and governmental meetings, while I wrote other news. We both sold advertising. Mother kept the books and waited on customers in the front office. Melvin wrote the checks, kept a keen eye on the bank balance, and worked in the composing room. No one had a specialty; we were generalists who could do whatever had to be done.

News was often routine. Readers enjoyed knowing who was in the "womanless wedding" staged by the Lions Club, when Dumas was going to get a new post office, who was going to run in the Democratic primary (tantamount to election), how the sports teams were progressing, who had died and who had been born, who was arrested and why.

Nearly 13 inches of rain fell in the first week of May 1958, putting 110,000 acres under water in Desha County and meaning a ruinous planting season. The Everett Norris family caught 24 fish while standing on their porch in Pendleton community. Mailmen couldn't reach rural areas for two weeks. A newspaper is bound to suffer in times like those, and we did. We could also serve, calling for opening a temporary trestle on a railroad bridge that had narrowed the opening in drainage Canal 19.

Also, we were focusing on economic change. The Puryear brothers, William (Doc), Glynn, and Buddy (Lynn), started a plant to build crib parts, ultimately attracting the Bassett Company which manufactured furniture in town for 27 years. Heicht B. Smith constructed a plant for steel building fabrication.

Governor Orval Faubus carried all 75 counties in winning re-election. It was obvious that we, who had dared to criticize him, were not his favorites. He sent an Employment Security Division representative to investigate our employment practices. The ESD investigator reviewed records in our plant for a week and couldn't find anything wrong. It was harassment, however.

The *Clarion* pumped a drive to build a town library, thus moving the books out of the City Hall's second floor. Editorially, we asked everyone to give $1 toward the project. We had organized a Community Council with representatives from civic organizations. Frances Rands (later Newton) worked with me and became a longtime friend. Our entry in the statewide community achievement contest won first, and the $400 prize later bought shelves for the new library. Winthrop Rockefeller, chair of the state's industrial effort, came to dedicate the new fish marketing plant here, and we had our first conversation with the distinguished philanthropist and statesman.

When another 13 inches of rain fell at harvest time, merchants depending on farmers were in as much trouble as the farmers. In nine months, Dumas had 60 inches of rain, equal to a year's total. In the midst of agricultural tribulation, good news came when Potlatch Inc. made it official: it would build a $35 million paper mill in Desha County. However, Desha voters would pay for a road to the site years before it became reality.

Sometimes the news came to us. Mother, sitting at our one desk in the front office, looked up one morning to see a Dumas citizen making a "citizen's arrest"—marching another man at gunpoint down the sidewalk. She did a quick dive under her desk for safety until the town marshal intervened.

Tackling Crises

Crisis years seem more the norm in the newspaper business, but late 1959 and early 1960 are remembered for very personal reasons.

After gall bladder surgery, Mother suffered a heart attack and was recovering at home. Melvin injured his back while delivering a desk and walked with difficulty.

In January 1960, John, six, and Sarah, two, were critically ill with an intestinal virus, and survived by the grace of God and the help of our good doctor, Guy Robinson. For eight days and nights, I seldom closed my eyes at the hospital, and Melvin was there every minute he could be. He drove to the Methodist church to summon Dr. Robinson on a Sunday morning when John went into convulsions. John passed through that awful crisis, but Sarah remained inert. Two days later, we knew Sarah was better in the middle of the night when she asked for "little beans." She was so weak she had to re-learn walking.

How we ever published a newspaper through that nightmare, I will never know. We did through pure grit and the compassion of our community.

An orthopedist called surgery a must for Melvin but said he still might be in pain after the operation. That sealed Melvin's decision. He called off surgery, determined to get better through exercises. It was a slow process.

Somehow, I kept home and business going. At the end of August, I realized that no posting of accounts had been done because of family illnesses. "I will get out the bills," I declared, settling in for a non-stop weekend. Friends were sympathetic. Amy Frank helped with the children, and Louise Loyd sent in a full day's meals. The bills went out on time, and the income allowed us to continue.

Meanwhile, Dumas was attracting state attention with its efforts at self-development. After the Community Accomplishment Contest, Merle Peterson, Mayor Billy Free, and I were summoned for a TV appearance. "Don't let it scare you when they bring the camera in close," Billy said. That was laughable. With the TV cast totally relaxed and drinking coffee, I quaked through the entire interview.

Dumas progress was ongoing. John Puryear pushed development by buying 100 acres from R. A. Pickens Co. to develop a residential subdivision east of Highway 65. By 1960, 13 businesses had been constructed where none had been at the decade's beginning. Elsewhere, there was a sad note. An October fire razed a corner of the historic Arkansas City downtown with its 1880s-era bank building.

While the *Clarion* front page had looked much the same for six years, we began making changes in the 1960s. We floated the nameplate, used larger headlines and four-column stories, and re-designed heads for the standing columns. *Arkansas Gazette* cartoonist George Fisher designed the "Clarion Chatter" column head of a young woman pounding out reams of copy. I explained how re-design occurred. Melvin and I went to an Arkansas Press Association seminar led by the famed newspaper designer, Ed Arnold.

We threw out the 30-dashes (—30—) used to signal the end of stories. Fisher designed a new nameplate, which included a cameo of Dumas's location in Arkansas, and a new head for "Desha Dispatch" with an outline of our county. Ed Arnold urged us to go down-style on headlines—using capitals only for the beginning of a headline and proper names—but it took some years for us to make that change.

Adopting new correspondence heads, we tried to improve the printing, but it was almost impossible with the early-1900s hand-fed press used every week. We added more photos, then sent them to an engraver in Little Rock.

Later, we dispatched photos for processing on a Photo-Lathe to Guthrie, Oklahoma, meaning that Melvin had to meet the evening passenger train to get the pictures in a small mail pouch. He did this so frequently that a townsperson stopped him and asked, "Say, have you got a second job working for the railroad?"

However, our prime objective was not the "look" of the *Clarion* but its content. We thought ourselves to be recorders of history. As such, we reported the last run of the Delta Eagle, a streamline train operating from Tallulah, Louisiana, to Memphis—and later from McGehee to Helena. J. Q. Haisty, a railroad engineer for 48 years, took it on the last trip, and told us that the first run from McGehee to Helena was made in 1906 with Jack Weinsing as engineer. The Delta

Eagle, always a pleasant way to travel, originally had an engine, a mail and baggage car, two passenger cars, and a dining car. The streamliner stopped at the tiniest towns, and for a while, it also served as a school bus, taking children to and from school in Snow Lake.

We also reported that ferryman Floyd Christman, Alton Farmer, Dr. J. H. Hellums, and Clay Cross Jr. drove to Memphis to bring back a new tugboat for the Pendleton Ferry on the Arkansas River eight miles east of Dumas. Dr. Harry Cogbill, dentist, made a special delivery to them as he flew his airplane over the ferry and dropped a copy of the *Arkansas Gazette* and a roll of Tums.

Human interest items were always covered, but so were the important stories, such as the Dumas population rising to 3,530—a gain of 1,018 in the decade. Celebrating progress, we received two awards at the National Editorial Association convention in Atlanta. In our first NEA convention at Hot Springs the year before, I was among four women editors on a panel and Melvin headed the resolutions committee. Being among well-known publishers from all over the nation was "high cotton" for country editors—high cotton then being a superlative for good crop prospects in the Delta.

Our old Chevrolet wouldn't make the trip to Atlanta, but Merle Peterson said, "Drive this new Mercury down there and back. Don't worry because it is insured." We rode in style in a sleek blue-and-white Mercury Marquis with which we fell in love. Melvin won a fishing boat and trailer, but with no clearance to tow it home, he sold it there and we put the $225 on the purchase of that Mercury. I became very ill with food poisoning when we stopped in Tuscaloosa on the return home, causing anxiety since I was pregnant with our third child, but I recovered in a short time.

Always I dreamed of new opportunities for our area. My editorial proposing a five-point program for Desha County, including councils on agriculture, industry, tourism, sports promotion, and advertising, drew state attention. TV Channel 7 came to Dumas to interview me in our front office. I was greatly concerned about the background—the weathered lattice-work which separated our front office from the composing room. How would that give anyone credibility? I guess it was acceptable, as two tourists stopped by later "to meet that earnest young woman we saw on TV."

Politics had always fascinated me, and the *Clarion* tradition of posting of election returns as they came in, however slowly, began in 1954. At first, we had a large blackboard; later on, we used poster boards we frequently updated. To get the returns, Melvin phoned election officials in each precinct and asked them to phone results collect at Evergreen 2-4925. Posting the vote was immensely popular, and by 1960, several hundred people typically gathered in front of our office to see returns. We managed to have the local returns far ahead of those reported to Little Rock.

The *Clarion* increased in size to 16 pages, developed a regular sports page mostly written by Melvin, and provided a popular column of reminiscing by Mother.

Our son Stephen Maurice (named for his grandfathers) was born October 26, 1960, in Desha County Hospital (on press day, of course). I wrote my part of the paper ahead of time and wrote in the hospital where we were required to stay several days. I never missed editorial responsibilities.

We had finally installed our second linotype to cope with an increasing flow of news and advertising copy. We bought the used Model 8 from the *Arkansas Gazette*. For six years, using a Model 31 linotype, we had to operate it from 6 a.m. to 9 p.m., with Melvin putting in overtime before and after regular operator Linnie Stuart's shift. He also handled maintenance of the machine with its multiple parts and became so adept he was offered a job by a linotype representative.

Editorially, I commented on a wide range of subjects, including the election of John F. Kennedy as president. I reflected: "Americans could have learned two very great lessons from the election last week.

One, that every vote does count as there was just a 300,000 vote difference out of 70 million total between the two candidates, and two, free elections are the greatest blessings which countries can enjoy."

Local political loyalties were strong. After a pre-election wager, C. W. (Rock) Meador and Clay Cross—Yellow Dog Democrats (the strongest kind)—found themselves being pushed in a wheelbarrow by Mr. Republican, Bob Stimson Sr. A band played for the event. "As close as the vote was, it was well that the winners waited a couple of weeks to see who was pushing whom," we reported. Mr. Stimson reminded them that he rode a donkey prodded along by Messrs. Meador and Cross when Dwight D. Eisenhower won.

Then, political differences were not bitter and were often enjoyed with jovial jibing.

12.
They Were Family

A weekly newspaper's staff, mixing tasks and responsibilities since it is few in number, becomes like one's family. It certainly was in our case.

Jerry Kozubski, our composing room foreman, and his sister, Kristina Kozubski Weaver Poole, our office manager, were the deans. Others notching more than 25 years were Ola Tillman, Joyce Russell, and Debra Conrad. Terry Hawkins, who was later to become the *Clarion* publisher, was associated with us on three different stretches totaling more than a score of years.

If our staff always seemed like family, our country correspondents were our "cousins." These volunteers, paid little by the inch for their work, recorded the heartbeats of their communities. For the most part, they wrote news dispatches by longhand and sent them by mail. Largely, these reports were the comings and goings in the community, occasioned by funny stories or editorial comment on the weather and crops. Long ago I discovered that while country correspondents might not be able to spell correctly or write grammatically, they always told the truth.

I also found that something humorous to me isn't always funny to my readers. Consider this item:

> Card of Thanks
> "We are so sorry to hear about the terrible misfortune which happened to the Jones family Tuesday. The whole community sympathizes with them in their loss. Three shoats belonging to the Jones' ate cuckleburries and passed away."

It isn't a bit funny when one loses the family's winter meat prospects.

Our correspondent with the "best nose for the news" was Ruth Thurman, who covered Kelso and Kurdo communities east of McGehee. She had neither telephone nor car. When a young man saved himself and two others from drowning after two others were lost, she knew she had a big story. She sent her husband and the young hero hitchhiking a dozen miles to town so that I could write the story and break it well ahead of the state daily newspapers.

Mrs. Thurman saw the funny side of life, and years later, I still laugh at some of her reports, including one about a wedding when times were more traditional and formal. For the purposes of protecting identities, I use fictionalized names in these reports by Mrs. Thurman:

"Dear Editor (which she could spell more easily than Schexnayder), will you please fix this wedding write-up to sound as well as possible. If you ask me, it was a mess."

Her story:

"Mary Brown and Huey Jones were married Sunday afternoon in a beautiful ceremony at the local church, which was decorated with red dahlias (a no-no). Mary came down the aisle with the best man, and poor old Huey came out of the Sunday School room all alone."

Another time, Mrs. Thurman wrote:

"Here is a snake story and believe me it is a jim dandy. Last Sunday, Polecat was burning some brush north of his house on the bayou and found a big diamond back rattler and killed it. He said it had 10 rattlers and was 6 and ½ feet long. Several people saw the snake and claimed it was the largest they had ever seen—although some things Polecat tells is quite a bit out of line. But he should be an honest man. He is a justice of the peace and a deacon in the church. Don't print all this for he would beat my ears down with his walking stick!" Another time, she wrote about a gasoline truck running into a bayou, with the spilled fuel killing all the fish. Her comment: "Now this community is sure a sweet smelling place!"

In the days when domestic living arrangements were more formal, I faced an irate reader one afternoon. She stormed into my office and demanded, "Ah wants a correction!"

"About what?" I replied in a calming voice.

"Well," she said with great disdain, "your correspondent had Mr. and Mrs. Sam Jones of California visiting here. He's my brother and she ain't his wife. They're just living together. Ah wants a correction!"

In one social item reported by another correspondent, we learned: "Miss Judy resided at the punch bowl. The table was centered with bowels of pretty pink roses." Spelling certainly was not that correspondent's long suit.

Mrs. E. G. Sponenbarger was our trusted correspondent from Arkansas City for years, and she always called the paper "Our Clarendon." She sniffed out every bit of news and when mail delivery was tardy, she dispatched her report by a county official coming to Dumas.

The name of the correspondent doesn't matter, but the truth does in this item filed:

"GAME FORFEITED: Watson forfeited the football game they had matched with Gould on account of not being in condition to play. Gould came to play all right, but the Watson boys said they just couldn't play after they seen the size of the Gould team."

Truthfully, I loved the day the country correspondence came in, as it sometimes afforded a laugh, a tear of sympathy, or just a chance to finger the pulse of a community. In fact, every summer I looked forward to hearing from Neal Community where there was great excitement because a "panther" had been sighted again. Large wild cats did exist in those times, and the correspondent dutifully reported that the public must be aware. She also warned of other dangers. Speaking of the cotton crop, she reported "boll weevils are fearce"—many farmers did indeed fear those infestations.

Arkansas has its mountains and people we then called "hillbillies," and its flat Delta and its residents then called "swamp angels."

Sometimes the two didn't mix. Once, a correspondent wrote: "Due to unforeseen conditions, Rev. Joe Brown who has been appointed to our church has been unable to accept the appointment. They've been living in the hills, and they say his wife refused to live in the Bottoms."

In typing and editing the correspondence, I came to feel as though I knew the people of the community better.

There was added pleasure when other readers dropped by our office with a kindness. Carl Smith had no car but every spring, he picked a bouquet from his yard and walked a long way to present it to our staff.

Not all customers were so thoughtful.

One day a man walked into our office and asked: "Is this where you make the *Dumas Clarion?*"

"Yes," we replied. "May we help you?

He rapped his knuckles sharply on the front office desk and demanded, "Make me one!"

I dared not criticize anyone, because typos often haunted us. For example, when an L was substituted for a D, the sentence came out, "The singing was hell in the fellowship hall." And I dreaded the possibility that the linotype operator would leave the "r" out of shirt. In the linotype era, each line of metal type was on its own potentially an errant embarrassment. Elimination of lines might be just as troublesome.

Early in my career, I left to sell advertising while the printer was relegated to proofreading. Imagine my chagrin when I returned to find lines omitted from a wedding write-up, and the bride's costume was thus described: "The bride wore a string of pearls, a gift of the groom."

And there was the time a prominent man died, and his survivors included some naughty grandchildren. It did not help the paper's image when lines fell by the wayside, and the obituary declared, "The funeral home was in charge of the grandchildren."

One of the self-proclaimed duties of a correspondent was to report on the health of community residents. One wrote: "Mrs. Essie are in bed again. Miss Jane are mending. Mrs. Annie can walk a little. Lutie is up again. Mrs. Julie has some good days but mostly stays week. There are a few cases of measles yet."

Country correspondents were the bread and butter of weekly newspapers. In our second issue of publication, I lifted one item for a front-page column because it was surely thorough:

"Folks in Gould have been playing House-Changeabout. Mrs. Price Smith, our country correspondent there, reports: The Sandsteins moved to St. Louis; the Overtons moved into the Sandstein home. The Sid Mosses to the Overtons; the Bob Murphys to the Moss house; the Shurdens to the Murphy home; the Outz family to the Shurdens; the Stephens to the Outz, and Herbert Jones's tractor driver to the Stephens."

Over the years, many of our correspondents passed away or resigned, and we lost some of the rural flavor and keen interest along with them. Being a community editor placed me close to the people, who came to depend on our newspaper. I also found fun in the everyday experiences.

I loved calling Circuit Clerk J. T. Henley and his wife, Deputy Clerk Marguerite Henley, to get the courthouse news. This saved us the 60-mile round trip to the courthouse in Arkansas City, and I often had a chuckle or two from the filings.

On one occasion, a petition was filed to change a name from Whithawatha James (Smith). I wondered all week what the name change would be, and the next week I found out: Whithawatha James (Brown).

Another time, a judge was hearing a highly contested divorce case. He inquired of the woman plaintiff: "How long since you've seen your husband?" She thought a minute and said, "Which one?"

Routine there was, but no days really were alike in the community newspaper office, and I thrived on the diversity.

For many years, Dumas had no resident psychologist. That was a role into which I was thrust. Whether it was counsel on marriage or money difficulties, ire at the government or problems with children, I offered an ear at the editor's desk

My advice was free, which made it so often sought. One Wednesday afternoon, as I was putting the finishing touches on the front page, the phone rang and the caller asked for me. "I told her you were busy," my receptionist-bookkeeper said, "but she wouldn't speak to anyone else." Must be important, I thought.

Said the caller: "Mrs. Sharksnider, I am writing a book. Is it all right if I write it on notebook paper?"

The requests reached from grammar referee to the ludicrous. As I was pondering an editorial one day, a businessman called and asked to speak to me.

He explained: "I am writing a business letter. Is sausage plural or singular?"

My comeback: "Depends upon how many you are eating."

Once, when a customer demanded to speak only to me, I had this request: "How much would you charge to cut two rolls of toilet tissue in two?" All I could think to ask was: "What do you want them for—streamers?"

I always tried to talk with whomever called or wanted to see me.

Doing double time in trying to get away for our first cruise, I was informed that someone "must see you."

I found a black woman in tears, and she told me a sad story of how she had to post $100 bond when she failed for pay for $1 in gas at a self-service station. "That's all the money I had to feed my family for two weeks," she wailed.

I took time to dig and found the woman was an excellent worker who had been employed at our largest industrial plant for seven years. She had pumped gas and forgotten to pay for it before driving just across the highway to a drug store to buy medicine for her sick children. When she returned to pay for the gasoline, the clerk refused her money, and the police required the woman to post $100 bond. That lack of understanding was corrected when I confronted city hall.

Our days were never dull!

13.
Our World Expands

In March 1961, I wrote an editorial on "How to talk ourselves into a recession," citing Dumas manufacturer Harold Jones's experience in trying to obtain sewing materials when others quit producing them. My comments were reprinted in the *Dallas Morning News*. With a new baby, a three-year-old, and a seven-year-old, this editor was delighted with outside recognition.

Often writing from home, I focused on editorials, columns, news acquired by phone, and occasional book reviews. Melvin covered meetings, sold advertising, managed finances, and kept the newspaper shop going.

On a week when a friend, Berzent Blagg (later Lincoln County judge), brought me a bucket of square nails from a pioneer homestead, another reader arrived with a copy of a newspaper published the day World War I ended. This caused me to write: "Someday, as our dreams go, we will see a museum erected here to preserve historical collections so that future citizens may know of the past and take pride in it." I was to see that dream realized.

I also wrote a review of the performance of Dave Rubinoff, a famed violinist playing before huge audiences before taking tours, one of which brought him here for a wonderful evening before several hundred people. He thrilled us with a Stradivarius, and when an ivory flew off our ancient piano used by his accompanist, he joked that his violin was made in 1731, but the piano probably was made 500 years before!

Although we owned and published a small newspaper, we were beginning to gain some recognition. I was named credentials chairman for the National Federation of Press Women convention in Little Rock in 1961. As vice president of the Arkansas Press Association, Melvin gave the official welcome. I also presided at the NFPW awards banquet. We took the family to Little Rock, and Mother kept the little ones at the Albert Pike Hotel.

A stately residence hotel, the Albert Pike offered "duebills," by which we could exchange advertising for accommodations, giving our family outings. One weekend, we celebrated liberation from measles which had afflicted our home and went to Little Rock. Visiting the zoo, Sarah, then four, was perceptive. Seeing the leopard, she exclaimed, "Look, he's got measles!"

A press meeting took us to Hot Springs where we had a duebill at the Majestic Hotel. The only accommodation available and offered was the presidential (owners') suite. That turned out to be quite an elegant and challenging weekend. Describing the adventure in my column, I wrote, "It was good to return to our humble home. In the Majestic suite, it was no little job keeping up with Sarah, 4, and Steve, 1, in a place with 3 bedrooms, 4 baths, 2 kitchens, 2 living rooms, a long hall, and 14 closets—to say nothing of a balcony with a five-story drop."

Equipment was improving at the *Clarion* office. In July 1961, we bought a new Heidelberg press which came in such a fancy crate that several locals would have paid more for the crate than the press. However, we placed the trade-in in the crate and shipped it to Houston in the deal. The Heidelberg speeded our commercial printing operations, then accounting for about 20 percent of our gross.

For a while, a succession of printers entered the *Clarion* much the same as characters come and off a stage. In a time when itinerant printers moved from place to place, a man named Jake appeared at our door seeking work. Melvin needed help; we immediately hired Jake. Several months later, Jake said he was sick one morning and thought he was having a heart attack. Mother felt sorry for him and said, "Take some of my bottle of Geritol. It will make you feel better." Jake did not come back to work that day. The following day, a paper company salesman stopped by and observed, "Say, I saw your printer working at the Monticello paper." Mother was indignant. "I didn't mind him leaving," she exclaimed. "But he took my bottle of Geritol!"

In the ongoing cast of characters at the *Clarion*, I was Salty Old Editor, which my family sometimes called me. If I perceived some wrong, I would exclaim with fire in my soul: "I am going to write a hot editorial!" Often I pushed for town change with the same fire in my soul.

The *Clarion's* editorial page continued to create interest, and one of our visitors had read one of my editorials reprinted in the *Arkansas Gazette*. He was W. R. (Witt) Stephens, then president of Arkansas Louisiana Gas Co., which was bringing natural gas to Dumas. He and his brother Jack Stephens were to found the largest investment firm outside of Wall Street.

When I asked Mr. Stephens about his success, he credited his parents, who taught him three principles he still followed: "1, go to church on Sunday; 2, work hard; and 3, save money and invest it wisely."

In keeping up with visitors, some great stories turned up in our small town. Stopping overnight at the Delta Inn, our first motel, was Dr. Arthur Wachmann, director of the observatory in Hamburg, Germany. He consented to an interview, considered a scoop for us since he had discovered four comets and a "flare star."

Our readers became reporters, and when they thought a good story might be involved, called in a tip. Several months after the Wachmann interview, we received a call from Grover Dancer, manager of the Delta Inn.

"Does a No. 2, U.S. House of Representatives, license plate mean anything to you?" he asked.

"It surely does," Melvin replied. "Hold him till we get there."

No. 2 was Charlie Halleck, Indiana congressman and Republican leader in the U.S. House of Representatives. He had come to southeast Arkansas for duck hunting and was staying overnight in Dumas. Thus, we scooped the entire state press with an exclusive interview in which he said that "a two-party system would be the best thing that could happen to the [then Democratic] South."

Congressman Halleck was a familiar figure because of the "Ev and Charlie" TV appearances in which he teamed with Senate Leader Everett Dirksen to present the Republican side of issues on nightly newscasts.

Melvin, Mother, and I were doing two and three jobs apiece. John, at nine, stood on a soft-drink crate and "killed out type," so it could be melted for re-use.

Melvin was elected president of the Arkansas Press Association, taking office during the January convention. A seven-inch snow fell and the mercury dipped to five below zero, but Melvin boarded a northbound bus going through Little Rock to Hot Springs—a 5½-hour trip. As APA president, Melvin had new experiences. In 1960, he had been invited to escort Governor Orval Faubus to the State Democratic Convention podium, even though we were never Faubus supporters. In 1962, the Arkansas Republican Party invited us to their convention, even though we definitely were not Republicans.

Space exploration continued to intrigue all of us. I wrote on February 21, 1962: "The linotypes and typewriters continued their pace and the first four pages of the *Clarion* rolled off the press yesterday, but uppermost in our thoughts—and those with whom we had contact—was the prayer that John Glenn would make it safely back to earth after his successful lift-off and flight. It seemed countless ages after his capsule dunked in the Atlantic before we heard for sure that he was aboard a recovery ship and A-OK."

An appealing facet of a weekly newspaper is that no two days are alike. Being a part of the human drama and holding a key role in a town always fascinated me. We always were amused at the requests we had and the visitors who made them. One day, a man, slightly uneasy on his feet, arrived and asked, "Pardon me, but would you give me the price of a cup of coffee so I could buy a bowl of soup?" When we said no, he staggered next door. In a line of businesses including an appliance store, pharmacy with soda fountain, furniture store, butane gas dealer, and shoe repair shop, we were used to odd requests when folks wandered by.

Sometimes it is semantics. One customer pondered a few minutes before saying: "I want a prescription." He pondered some more, saying, "I want a postscription."

"No," he continued, "I want a perscription."

Exasperated, he said, "Oh, Hell, just give me the paper for a year!"

Mixed into the mundane were exciting experiences afar. In our first 15 years as publishers, we limited vacations to the Arkansas Press Association convention weekends. We worked six days, and even if needed, some Sunday afternoons. When Melvin, as APA president, was invited to a U.S. State Department conference featuring President John F. Kennedy, we were mesmerized into believing we all could go to Washington—Mother, the children, and I for the first time, although Melvin had been there in World War II. The National Editorial Association's second Government Affairs Conference was scheduled at the Roger Smith Hotel. Mother said she'd care for the children so I could join Melvin in some sessions. How would we manage at the *Clarion*? We would do as much as we possibly could ahead—and catch up on return.

So, in March 1962, Mother, Melvin, John, Sarah, Steve, and I began the adventure with Melvin driving our big blue Mercury. Spring and the Schexnayders arrived at the same time, and neither auspiciously. It was a dark, damp day, and we were limp from the 2½-day trip, with overnight stops in Huntingdon, and Rutledge, Tennessee.

Along the way, we stopped at public telephones, where I tried to edit the *Clarion* and solve problems.

At the NEA reception, I managed to break the men-only domination of the National Press Club. We didn't know women weren't permitted there and took the elevator to upper floors in search of Mrs. Catherine Norrell, congresswoman from Arkansas's Fourth District.

Observing a man asleep and a party in progress, we decided Mrs. Norrell wasn't there. When we descended to the ground floor, she was there to greet us.

"Where have you been?" she inquired.

"Upstairs to the Press Club," I replied.

"Oh, my," she exclaimed, "women aren't permitted there!"

Maybe not, but it was one of the first barriers I was to break.

I also attended a briefing in the Indian Treaty Room featuring presidential aides McGeorge Bundy, Ted Sorenson, and Under-Secretary of State Chester Bowles.

While Melvin met and met, the rest of our family toured the Smithsonian Museums, Embassy Row, National Cathedral, National Gallery of Art, Arlington National Cemetery, Custis-Lee Mansion, Mount Vernon, and the Capitol. We visited the offices of Senator J. William Fulbright and Congresswoman Norrell, and watched Speaker John McCormack bring down the gavel in the House of Representatives. We toured the White House and a policeman told me I could take eighteen-month-old Steve only if he were quiet. Steve was so awed that he never uttered a sound.

Melvin and I reveled in the historic artifacts at the elegant John Adams Room of the State Department where an NEA reception was held. He glowed over hearing President Kennedy's speech, and I also saw the president and poet Robert Frost on the White House grounds. We had lunch at the Pentagon for less than a dollar each, but I noted that such a bargain was unusual, as Washington was "a city of the out-stretched palm."

Managing limited finances, we had breakfast in our rooms, lunched at restaurants, and used the nearby deli for the third meal. Would we dare try this again? Heavens, no! Only the young have such stamina.

I pronounced Washington as "a city of superlatives." A half-century later, after many visits there, I am still charmed. The return trip included a visit to the Hermitage, Andrew Jackson's home near Nashville, Tennessee; Williamsburg, Virginia; and the Smoky Mountains. We had travel copy for weeks. Another highlight for Melvin was an invitation to join other publishers in a two-week tour of Ontario, Canada.

At home, I supervised the newspaper operation. When an employee sought to repair the linotype and removed a critical screw, it literally fell apart. Also, when I rose to check on the children in the night, I ran into the breakfront and broke a toe. I proclaimed that the drama included a balky linotype which wouldn't run, a press trapping the newsprint in the rollers, and a folder with belts that broke constantly. It was aptly entitled "We never sleep!" We produced the newspaper, but I didn't rest until Melvin returned and settled the routine.

We always took time to participate in the Arkansas Livestock Show Press Day, and 1962 was interesting as *Bonanza* stars Lorne Green and Dan Blocker greeted us. The midway and rodeo were major attractions for the children, and we enjoyed Les Paul and Mary Ford at the grandstand. Owning a small newspaper opened many doors.

Taking trips was fun, but those were also serious times, on which I commented in the *Clarion*: "The cold feeling we have this week stems not from the cool front which moved through here Tuesday. It follows the perilous course this nation faces in meeting the challenge of Soviet-based missiles in Cuba. We totally support the seven-point program of President Kennedy, believing, as one Dumas citizen put it, that we face this challenge to our freedom before it is too late." A nuclear missile attack launched from Cuba left no place to hide.

The travel bug having bitten, we took our family to the national convention in St. Louis. Melvin dined with Stewart Udall, secretary of the interior, and John and I toured. The year greatly expanded our view of the nation and neighbor Canada.

For the APA convention where Melvin would preside, we had a suite at the Arlington Hotel in Hot Springs. The weather was almost a repeat of the previous January. Snow gently coated the mountains, creating a fairytale view of the Central Avenue valley. Hot Springs casinos jingled full blast at that time, and convention banquets always adjourned early enough for revelers to work the slots.

We gathered and implemented ideas from press meetings, but our prime focus for '63 was The Big Move. Seeking a building of our own with expanded space, we had considered several locations without success. Alton Farmer, an appliance business owner across Waterman Street, offered to build a 29' x 100' structure adjoining his business and to give us a long-term lease. It was our best opportunity, and for months we planned to re-locate to a climate-controlled building, a notable first for us.

City progress encouraged us, with Merchants & Farmers Bank building a new structure three blocks away and a new Sterling Variety Store opening downtown. Moreover, a $400,000 bond issue was proposed to expand the Desha County Hospital in Dumas (now Delta Memorial).

Key to the new building would be a place for a better press—not new but better. We sought a used Model A Goss rotary press, an improvement over our hand-fed operation. The 24,000-pound monster required a four-foot pit, and we came to think of this as a quick storm shelter although a press collapse would hardly have protected anyone.

A moving date of July 4 was set because of less downtown traffic on that day. Offering moving help were F. H. Collins, Merle Peterson, pressman Earl Lewis, and even bystanders. Under the careful supervision of Melvin, forklifts ferried two linotypes and three job presses across the street (Highway 54) in 104 degrees. The equipment had to be ready for business in three days, and we couldn't afford to see anything dropped.

Installation of the newspaper press, erected piece by piece, was ongoing for two weeks. Alas, the press proved to be a big disappointment as the printing quality was poor and our knowledge of it was limited.

Staying up most of the night to get the paper out, Melvin and I eyed each other with trepidation. Steve, then 2½, summed up our dilemma: "Know what, Gram? The paper on the big press went 'pop,' and Mama and Daddy don't know what to do about it."

The new building offered private offices for Melvin and me. Mine had a window so that I could keep a good eye on the commercial shop. We had expanded the "front office" to include a growing inventory of office supplies, cards, stationery, books, and gifts. If advertising sales were down, we could count on other revenues from commercial printing or office supplies and gifts, as there was demand for both.

Our new locale included a flagpole, and an editorial on U.S. freedoms told why it was important for us to fly Old Glory: "Because on numerous occasions we have criticized the administration in power during our 20 years in the newspaper business, we value most our freedom of expression."

Our improved facilities called for celebration. At our open house Sunday, August 11, several hundred came, including visiting publishers. We also honored our correspondents at a Hotel Dumas dinner. That was appropriate, as Hotel Dumas, operated by the gracious great cook Ruby Borland, was a fixture in our lives. In addition to its coffee shop with plate lunches and memorable pies, the two-story brick building offered small apartments and rooms, mostly for senior citizens. From a plate-glass window across the east front, Mrs. E. S. Terral, fondly known as Aunt Carr, surveyed and reported.

My work schedule was interrupted in late September for needed surgery, causing a 10-day hospital stay resulting in reading and writing time. My caring neighbor Ora Lee Godfrey joined Melvin in taking our children to the State Fair where they met Granny and Elly May of the *Beverly Hillbillies*. Son John, 10, chronicled the experience for the *Clarion*.

Tragedy most marked 1963. We'll never forget the November 22 assassination of President John F. Kennedy. Melvin, selling advertising, came home and we wept together. It was the first time I remember seeing him cry.

At the *Clarion*, we published a black-bordered front page on the unthinkable loss—proclamation of mourning, coverage of local services, and an editorial along with photos. My editorial included this comment: "His commitment for his fellow man, his devotion to his country, his brilliant and expressive mind, and his example as a husband, father and son are among the attributes we value so belatedly. May the eternal flame at his graveside in Arlington cemetery be a constant reminder that while a patriot may be felled, his ideals will inspire generations to come."

In the front office, we arranged a window display of red roses, U.S. flag, and the president's photograph. People stood before the window and mourned. Community churches held memorial services, and at every available time, we joined in the national mourning unfolding before us on television.

14.
Politics: No in '64

Politics felt ingrained. Daddy had always stayed up all night for election returns, and even though he died when I was barely eight, I always remembered the political conversations. "Civics" or politics constituted prime mealtime conversation.

In 1964, when I was irritated by some governmental decision, I mused at breakfast: "If I had the money, I would just run for state representative." Mother didn't blink. "Honey, if you want to run, I'll give you the money," she quietly said. Melvin joined me in laughing at the incident, because it all seemed so impossible. He was still laughing when he repeated the conversation during coffee with cronies at Hotel Dumas.

The grapevine was fully at work. Later that day, he was approached by a friend who said, "Hey, I hear you're selling the *Clarion* and getting into politics!"

To quell a rapid rumor, I wrote in my column: "Last week we were quite amused to hear a rumor that we were going to sell out and enter politics. As well as we like politics, we never intend to be a candidate for we feel that holding office and being an editor don't mix well."

Twenty years later, I would have a second thought.

I was busy enough with editing a newspaper and caring for three young children and my mother, who was troubled by arthritis. John was in the fifth grade in Dumas, and Sarah, who barely missed the public school age deadline, was enrolled at St. Mary's Catholic School in McGehee. Melvin drove the 40-mile round trip each day to take her to school, where the nuns were most kind. A scramble to get our children off to school each morning was reflected in Sarah's card: "Happy Mother's Day. I love my mother. She helps me find my shoes. I pray for her."

I managed a Terry family reunion to honor Mother's 72nd birthday. She was still anchoring the Dumas social news coverage, generally two full pages in the *Clarion*.

June brought another challenging trip, and a very sentimental one for Mother. In 1904, her parents had taken her to the World's Fair in St. Louis. Sixty years later, we planned to take her to the New York World's Fair.

Again, we settled into the big, blue Mercury and headed out for the long drive to New York City. Arriving in the midst of the theater district rush hour, John, not yet 12, confidently guided Melvin to the Commodore Hotel.

We had taken five days to get there, with the first stop at Mammoth Cave even though claustrophobia bothered Mother. We rolled on, crossing the Ohio River and causing Steve to wonder, "How did dem fill it up?" On to Gettysburg and Philadelphia, historical stops to delight us. Once in the Big Apple, we enjoyed the Radio City Music Hall, United Nations, Statue of Liberty, and other sights—along with attending the National Editorial Association convention.

We took the children to see the automat, where they could put in their coins and get treats. Three times, a man passed our table. Finally, he stopped and said, "You must be Melvin Schexnayder I knew in engineering at Louisiana State University." On leave from his work in Iran was Louis Acosta, and he and Melvin enjoyed a small-world reunion.

On a Sunday morning, we went to immense St. Patrick's Cathedral prominently displaying our press badges. An usher motioned for us to come down front and unlocked a seventh-row pew for us. We stumbled into the pew and knelt, with Melvin whispering to me, "Why are we in this pew?"

"I haven't the faintest idea," I replied. The children looked around in awe. A large crowd stood at the back of the cathedral. Soon it became even more interesting. Francis Cardinal Spellman entered and welcomed Francisco Orlich Bolmarcich, president of Costa Rica, and his party. Apparently, they looked at our press badges and assumed we belonged in that delegation. Marveling at our newly found and unexpected prominence, we exited on cue with the delegation.

Living in a small town of 3,000, we took New York in stride. Riding the subway, we were among NEA delegates traveling to the World's Fair, which was dominated by its Unisphere. At the fair, Melvin pushed Mother in a wheelchair, I guided Steve and Sarah in a rented stroller, and John walked beside me. It never occurred to us that a family, ages 3 to 72, couldn't take in the fair together, and there was great pleasure in seeing Mother enjoy comparing fairs 60 years apart.

Our return was by Aberdeen Proving Ground, Maryland, where Melvin had received his army commission 21 years before. On to Washington DC, where we observed President Lyndon Johnson officially welcoming the Costa Rican president and went to Arlington Cemetery to see President John F. Kennedy's gravesite. Then to Fredericksburg, Richmond, Williamsburg, Jamestown, and Norfolk, where we stopped to dip toes in the Atlantic Ocean. Before heading home we went to Emporia, Virginia, to visit Don and Betty Tillar, only recently discovered members of the Tillar family, and to see the grave of ancestor John Tillar, who emigrated from Wales in 1690. Crossing the Blue Ridge Mountains, we stopped in Asheville before returning to Dumas—a 3,400-mile marathon.

Jack Halter, a former newspaperman, came out of retirement to help our staff during our tour. I had copy for weeks in the *Clarion*, which usually included two sections and three on occasion. Subscriptions were $3.50 a year, and single copies were 10 cents. Our paper boys paid 5 cents a copy and doubled their money on street sales, totaling 1,500 to 1,700 copies weekly.

Legal notices boosted income, particularly proposed state constitutional amendments and acts. Large grocery ads from Lee's Supermarket, Nichols Food Market, and Failla, and national car advertising also were mainstays. Political advertising was vital, and the race between Gov. Orval Faubus and challenger Winthrop Rockefeller made for a successful fall.

We acquired a large Ludlow type-casting machine. It never quite matched the handset type we used, but it was much faster. We also bought a Photo-Lathe for light metal photo engravings later mounted on wood blocks.

Politics provided major news coverage. The Arkansas Supreme Court upheld Senator Merle Peterson's 16-vote win in re-election. Politics were part of home, too. John distributed Lyndon B. Johnson bumper stickers, and Steve, almost 4, noted that there were three kinds of water: "Hot water, cold water, and Goldwater."

A December election was scheduled for Dumas citizens to vote on the industrial district. The Dumas economy was rapidly changing. Mechanization of agriculture reduced many of the farm jobs, and industrial payrolls were badly needed to take up the slack.

Our involvement in national press associations had continuing benefits. On February 27, 1965, we were invited to the Foreign Policy Conference at Southern Methodist University in Dallas. I reveled in hearing George W. Ball, under secretary of state, and Ellsworth Bunker, ambassador to the Council of Organization of American States.

Our newspaper supported expansion of the Desha County Hospital, an industrial fund drive, a 50-unit public housing project, and an industrial park. As usual, the people of Dumas were generous, giving $25,000 toward hospital expansion and raising $140,000 for an industrial site where Sunbeam Corporation would locate a plant. Foretelling the town's commitment, Dumas voters approved a $2 million bond issue for a Sunbeam building 742 to 25.

Melvin carried a heavy civic load as chairman of the Hospital Board and officer in the Chamber of Commerce and Lions.

Newspaper production was often a problem, but friends sometimes came to our rescue. When a major cog broke on the Duplex press and a substitute could not attained quickly, we turned to Cone Magie, who agreed to print the last eight pages at his Lonoke plant. Jimmy Humphries of Stuttgart volunteered to run the press. Melvin and foreman Earl Lewis took the heavy forms (150 pounds each) to Lonoke and returned at midnight. At 6 a.m., our crew was in place to insert sections and mail the papers. Since we most often printed eight-page sections, assembling the paper required extra help called "stuffers," who manually combined sections.

Before global warming, we had the problem of street sales in March snows. Three of four weeks saw our paperboys plodding through spring snow to sell the *Clarion*. Whatever the effort required, we responded. Many people depended on the *Clarion*. We always remembered an earlier letter from Genia Horton: "I am writing to let you know I did not get my copy of last week's paper...P.S. I missed it pretty bad."

We tried to cover local news fully, sadly reporting in 1965 the deaths of D. W. Gill Sr., respected superintendent who shaped Dumas Public Schools for 34 years, and our optimist neighbor, Mrs. Jennie Moss, who cheered us.

We sought human interest stories, such as our people coming to the aid of a father, mother with babe in arms, and four little children stranded along the highway. The family began hitchhiking after their car had broken down in Oklahoma, and although other towns had ignored them, Dumas people provided food, lodging, and bus fare to relatives in Alabama.

Only in a small town could there be so many willing crime fighters. When businesswoman Winnie Franks had her bank bag snatched by a youth downtown, Mack Burns stopped his car, left it running, and set out in pursuit of the thief. In sequence, he was joined by Superintendent Ben Stephens, Postmaster Alvin Bridwell, bank president Jack Frank, Odie Kirtley, Marvin King, C. A. Rogers, Jarrell Carter, and Jack Dowden. The youth dropped the bank bag and landed in the mid-section of Bridwell as others closed in. As we wrote, "Where else would a bookkeeper, bank executive, postmaster, school superintendent, businessman, car salesman, farmer and ginner form such an efficient posse!"

There always were interesting stories, including the saga of a man who came to dinner in Granada Hills, California, stayed there for a month (collecting credit cards), borrowed a Thunderbird, traded it for an airplane, and landed in jail in Desha County. Moreover, he threatened to sue me for libel because I published the story.

We worked very long hours, but we scheduled break times, including the fourth annual Journalism Days at the University of Arkansas. Association with bright young students there renewed our sense of purpose and presented an opportunity to meet future state leaders, including Skip Rutherford, Brenda Blagg, and Ron Robinson. Other welcome diversions were Press Day at the State Fair where we met Fess Parker (starring as Daniel Boone on TV) and a family trip to Dallas for the NEA convention.

National meetings put us in touch with newsmakers. Astronaut Gene Cernan, who had been on a voyage to the moon, joked that it was more difficult to get to the eighth floor of the Baker Hotel when the elevator was not operating. Visiting with oil tycoon H. L. Hunt, a southern Arkansas native, during a reception, we said we admired the 52-story bank building he had constructed and were sorry we couldn't see the closed observatory. "Oh, but you can!" he exclaimed. "Just tell the guard I sent you!" Magic words, for we accepted the invitation. Shy, we were not.

The mid-sixties were among Dumas's finest hours, showing the citizenry's cooperation and commitment. The Dumas Industrial

Foundation bought 140 acres of farm land from R. A. Pickens. When cash and pledges totaled $103,000 in January, the Industrial Foundation executed the purchase of 50 acres for the Sunbeam Appliance plant. The sum raised represented sacrifice. Some borrowed to give.

Residentially, Dumas was growing, with O. L. Puryear and Sons developing 200 lots in east Dumas, and the Low Rent Housing Authority locating a new block of multi-family homes in West Dumas. Notable among the new houses was the one bringing Jack and Amy Frank with Sue and Tommy next door. They became a grand support crew for us, through thick and thin. A marvelous cook, Amy prepared Wednesday night treats for years. She knew how demanding was press day.

Construction of the new Sunbeam plant and presentation of the first electric mixer off the line were notable highlights of 1967. The City of Dumas studied plans for a municipal airport. Construction was under way on Arkansas river locks and dams, feeding monies into the area. Also being built was the mammoth (later growing to 330,000 square feet) warehouse for United Dollar Stores. Where there had been two houses 12 years ago, now there were hundreds east of Highway 65. The State Highway Commission approved a bridge for Pendleton, replacing a ferry crossing and linking Desha County with Arkansas County.

As Dumas grew, so did the *Clarion*. Many weeks, we published three sections as we battled our press's poor printing. When a kindergarten class visited the *Clarion*, Kevin McGinnis, age six, pointed out, "They've got a mechanical marvel from outer space." Sometimes, we also felt that way about it. The Arkansas Press Association gave its "Man of the Year" award to Melvin, recognizing his leadership in establishing Journalism Days at the University of Arkansas. He also was honored for serving as state National Newspaper Association director and raising funds for its first legal counsel.

In 1936, the *Clarion* editor had written: "If you like to read the *Clarion*, do something about it. If money is scarce, we can use corn, potatoes, syrup, chickens, eggs, heater wood and corn licker." In the sixties, we still exchanged subscriptions for pecans, produce, and eggs. An elderly woman annually came by with a double-handful of pecans and said, "I don't know if I have enough to pay for the paper," to which Melvin always replied, "You have just the right amount!"

The *Clarion* gained our first original cartoon for our editorial page, with Craig Ogilvie, 21, of Batesville as the freelancer.

My home support included Archie Mae Poole, a good-natured African American woman with a hearty and infectious laugh. She fried the best chicken I ever ate, but otherwise I cooked our meals. Her job was to help with the children, later with Mother. We dearly loved Archie Mae, a true godsend, but I always was there as needed. When the mumps struck, I held Steve who was terribly ill for a week. I didn't remember having mumps as a child, and I endured his siege without having them.

For our national newspaper trip to Boston, we depended on Jack Halter and on Kersh Hall, University of Arkansas summer intern. "Killing out" or dumping type for resmelting was one of Kersh's occasional tasks. Instead of killing out stories never to be used again, Kersh misunderstood and threw in the whole church page. We all made mistakes and we were really glad to have Kersh, who later achieved a fine newspaper career in Forrest City and Pine Bluff. I still called in several times a day with advice, welcome or not.

These trips were more than vacations; contact with other publishers and editors over the nation inspired us to do better. These contacts were planting a seed for a changeover to offset printing and a vastly improved product.

Previous trips had left us so enamored with Washington DC that it was a "must see again" on our way to the NNA convention in Boston. We also visited West Point; Hyde Park, the Franklin D.

Roosevelt Home and Library; and the Vanderbilt Estate. In Hartford, Connecticut, we found some truly caring strangers when Steve became ill with a high fever—ultimately a strep infection. He made a good recovery, and we continued on to the convention.

Touring included Boston Harbor, the Wayside Inn, the frigate *Constitution*, Boston Museum of Fine Arts, the Boston Commons, Harvard, and MIT. My favorites were walking the Freedom Trail, visiting old North Church and Faneuil Hall, and hearing the Boston Pops perform in the St. Charles Band Shell. When we went to Concord, citizens served refreshments "on the green" while we savored the history. A kind lady asked if our children "would like a tonic." Mother thought she said "toddy," and replied, "I think they are a little young." "Oh, no!" said the lady. "It is just a soda!"

On the return, we took Mother to fulfill a lifelong dream of seeing Niagara Falls, and turned south to visit Detroit and Greenfield Village. Nearing home, Mother became ill with exhaustion. We hastened home, but Mother never recuperated and began a long decline.

Oklahoma City beckoned as host of the national newspaper meeting, with its cross-pollination of publisher ideas. We met E. K. Gaylord, then a spry 93, and he invited us to tour the *Daily Oklahoman*. Melvin presided at community service sessions. Although I had been on panels, women weren't in leadership roles for our association.

Politics enlivened the fall. Winthrop Rockefeller, Republican candidate for governor, brought his campaign bus to Dumas, and Police Chief A. L. Morgan gave him a parking ticket. I went to apologize for the parking ticket, which I considered politically motivated since we were a Democratic stronghold, and had a pleasant visit with Mr. Rockefeller. He ended Orval Faubus's 12-year tenure and changed the face of Arkansas politics.

I wrote a front-page editorial declaring voting machines were needed—after two boxes were purloined from the city jail where they had been stored. The theft made the polls in two Dumas precincts open nearly an hour late because no voting boxes were available. County citizens, in a later referendum, approved voting machines by a 39-vote margin.

In a troublesome time for us, our good neighbors Jack and Amy Frank were badly injured in an auto collision at Pickens Bridge, the accident killing three in the other car. I organized friends to sit with the Franks at our hospital, and helped their children, Sue and Tommy, and their grandparents, "Mammaw and Pappaw Frank."

Other times were happy. After three years of Mass in the living room of Art and Stell Mayer's house and eight months of church at the funeral home chapel, we Catholics rejoiced over the groundbreaking of Holy Child Catholic Church. On a spring Sunday, the funeral home roof rattled and suddenly prayer became more serious. We didn't know until later that it was a minor earthquake.

In the middle of all the long days, we found time for fun, taking our family to Little Rock to see Carol Channing in *Hello Dolly*, much in the same spirit that my mother had taken me to cultural events during the Great Depression.

Desha County was bustling, with Desha Central opening a new school and Dumas Methodists celebrating a new sanctuary with striking stained-glass panels from its old church. An Act 9 bond issue was set for the Puryear Wood Products' million-dollar expansion, later to become Bassett Industries for 27 years.

15.
Year of Transition

In newspaper production, 1968 was the year of our greatest transition. We scheduled an end to the cumbersome process of copy transformed into metal type, made up into forms weighing 150 pounds per chase, and printed on a monster of a press. We studied the transition for several years. First, we changed the operation to a paste-up procedure of type produced in paper strips, photographed pasted-up pages, and made the plates in our shop. Until we could install a new offset press, we planned to print the plates at DeWitt, already an offset operation. The grand plan depended upon financing.

I went to Merchants & Farmers Bank. "We need to borrow $60,000 for an offset operation," I said. Specifically, we required $52,547 for a new press, a V-15A manufactured by the Harris Corporation. That sounded like a million dollars to us in 1968, as well as to the bank.

Bank officers said they would have to put the request before a loan committee. I said I could get the money elsewhere, if necessary. By late afternoon, our neighbor, Jack Frank, the bank's president, came to our house and said that we could get the financing. The payments would be $830.53 a month, and they would come first out of the gross. By comparison, we were taking just $400 a month for our salaries. "We will repay every cent if we can keep our health," I told the bank. To insure the loan, both Melvin and I bought life insurance policies.

Many changes were occurring in Dumas as well. Sunbeam Corporation was adding employment at its new plant, and T.

Minter Carter announced a new shopping center at the Highway 65/54 intersection.

Significantly on the educational front, Thomas F. (Tommy) Shea was elected president of the Dumas School Board. Ultimately, he and Superintendent Harold Tidwell skillfully led the district through total integration of the schools.

The year also brought brushes with the famous, again proving that a small newspaper opened many doors. When Melvin and I went to the National Newspaper Association government conference, we read in the *Washington Post* that Attorney General Robert F. Kennedy would reveal his political plans. Melvin said that it would be a special occasion, as he had visited with the attorney general in his office in 1963 and still cherished a photo made then.

Our Arkansas delegation reasoned that we might get into the press conference. When we reached the hall outside the Senate Caucus Room, there were an estimated 400 people seeking entrance. I went to the policeman at the door, and said, "You don't know me from Adam. I publish a newspaper in Arkansas—and so do these other people with me. Here is my press card. We would like very much to attend Mr. Kennedy's press conference."

He said, "Go ahead, lady," and beckoned to the group with me, including Tom Dearmore, then editor of Mountain Home's *Baxter Bulletin*. Tom had been pushed from the platform by a Mutual Broadcasting System reporter when President Kennedy came to dedicate the dam in his home county. Tom saw a chance for revenge, took the seat marked for Mutual Broadcasting, and would-n't budge throughout the conference. We stood at the back where Melvin was on a small platform by CBS and NBC, giving him a place to use his reflex camera. Thus it was that Tom and Melvin showed up on TV coverage.

Robert Kennedy was accompanied by his wife, Ethel, and eight children to the historic room, where his late brother, President John F.

Kennedy, also had made his announcement. Totally at ease, Robert Kennedy handled barbed questions with intellect and wit.

From this peak of coverage, we were to descend into gloom. Soon after returning from DC, to our horror, civil rights legend Martin Luther King was assassinated in Memphis. And who then could have envisioned that Robert Kennedy also would be killed the following summer?

We continued to stress local news. On the first day of spring, a 12-inch snow overburdened and broke budding trees. A tornado killed five and caused heavy damage in Lincoln County. On a brighter note, Dumas attracted visitors from afar as Bob and Andy Stimson, shorthorn cattle barons, held the Mid-South Shorthorn Sale.

Ending our production tradition, 69 years of letterpress at the *Clarion*, we published the *Clarion*'s first offset edition in July 1968. I commented: "We're all for this conversion, but we found that we're not so great at 'eyeballing' which consists of trying to line type up straight in a layout. We also lost several headlines and a short story in the 'waxer' and found it a little difficult to exchange a make-up rule for a pair of scissors, but we're still pursuing the goal. At this juncture, we feel as Harry Truman did about the presidency when he declared 'it's like riding a tiger; you don't dare get off or you get eaten up!'"

Since our new press wouldn't arrive for several months, we took the plates to DeWitt for printing. It was harder to make corrections there, but we did. Frank Whitbeck, a Little Rock insurance man campaigning for governor, provided our lead story. Also featured was a photo from a fire destroying a 1908 home in Tillar. As the *Clarion* rolled off the DeWitt press, we scanned the front page and shouted "Stop the press!" Photos had been pasted in wrong and Frank Whitbeck's campaign picture was identified as "Tillar Landmark Destroyed by Fire."

Noting that 35 Arkansas newspapers already had gone to offset, I pointed out that the graphic arts business had progressed more in 10 years than in many previous years combined. "It is like going from the

Model T to the Jet Airliner," I wrote. "It gets you to your goal faster and better—if you don't wreck en route!"

No one wanted the old duplex rotary press, long our printing nightmare. Since the press was erected over a pit, we hired a welder to cut the monstrosity and pitch parts into the pit. To that we added a pouring of concrete. We had a hearty laugh after observing what archeologists might think of the pit in centuries hence.

The new press arrived November 20, 1968, and Jerry Drennen of the Cottrell Company was in charge of installation. Assembled with newspaper roll stands, the press measured 26 feet. Clearly above our production, it could print 15,000 copies—eight pages—per hour when our circulation hovered around 4,000. Conversion to offset marked the end to ink-stained fingers, which seemed our trademark.

Coverage of town grief always left me emotionally spent. Dumas lost one of its bright young men when Johnny Halsell died of wounds in the Vietnam War, and I shall never forget how a former classmate-pallbearer lovingly touched the American flag on his casket. Dumas people generally supported the war but were beginning to question the U.S. role there.

Dumas continued growth as a new swimming pool and nursing home were under construction. Puryear Wood Products built a plant later to become Bassett Furniture Industries. The Arkansas River Navigation project scheduled an October 4 dedication to mark the completion of the first six locks and dams. A new apartment complex was erected by Mr. and Mrs. W. E. Adams, First Methodist Church completed a new sanctuary, the Hellums Wing was added to Desha County Hospital in Dumas, and United Dollar Stores expanded its warehouse. Our newspaper also benefited, with strong advertising.

In a hectic news week, 10,000 bales of cotton burned in a $1.5 million fire at Federal Warehouse in Dumas. Awaking to the acrid smoke smell in the early morning, we soon saw a monstrous fire sending huge cinders funneling toward our house two streets west of the compress. Atop ladders, Melvin and son John manned water hoses spraying our roof. I ran to wake the neighbors and tell them that flaming cinders were landing on their porch and yard. Garden hoses seemed totally inadequate. We had fought cinders a half-hour when a Dumas policeman came driving up the street to alert us. "We know!" we rejoined.

Being young and determined to succeed moved us through challenges. Smudged printing in news files from those years reminds us of the struggle with offset. Notable, however, was the Christmas paper with a three-color nativity drawing. Since each press unit would handle only one color, an "s" wrap provided the third color. Color was in the future.

Selected Photographs

Charlotte at age three.

At 16, Charlotte poses with Tillar sign on Highway 65.

A last family photo, just weeks before Charlotte's father died, shows Jewell and Bertha Tillar with Julian (in airman helmet) and Charlotte with a doll at Christmas; 1930 in McGehee.

At Louisiana State University, the Reveille staff enjoys a fun moment. From left are Ed (Jersey) Smith, Juanita Greene, Vernie Pitre, and Charlotte Tillar.

Charlotte (second from right) and Melvin Schexnayder (to Charlotte's right) observe letterpress makeup of the Reveille at LSU.

As editor of the McGehee Times, *Charlotte Tillar receives the 1945 General Excellence Award for weekly newspapers by the Arkansas Press Association in a presentation by John Guion, president.*

Melvin John Schexnayder in his army photo when he was commissioned a lieutenant in the Ordnance Corps; circa 1944.

Charlotte and Melvin Schexnayder after their wedding on August 18, 1946. (Attempts at commercial photos of the grand occasion failed.)

Melvin and Charlotte Schexnayder become advertising manager and editor, respectively, of the McGehee Semi-Weekly Times in 1948.

Col. T. H. Barton presents the Arkansas Press Association weekly sweepstakes award to the Dumas Clarion publishers Melvin and Charlotte Schexnayder in 1957.

Charlotte straightens Melvin's attire for the 50th anniversary of Dumas's incorporation in 1954 as Charlotte's mother, Bertha Tillar, joins in.

Charlotte's mother, Bertha Terry Tillar, at her desk in the Dumas Clarion *office; 1963.*

Melvin Schexnayder checks the news and finance information at the Dumas Clarion; *1963.*

Young Steve clings tightly to his mother, Charlotte, while brother John cradles a healing arm in this backyard photo with Melvin and Sarah.

Tommy Gillespie, president of the Arkansas Press Association, presents the weekly sweep-stakes award for the Dumas Clarion to Melvin and Charlotte Schexnayder; 1971.

A winning newspaper family and staff gather in the Clarion *office. From left (front row) are Sarah Schexnayder, Steve Schexnayder, Charlotte Schexnayder, and Mary Frances Farabough; (standing) Melvin Schexnayder, Eva Price, Terry Stallings, Carolyn Moore, Roy Williams, Kristina Weaver (Poole), and John Schexnayder.*

At the 1970 National Federation of Press Women Convention in New Orleans, Charlotte expresses thanks for being chosen as National Press Woman of Achievement. From left are astronaut John Swigert, Melvin Schexnayder, Steve, and Sarah.

Charlotte interviews gubernatorial candidate Winthrop Rockefeller in downtown Dumas; 1970.

Governor David Pryor is greeted by supporters Melvin and Charlotte.

The Clarion *staff in the early 1970s. From left (front row) are Jerry Kozubski, Debra Conrad, Kristina Weaver Poole, Ola Tillman, Flossie Gilbert, and Ivory Bolden; (back row) Joyce Russell, Jane Sigmon, and Terry Hawkins.*

Charlotte, first woman president of the Arkansas Press Association, presides at a 1981 board meeting. Seated from left are Louie Graves, David Fisher, Tom Riley, Joel Irwin, APA manager Dennis Schick, Frank Robins, Ross Pendergraft, Orville Richolson, Cary Patterson, and Bill Whitehead Jr.

Elected to the Arkansas House of Representatives and taking office in 1985, Charlotte Schexnayder works at her desk.

Governor Bill Clinton explains his position on legislation to House freshman Charlotte Schexnayder; 1985.

Governor Bill Clinton signs the major ethics initiative on the shoulder of Rep. Charlotte Schexnayder as State Sen. Jay Bradford smilingly approves. The initiative was passed by Arkansas voters.

President Ronald Reagan greets Charlotte and Melvin at the White House.

Founding chair of the Ding Dong Days festival in Dumas, Charlotte is joined around the parade banner by festival leaders Paul Wilson, Mary Martin, and Michael Jones.

President William Jefferson Clinton and First Lady Hillary Clinton welcome Charlotte and Melvin Schexnayder to the White House.

Charlotte introduces General Colin Powell at the National Newspaper Association convention.

Arkansas members of the Electoral College in 1992 included Daisy Bates (seated), as well as (standing from left) Mary Ann Salmon, Skip Rutherford, Charlotte Schexnayder, Harold Jinks, and David Matthews.

Assistant speakers of the Arkansas House of Representatives in 1995, appointed by Speaker Bobby Hogue, were (from left) David Choate, Jerry Hunton, Charlotte Schexnayder, and Ben McGee.

Melvin took this photo of Charlotte, who was inducted into the Hall of Distinction at Louisiana State University in 1996. She is with their children, Steve, John, and Sarah.

The Schexnayder children entertained with a family dinner to celebrate the 60th wedding anniversary of Melvin and Charlotte on August 18, 2006. From left (front row) are Daniel Schexnayder, Allie Schexnayder, Annie Schexnayder, and Amy Schexnayder; (middle row) Dr. Steve Schexnayder, Dr. Rebecca Schexnayder, Charlotte and Melvin, Deanna Schexnayder, Sarah Steen, Emily Holden, and Lauren Holden Smith holding daughter Clara (Lauren's husband, Graham Smith, was unable to attend); (back row) Edward Schexnayder, Charles Schexnayder, Kelsey Schexnayder, John Schexnayder, David Schexnayder, and Mark Steen.

16.
Sorrow and Continuing Battles

Coping became our style, but family losses are never overcome. Melvin's mother, Rose Meaux Schexnayder, suffered a stroke and died February 13, 1970. "Mom-Mom," as we called her, was a model of humility, kind and caring for all she knew. Mothers leave us, but their spirit and inspiration remain ingrained.

In a sorrowful time, our prime responsibility was to our citizenry and there was some comfort in hard work. Pivotal to the peaceful integration of Dumas Public Schools was the March 5, 1970, vote on a new high school building. However, for Melvin and me, it was hardly peaceful. As we joined school board and city leaders urging a new school, we heard veiled threats and saw advertising withdrawn.

While the Dante and Tanenbaum families generously provided a 40-acre site at no cost for the new high school, opponents to the proposed million-dollar bond issue questioned "the remote site" in a new city addition. Increased taxes and safety (students having "to cross a busy highway") were other perceived deterrents. For some, the real problem was a new building to provide ample facilities for total integration. Until then, schools were divided into white and black facilities, semi-desegregated through the "freedom of choice" program.

Overcrowding meant that 175 students packed into gym bleachers for study hall at Reed High for African Americans, and 600 were using a Dumas High building designed to accommodate 200. Some pitiful frame buildings came from hastily constructed facilities at the

Rohwer Relocation Center, which had interned Japanese Americans during World War II.

At one point in overcrowding, a fight broke out between students. Response was a line of pickup trucks (guns in racks) parked at Dumas High. Melvin and I drove to the hospital grounds nearby, and he admonished me to remain in the company van. "Think of the children," he said. "Both of us should not be out on this line."

In another brave stand, he brandished a camera as he walked along the line of trucks. Most there did not wish to be photographed. The fracas was settled peacefully, but school board resolve and Melvin's courage counted.

I pushed editorially: "Dumas does need a new high school, despite the misinformation being circulated, and the whole future of the city and its young people hinges on the March 10 school election."

A heavy rain flooded some classrooms in the 1927-vintage high school just before the vote, but it swayed few. Despite our editorial efforts, the bond issue was defeated by a 1,243 to 498 vote. However, the issue would not vanish. Neither would our editorial perseverance. I examined the Dumas School Board's predicament—whether to patch up old facilities or try again on a bond issue the next year. Once, upon entering Meador Pharmacy, I heard the comment: "Those ******* Schexnayders just won't give up." No, we wouldn't.

Alton Farmer's agreement to rent us another portion of his building made room for newsprint and printing supplies as well as expanded office supply inventory. A corner was reserved for office space. I wrote: "The new office space might aptly be called Charlotte's Hideaway, because my editorial comments often have put me in a position of needing to hide."

Hide, I never did. Seeking both news and advertising, I walked downtown and frequently took on the verbal challenges. I often rode my bike and stopped to chat, as I did not drive at that time. Often was I asked for advice, not always on editorial issues "Mrs. Shenanigans," said one caller, "If you wuz my son, would it be better to be GRAFT-ED or PREFERRED under the new law?"

I pounded my old manual typewriter with conviction: "We believe the great majority of the patrons of the Dumas School District sincerely want their children to get the best possible education under circumstances conducive to learning. We hope that responsible citizens of both races will stand behind the School Board in its efforts to achieve a unified school system with this goal."

Dumas marked a new high in population—4,601. United Dollar Stores, based in Dumas, grew to 200 stores, and the Pendleton Bridge across the Arkansas River was completed. McGraw-Edison came to Dumas to look at the possibility of purchasing 70,000 square feet of space from Federal Compress and Warehouse. No deal could be made, but Merle and Deloris Peterson, Dumas's most solid supporters, agreed to build a 125,000-square-foot building. McGraw-Edison located here, providing 250 jobs and spurring additional growth.

A signal honor awaited me. Mary Louise Wright of DeWitt nominated me for National Press Woman of Achievement. To my great surprise, I won and shared the evening's podium with astronaut John L. Swigert at the convention in New Orleans. Bringing joy to my heart by being there were Melvin, Sarah, and Steve. John was enrolled in the University of Arkansas summer honors program. Mother relished a later report.

Invited to appear on TV, I sat 30 minutes in the deep freeze studio. I don't know what was worse: chilblains or jitters. I was just warming up when hostess Mary Connell signed off for "Eye on Arkansas."

Weekly newspaper opinion was considered important. Politicians made a beeline to weeklies in hopes of free publicity. Thus, our interest was constantly whetted.

When Dale Bumpers came to speak outside at John Puryear Deer Camp, women emerged from the clubhouse and listened intently. Melvin observed, "He's going to win—look at all the support he has from the women." No surprise to us that Mr. Bumpers defeated Winthrop Rockefeller in the general election! I was excited because it was my first time as a delegate to the State Democratic Convention.

State politics were considered an interesting sideline, but our principal focus was local. Our courageous school board served notice again: the million-dollar bond issue for a new high school again would be on the ballot. I editorialized: "It is not the responsibility of the school board to convince patrons of the need. The patrons have only to open their eyes and spend a day in the school system to see the overcrowding."

Although the opposition was not as vocal as previously, the divide remained great. We gave all the information we could: teacher pleas, editorials, drawing of a new high school, polling places, and even our son and fourth grader Steve's plea for bond issue passage.

The banner headline of March 10, 1971, said it all: "High school bond issue approved by 3 votes." Of course, litigation followed. Citizens challenging the vote and seeking a recount were Patrick Dillon, E. R. Henry Sr., Harry Norris, and Charles Taylor, represented by attorney Jay Dickey Jr. of Pine Bluff. County election commissioners C. C. Stuart, Noel Newton, and Bert Southard heard witnesses and unanimously turned down the recount petition. Melvin reported the proceedings for the *Clarion*, and his notes later became important affirmation.

Our editorial supported the integrity of election officials. I defended the school board, commenting, in part: "They have been faulted for desiring to place a new school on as many as 40 acres; for putting only three, and not four, grades there, to accepting a site on Highway 54; for not putting more buildings on present campuses, for nearly every reason that could be thought up. Oftentimes, the reasons given for opposing a new high school are used to cover up either prejudices, by both whites and blacks, or economics, raising of taxes."

Prejudice fueled most of the fight. We lost significant advertising and a few subscriptions. Circulation of the paper, however, did not really decline. People were too curious, and they would continue to buy papers on the streets.

Two suits contested the election. One asked for a recount. Another challenged five votes cast. Several days later, a third suit was filed—against County Judge Bonnie Zook, who had certified the vote after it was forwarded to him by the election commission.

In one column, I wrote: "If I had a dime for every rumor circulating about the school bond election and a quarter for every complaint on the new city occupation tax, I would be a wealthy woman." Knowing controversy would never leave our occupation, we remembered that President Harry Truman said, "If you can't stand the heat, stay out of the kitchen." We were in the kitchen for the long run.

Amid the school bond election controversy, we focused on news coverage including Al Eastham (later to become an ambassador) being the first from Dumas to register when the voting age was lowered to 18, as well as the merger of Watson and Desha Central schools. We covered an archaeological dig on Indian mounds beside Amos Bayou near Tillar and the formation of a Helping Hand to assist the less fortunate.

Then came the ruling by Circuit Judge Randall Williams, denying the plaintiffs' petitions. He wrote: "An election is expensive and affects a large number of people. It should not be set aside except for specific grounds and proof." Attorney Dickey announced an appeal to the Arkansas Supreme Court.

Amid controversy came an especially proud achievement. Our son John and Susan Phillips were Dumas High co-valedictorians. Named a National Merit Scholar, John had many scholarship offers and chose our alma mater, Louisiana State University in Baton Rouge.

The same May, the new bridge crossing the Arkansas River at Pendleton was opened to traffic. Thus came new opportunities, new friendships, and new business dealings for Desha County and Arkansas people, who had long contended with a ferry crossing.

Taking a break, Melvin, Sarah, Steve, and I flew to Phoenix for the National Federation of Press Women convention. At Camelback Resort, we heard luminaries Barry Goldwater and Arizona judge Sandra Day O'Connor, who later became the first woman on the U.S. Supreme Court. We visited the Frank Lloyd Wright complex, Taliesin West, where Mrs. Wright and young architectural interns greeted us.

John remained home to help the *Clarion* staff and Mother, then aided by devoted caregivers Archie Mae Bealer and Nellie Mae Young. We came home to joyful news that the *Clarion* had won Arkansas Press Association contest sweepstakes.

Meanwhile, the Dumas School District proceeded with plans to sell the school bonds, but on advice of counsel, decided to delay the procedure. Throughout the process, board president Tommy Shea provided strong leadership.

In August, Melvin was hospitalized with a severe kidney infection. Until then, he had never missed *Clarion* duties because of illness, even working while on crutches. Our family again filled in. When an airplane crashed into Amos Bayou, Steve, age 10, and I donned boots and sloshed through water moccasin–infested mud. Steve photographed the airplane hanging in a tree. Amazingly, the pilot had escaped injury.

On August 18, I wrote: "This Wednesday marks our 25th wedding anniversary. Since 23 of these 25 years have been spent in the weekly newspaper business, perhaps it is symbolic that our silver anniversary occurs on PRESS DAY—but it doesn't leave much time for celebrating…"

And I went on to say, "There are some irrevocable rules about Press Day, as gained from our many years of surmounting them, such as:

1. If something breaks down on press day, then at least three other BAD THINGS will happen.

2. If we are sailing along and about two hours ahead of schedule, something is certain to happen, like the plates going bad on the press or a part breaking. All of a sudden, we are two hours behind.

3. The most startling story of the week happens 15 minutes after the papers are out on the street.

4. At least three people have searched for errors, but just as the last paper rolls off the offset press, we discover a glaring error in a headline."

Melvin was recovering and I had work responsibilities, so John and Sarah prepared our anniversary dinner. Steve joined them in pooling resources, and with the help of Betty Jane Oldner, they bought a chandelier from John Puryear Hardware.

Our family accompanied John to enroll at LSU, especially traumatic for Steve, who snubbed back tears and declared, "I didn't think John would leave me."

Clouding the fall was the court case hanging over the Dumas school bond vote. In November, the Arkansas Supreme Court remanded one of the suits back to Judge Williams and ordered the Desha County Circuit Court to hold a hearing on allegations by a group of Dumas area taxpayers that the county board of election commissioners refused to act on their petition for a recount.

In other rulings, the high court said that a suit contesting the school election should be filed against the school board instead of the election commission, and it dismissed the suit alleging fraud.

Judge Williams convened a Circuit Court session December 8, 1971, to determine whether the election commission had held a proper hearing. Melvin was subpoenaed to appear and bring his notebook on the election commission hearing. Sensing the importance of those notes, we had kept the notebook in a fireproof file. Also summoned witnesses were election commissioners. The judge ruled that the election commission had considered the petitions, and entered a court order to that effect, thus clearing another hurdle to the building of a new high school.

The final ruling came on December 20 when the Arkansas Supreme Court, without comment, refused a rehearing petition by the plaintiffs.

At the *Clarion*, we dispensed with those awful "Justowriters"—a mix of typewriter and computer that often didn't work. One Wednesday, the Justowriter jammed, and Melvin couldn't fix it. In desperation, he slammed his fist against the side of the equipment. The Justowriter clattered again … and jolted to action. Melvin said he got its attention.

We installed a new Compugraphic system. Our compositors, Carolyn Moore and Shirley Smith, now punched a tape fed into a computer which could hyphenate, paragraph, and boldface. What a grand change! Typo errors continued, but we could produce the type much more easily.

Always seeking human interest stories, we made great effort to get them. In 1972, we learned that the *Delta Queen*, once a prominent steamboat on the Arkansas River, would make a voyage upriver to Little Rock. We drove to the Pendleton Bridge area in mid-afternoon and waited at Clay Cross's marina. I reminisced about having gone to Arkansas City in the late 1930s for an evening's excursion on the *President* paddlewheel. News came that the *Delta Queen* had reached Dam 2 and its smokestack had to be lowered for it to proceed. At 10:30 p.m. the *Queen* approached and we had a shot of the lighted steamboat going just under Pendleton Bridge—calling it a ghost from the past. We thought it worth the six-hour wait.

Publishing was hands-on, but politics often occupied my thoughts. I wrote: "We believe that the next few years will see more and more women seeking office and becoming involved in the work of political parties. At the present time, there are only three women in the State Legislature, and certainly, there are many women qualified to run for these positions."

My long advocacy for women in government was bolstered by my appointment to the Arkansas Commission on the Status of Women by Governor Bumpers. I admired First Lady Betty Bumpers for her leadership in childhood immunization and later in national Peace Links.

Our family life was saddened by the loss of our dog, Honey, who most loved to crawl into the *Clarion*'s yellow van, stretch out, creep up, and rest her head on Melvin's shoulder as he drove. Given a chance, she would dash into the *Clarion* office and lie under his desk. A lovable dog who had to be petted before she ate, she had two problems: chewing on everything in sight and chasing cars. The latter resulted in her death.

As Dumas was a frequent stop on Arkansas's campaign trail, Governor Dale Bumpers and Ted Boswell sought votes here the same week. Thinking about politics of my own, I was urged to run for an office in the National Federation of Press Women.

Meanwhile, our volunteer reporters alerted us that the *Batfish*, a World War II submarine, was being towed up the Arkansas River toward Catoosa, Oklahoma, where it would become a Maritime Museum. When it stopped at Pendleton for re-fueling, more than 200 land-locked school students turned out to see history passing.

And on invitation, we were in Russellville to tour the Arkansas Power & Light Co.'s nuclear power plant under construction, creating a special page in the *Clarion*.

A simple postage-stamped request to the National Aeronautics and Space Administration brought us regular photos, and thus our small newspaper had photo pages of space exploration, including *Apollo 16*'s journey to the moon. We believed our primary mission was to cover the area news, but we never shied from the chance to give our readers extra coverage on the national scene.

A nationally known civil rights activist, Mrs. Daisy Bates, came to Mitchellville, the small African American town a mile north of Dumas, and worked toward a community center and a fire truck. We found her pleasant as we covered the activities, but I never dreamed that she and I one day would become presidential electors at the same time.

Political advertising was thriving in the primary season. We were critically interested because we supported Representative David Pryor, seeking to unseat Senator John L. McClellan. At an Arkansas Press Association meeting in Hot Springs, David assembled a group of newspaper people, asking if we thought he should undertake the race. We all said, "Go for it!" The Democratic primary of June 1972 was the only time that candidate Pryor ever lost. Thereafter, I hesitated to offer political advice.

Our family came to a difficult crossroads. My mother, who had made her home with us for 27 years, was so feeble that she required around-the-clock assistance. Even though we had help, she constantly called for me and it was difficult for our family to sleep. I faced my most painful decision. With her agreement, we moved her to a private room in the Dumas Nursing Home with Nellie Mae Young to be the "night sitter." We said, "We'll try it for two weeks," but we knew it was likely permanent.

I was an Arkansas delegate to the Press Women's national convention in Seattle, so Melvin and I decided to take the family, fly to Denver, and then drive through Yellowstone en route to Seattle. When we reached Colter Bay cabins near Yellowstone, Sarah and I stayed up most of the night while gazing at the majestic Teton Mountains. We awoke to a fairyland from an overnight snow, and we toured Yellowstone when it was too cold for bears. Snowball fights in the mountain passes offered a treat.

Big sky Montana and impressive Seattle were favorites, as was a ferry trip to Victoria, British Columbia, to enjoy the Butchart Gardens and crumpets, fruit, cake, and tea at the Empress Hotel.

FBI agents boarded our plane on our return flight, but we noted that we were not suspect with a family of five, 10 pieces of luggage, three cameras, five coats, a large sack of souvenirs, and a bag of pretty rocks we'd collected.

As a mother, it was one of my busiest times, with a son in college, daughter in high school, and son in elementary school. As a daughter, I made daily visits to my mother in the nursing home. Challenges galore. We took time to attend the 25th anniversary of Melvin's graduating class from LSU, visit John, and attend performances of Bob Hope and the Temptations.

Our focus was enlarged to cover noteworthy national news including the death of former president Harry Truman on December 26, 1972. We placed a large American flag, flowers, and his portrait in the *Clarion's* front window. Many stopped respectfully at the window, acknowledging that Harry S. Truman, though hardly popular while in office, was a great president.

17.
True Bear Tale and Other Adventures

An unusual story came on press day, January 3, 1973. Eyeing front-page makeup, the last page to be turned back to the cameraman, I heard my phone buzzer.

"Mrs. Schexnayder," said the caller, "would you think I was drunk if I told you there was a bear under my trailer?"

"No, ma'am." I replied, "Just hold it till we can get there!"

She added, "I called the police and they said I was drunk. I heard dogs barking, went out to check, and there was a bear." Knowing that Mrs. Zerlene King was fully sober, and sensing a great story, I yelled to Pressman Jerry Kozubski, "Hold everything; we've got a bear in town!"

Melvin and assistant editor Lynn Vance grabbed cameras and raced to the mobile home park near the nursing home. I began redesigning the front page.

The *Clarion* duo indeed found the bear under the trailer. The bear shot out from hiding, with police, wildlife officers, two *Clarion* photographers, and bystanders in pursuit.

A tranquilizer dart hit the bear but did not slow her. Jody Wilkin tried to lasso the bear, but the bear eluded him and climbed into a nearby hackberry tree where some 2,000 witnesses gathered. Melvin photographed the bear in the tree, and we featured it on the front page of that week's *Clarion*.

"Darn," said businessman Jerry Tanenbaum, upon coming into the *Clarion* office to buy a paper. "You cost me $5! I bet someone you wouldn't get the bear picture in today's paper, but here it is!"

After several hours, the bear came to a sad end. While Game and Fish officers and veterinarian Lewis Partridge were trying the tranquilizer approach, the bear fell from a limb and broke her neck. Police Chief A. L. Morgan collected donations to have the bear mounted, and it's now a popular exhibit in the Desha County Museum.

While most coverage was local, we always included noteworthy national news. In January, we arranged another memorial window at the *Clarion* when President Lyndon Baines Johnson died. In a lengthy editorial, I commented on the civil rights, Medicare, and Housing and Urban Development plans he implemented, concluding, "The legislation passed during President Johnson's term of office mirrored that which he truly was—a man of the people, all of the people."

When Sheriff Robert S. Moore died from a vehicle accident on March 12, we lost one of our strongest political forces for Desha County and a resolute law enforcement officer. His widow, Dorothy, was appointed to fill out his term and served with grace and dignity.

Heavy spring rains brought the Mississippi River to its highest level since 1937, and wildlife seeking higher ground attracted a steady stream of cars to see deer, turkeys, possums, and rabbits seeking refuge on the levee. Gates on Dam 2, Arkansas River, were opened wide enough for engineers' boats to pass.

Dumas leaders began a $600,000 drive to build a medical clinic, to be operated by our hospital, on Highway 65. In typical generosity, Merle and Deloris Peterson gave 10 acres of land to be sold for the benefit of the clinic project, with stipulation that the clinic be named in honor of the late Sheriff Robert Moore. Also planned along the highway was the new Brookhaven Shopping Center, to be constructed by Pudata, Inc., owned by the Puryear, Dante, and Tanenbaum families. Plans included a new theatre, long after the old Gem Theatre closed.

My days were brightened by calls from our collegian at LSU, including the statement, "I am going to the Student Union for fried chicken and watermelon." Several days later, I inquired, "How were the fried chicken and watermelon?" Came back illumination for me, "Mother, that is the name of a rock group!"

In June, Leonid Brezhnev arrived amid pomp and a 21-gun salute in Washington DC, while our family, vacationing in our new Mercury, spent an hour and a half circling the U.S. Capitol in an effort to find parking. It was an updated visit for our children, who had been much younger on their last visit. Congressman Ray Thornton escorted us from his House office through the underground tunnel to the Capitol, the first of many times I was to use this route later in lobbying for the Great River Bridge. Our homeward trip included visits to Charlottesville, Virginia; the Monticello home of President Thomas Jefferson; and Colonial Williamsburg.

We returned to cover a new festival. In an era when civic clubs flourished in Dumas, the Jaycees successfully staged a Ding Dong Daddy Water Festival at Pendleton on July 4, and the Optimist Club worked on many youth projects.

With the newsprint shortage affecting the country because of Canadian rail and paper mill strikes, we editorially assured our readers that we had sufficient paper supply until January. We then bought it by truckloads and borrowed a forklift to maneuver it into the *Clarion* storeroom. Shortly after our announcement, our supply was cut 30 percent, resulting in downsizing to assure production. However, as had been our tradition, the editorial page would not be cut.

Changes were coming to the Dumas business community as Continental Telephone purchased Lincoln-Desha Telephone Co. from Kay and E. G. Van Train. Kay and her late husband, Ted Adair, bought the system in 1952 and had supervised many improvements, including transition to dial. Also, the city bought property for an airport.

National Newspaper Association membership took us to Hot Springs where I spoke on a panel and Melvin served on a committee. Governor Dale Bumpers was a smash hit and witty as usual. He said, "I make $10,000 a year, the maid saw the check, thought it was

hers and quit." A Texas publisher commented, "He must be kid-
ding." No, he wasn't.

Among the first women elected to the Little Rock Professional
Chapter, Society of Professional Journalists (previously Sigma Delta
Chi), I became its first woman president in 1973. In our delegation to
the national convention in Buffalo, New York, were Melvin and me,
Bob and Georgia Sells, Bob and Muriel McCord, Roy Ockert, and
Larry Odell. Convention show stopper was a panel on Watergate,
emceed by Bill Smith, CBS vice president, with panelists John
Chancellor of NBC, Ben Bradlee of the *Washington Post*, and the
public relations counsel of Archibald Cox's staff. Bradlee opined that
the scandal "had not bottomed out." He was right! Particularly entertaining was Charles Kuralt, noted TV journalist, who said one of his
favorite stories was of "a black man who built a library in the piney
woods of Arkansas."

In a mix of hard work and pleasure that year, I made an unsuccess-
ful run for vice president of the National Federation of Press Women at
the Detroit convention, losing by only a few votes. I then accepted the
tough job of being national contest chairman for two years.

As I neared my 50th birthday on Christmas Day, I became very ill
with influenza and worked with 103 fever until the family sent me
home. Steve took over the medical routine for me. Those days foretold
his future career. With talent for both, he would choose medicine over
journalism. My illness escalated to pneumonia. Hospitalized for a week,
I survived because of antibiotics, unavailable when Daddy died in 1931.

I recovered enough to attend the Arkansas Press Association
when I was elected the first woman on the board. Frank Robins, publisher of the *Log Cabin Democrat* in Conway, nominated me and long
remained a supporter.

Growth and inflation affected our economy. Magic Mart became
anchor for the new Brookhaven Shopping Center, also including
Piggly Wiggly Supermarket, Geno's Pizza Parlor, and Pets 'n Stuff.

Dumas State Bank opened with Ernie Ashcraft as president and Merle F. Peterson as board chairman. Lurking economic hazards were the rising price of gasoline and the OPEC embargo.

Governor Dale Bumpers, in a speech here, stressed the need for U.S. leadership, a tip-off that he was planning a race against Senator J. William Fulbright.

Late one afternoon as I wrote and Melvin made up pages, we heard a knock on the front office door. We found Senator Fulbright motioning that he wanted to come inside. The senator seemed both exhausted and resigned. He talked of the race, and then, out of the blue, observed, "If the voters of Arkansas don't want me any longer, that's all right. I've had a wonderful career." I was shocked, as I had considered Senator Fulbright unbeatable. Dale Bumpers was to prove me wrong.

In the early morning of April 23, 1974, we had a great scare. Separated by an alley from the *Clarion* building was the vacant two-story Hotel Dumas, once Dumas's hospital. City officer James Daniels spotted a curl of smoke from the building at 3:50 a.m. and sounded the alarm.

Our phone rang at 4 a.m. Said Smitty, the radio operator, "The hotel is on fire. I thought you ought to know."

Melvin, Sarah, Steve, and I donned essentials and dashed to the *Clarion* office to remove whatever we could. Volunteer firemen battled, and we began ours. Bystanders came to help pull out composition equipment and records. Sarah lugged a filing cabinet she could not have otherwise moved.

In the midst of the conflagration, I re-entered the *Clarion* office and saw Steve.

"Did you get a fire photo for tomorrow's paper?" I asked.

"No, ma'am," he replied as he struggled with an armful. "I have the accounts receivable."

Bless him! At age 13, he had real business sense. I was still a journalist first. Jack and Amy Frank, our neighbors, rushed up to help.

Amy demanded, "Where are the contest entries?" As contest chairman for the National Federation of Press Women, I was responsible for 2,500 entries, waiting to be judged. Thankfully, those entries had covered our home dining room, and we didn't have to evacuate them.

Sarah and I perched on the sidewalk across the street and prayed. Steve was busy with his camera, and Melvin watched anxiously. A heavy fog came to our rescue. The hotel wall threatening the *Clarion* office collapsed inward, as firemen pumped cascading water to save the *Clarion* building.

Providence and the brave Dumas volunteer firemen had spared us.

We were back to work at once, but politics most dominated the spring of 1974, leaving a long imprint on Arkansas. Governor Dale Bumpers ousted U.S. senator Fulbright. Congressman David Pryor clipped former governor Orval Faubus in the Democratic primary.

Melvin and I had long shouldered the work of several persons each, as we wrote, sold advertising, led civic careers, and managed the *Clarion* operation. We needed help, and the *Clarion* operation had grown enough to afford a news editor. Martha Ballard Hawkins, then alumni director at Arkansas A&M College, and I were former classmates. I wrote to her, asking if she knew someone who might be interested. Joining us in June 1974 was her son and recent A&M graduate, the talented Terry Hawkins—ultimately the next generation in *Clarion* management.

Our year was saddened by the death of Melvin's father, Maurice Schexnayder, in New Iberia, Louisiana. Kind and thoughtful Pop had been a wonderful part of our lives. Melvin's sisters, Duce Judice and Mabel Darcey, lived close by and had cared for him, and we had visited as often as we could.

Later I decided a change might help Melvin's depression. Instead of my planned flight, our family would drive to Bismarck, North Dakota, for the convention of the National Federation of Press Women. In our last long family vacation, we found the Midwest appealing and the people friendly. We felt at home in the small city of Bismarck. A day trip to the badlands at Medora provided another highlight. When our NFPW president called a board meeting there, a park guide snorted in disgust, remarking, "Those women are holding a meeting after riding all those hours just to get here!"

Students moved into Dumas's new million-dollar high school in September. Soon citizens who had fought to defeat a bond issue for the building were proclaiming it to be "our fine new school." Newspaper editing taught me much about human behavior.

Dumas had its first resident psychologist in late 1974, and I was able to abandon my unofficial position. For years, citizens had come to my desk and poured out their problems. Seldom could I offer a tangible solution, but I always listened to the problems: marital, financial, grudge, children, insecurity. Perhaps it made folks feel better just for having someone to listen, if not to provide professional counseling.

But before we had a psychologist, I had all kinds of requests.

For instance, an elderly African American man arrived in the front office one day and asked to see the editor. When I greeted him, he said: "Lady, somebody told me you would help me. My brother died, and I ain't got no suit to bury him in." Pushing back tears, I told him we would get a suit for him, and we did.

Another time, as I worked on page makeup, a young stranger appeared at my elbow. He had come in our open back door. He said quietly, "I heard you might help me. We had a little too much beer last night, and my friend and I landed in jail. I am out of jail, but I am afraid of the police. I have the money, and I need you to bail my friend out of jail."

I questioned whether the police had been brutal and learned the young man found them threatening. So I walked with him to the jail across the street and said, "This young man needs to bail his friend out of jail, and I am here to help him." Both young men were given their belongings, and they departed. I never knew their names, but the next day, the local florist delivered an African violet to my office. A note said, "I will never forget you."

My first venture outside the continental United States came in November 1974, when neighbor Amy Frank joined me in flying to Honolulu for the National Federation of Press Women's fall meeting. I aspired to NFPW office. On a free day, we accompanied Mary Louise Wright and Thelma Butler of DeWitt to the Big Island of Hawaii where we rented a car to circle the island. Amy and I were so charmed that we ventured into a real estate office and asked the price of a generous-size lot. "$8,000," came the answer. Amy pondered, "Do you suppose we might convince Jack and Melvin to relocate over here?" Laughing at this absurdity, I was still imbued with travel fever.

As the national bicentennial approached, in 1975, Mayor Billy Free, Carolyn Porter, and I were members of the Desha County Bicentennial Commission. Kay Canada, president of Women's Service League, noted that her group planned to begin an annual Arts & Crafts Fair and also would support a museum, a project I had pushed for years. Civic leaders agreed both projects were needed.

One April afternoon, a phone call from Governor David Pryor summoned me. Melvin and I had been friends with David and Barbara Pryor since they published the *Ouachita Citizen* in Camden and had supported him in all his races. When David Pryor was running for Congress, Melvin took him to the grassy strip serving as our airport and handed him a check for $200, half of our checking account. We surely weren't as generous with other candidates!

On that April 9, Governor Pryor said to me: "I would like you to think about something and give me a quick answer. I would like to appoint you as the first woman on the parole board, and I want to make the announcement when I come to Dumas tonight."

I was stunned beyond response, but managed to remark, "Let me think about it. I have a conflict of interest because of the newspaper. Why me?"

"You are tough and fair," he replied. "We need you." I called Little Rock friends, including Robert Fisher and Bob Sells, and asked their opinion. They already knew the governor's intention and urged me to take the appointment. Soul-searching and conferences with Melvin went on for several hours, and I finally called the governor to accept. At no time then, however, did I realize that appointment would lead me into a joint career of politics and journalism. Nor did I realize how much it would teach me about the lost in our society.

Governor Pryor was accompanied on his flight here by a *Newsweek* editor, Mel Elfin, who had an apprehensive surprise when the governor announced they would land on a grass strip.

The evening sparkled for me. Arkansas Supreme Court justice John Fogleman of West Memphis presented me with the George Washington Honor Medal from the American Freedoms Foundation. He had nominated me for the honor because of my July 4 column, "An American Creed."

There were more immediate challenges at hand. As Press Women contest director, I had to enlist volunteer judges to gather in Memphis. Two weeks later, we went to Oxford, Mississippi, for the regional meeting of the Society of Professional Journalists and then it was to Fayetteville to present the *Clarion* scholarship at Journalism Days. As Melvin kindly drove, I often penned columns and editorials.

Dumas State Bank announced a grand opening celebration on the same week that McGraw-Edison Co. said it would close its plant here. Dumas had another challenge to find a successor to McGraw-Edison, but had a good track record. In addition, we had great boosters in Merle and Deloris Peterson.

In 1975, Dumas High School was ready to graduate its first class from its new building, and we proudly beamed when our daughter Sarah, an honor student, received her diploma. It was double pleasure when we then raced to Baton Rouge to see son John and 2,046 others awarded degrees from Louisiana State University.

John and his fiancée, Deanna Tassin, planned to marry on May 24 in Edgard, Louisiana, and we excitedly planned another celebration. On the wedding day, Steve had a 102 fever from a sinus infection but managed to escort me down the aisle. Melvin served as best man, and Sarah was a bridesmaid. John and Deanna left for Charlottesville, where he had been accepted into the University of Virginia Law School.

In our ever-busy life, Melvin was president of the Dumas Chamber of Commerce when he was elected chairman of the Desha County Hospital board. For the summer, we managed to bend the budget enough to send Sarah with enthusiastic teacher Alyce Smith's group for six weeks' study in Europe. Steve, then our newspaper photographer, headed for band camp. A first taste of an empty nest.

We were still answering news calls at all hours. When we heard there had been a train derailment with escaping chemicals in Tillar, Melvin and I drove there for photos. Tillar and Reed were being evacuated. The quick action of citizen Frank Poe, using his garden hose to extinguish the fire beginning in a ruptured tank, prevented a calamity. Unassuming, he "just thought it was the thing to do."

A challenge of the summer was the transportation of the Press Women's contest entries to Idaho. We took 13 boxes, plus one bag each for Melvin, Steve, and me, and flew to Denver where we rented a car. From then it was a scenic trip through Wyoming to Sun Valley, Idaho, with a new experience, fly fishing for our dedicated angler Steve. Our return trip was through the glorious Colorado Rockies.

Returning to the routine of gathering news, we had several months without spectacular news. Then came a McGehee fire in September 1975, when three volunteer firemen, David Dupwe III, Michael Hunt, and Russell Leonard, were killed as the roof fell and walls blew out on them. Tragedies one writes about are indelible memories.

I wedged work and home duties between frequent visits to the nursing home, where my mother was in decline. I was torn between responsibilities, but coped with help from caregivers Nellie Mae and Archie Mae.

November brought the first annual Delta Arts & Crafts Fair sponsored by the Women's Service League, and the Otrabanda River Raft Revue, a Bicentennial troupe from New Orleans, performed in a nearby tent. Dumas also welcomed the *Sergeant Floyd*, a tow boat celebrating the Bicentennial and docking at Pendleton.

In late 1975, we added a new feature to the *Clarion*—an eight-page tabloid of features and photos produced by University of Arkansas journalism students. We printed the section on newsprint although book stock would have made a slicker publication. One notable issue featured Bud Adams Mercantile where we all enjoyed buying summer sausage, cheese, and crackers. Our downtown area was changing with a newly renovated municipal building and fire station, but the business area was stable.

Our staff had an intern from afar. Joe Stroud, editor of the *Detroit Free Press*, asked if his daughter, Kim, could intern for us as a high school project while she lived with her grandmother, Marion Stroud, in McGehee. As I wrote, "Kim is observing—and contributing, too. You'll see her accompanying us on our news and advertising rounds—and behind the scenes, she is proof-reading, researching, writing and even drawing some ad illustrations. She probably agrees with the humorist who called the weekly newspaper a venture in 'organized chaos.'" Chaos it was, as the typesetter roared like a tank, and a borrowed motor, installed backwards in haste, emitted type appearing to be Greek!

Aside from production problems, our focus targeted the Bicentennial celebration. Dumas called on native son Jerry Wilson, who had been in France as an assistant to Marguerite Yourcenar, famed novelist. He wrote and filmed a documentary on the American South's gospel music, and his work was highly acclaimed at a festival in Europe. Based on African American spirituals with photos from churches here, the multi-media show became our Bicentennial signal event. Governor Pryor joined us, black and white, arm in arm, to sing choruses led by the powerful gospel star Marion Williams.

Rain did not deter the old-fashioned Fourth celebration and parade, even though our newspaper float, featuring son Steve and printer's helper Ivory Bolden with a hand-operated press, was dripping wet and soggy. Steve and Ivory also went with us to the Arkansas Post celebration and printed souvenir copies of the Declaration of Independence. We believed the *Clarion* had to be a part of all the major celebrations.

Boundless energy carried me through family illness and sorrow, an always fulfilling career, and mounting civic responsibilities. Demanding my full attention were the monthly meetings of the Arkansas Parole Board, which held sessions at Cummins, Tucker, and Pine Bluff prisons. I served with James Gardner, thoughtful and genial Blytheville attorney; Bob Wells, conservative Paris businessman; James Hannah, serious Searcy attorney later to become chief justice; and Bill Hamilton, Little Rock educator and activist. Later, Little Rock schoolman J. J. Lacey served with us. Although they sometimes remarked that I always brought out a woman's viewpoint, they accepted my being the first woman board member and ultimately handed me a role as clemency reviewer. ("She will be tough on rapists," they declared.)

We received $25 a day, later getting expenses, and several years later, being paid $50 daily for three days of work. A week before our monthly meetings at three prisons we received a bulging board book with information on inmates we were to interview. Never were the decisions easy; never did I feel competent in that role. I simply tried to do the very best I could in preparation, listen intently, and judge fairly.

I learned that many are in prison for having lost control of their lives in an instant, to be regretted thereafter; that some are truly "con artists"; and that some never had a chance. Once while interviewing a 16-year-old at Tucker Prison, I asked, "If you are granted parole, where will you go for a home and a job?"

"Ma'am," he replied, "I ain't never had no home. I will just find some place to stay and try to find me some work."

When I first joined the parole board, women prisoners were housed in a former chicken house at Cummins, but they soon had model facilities at Pine Bluff. I often tried to see beyond the board interviews and observe their activities there. Yet I learned that women can be good con artists as well. Once I asked why a woman had gone to prison for forgery, and she declared, "You can just blame it on Nixon. I was working for a carnival in Hot Springs when our president got into trouble, the economy went sour, and I started writing bad checks. You can just blame it on President Nixon!"

Often, an inmate blamed his/her troubles on having gotten into the wrong crowd. On the parole board, we thought, "If we can catch the wrong crowd, we will have fewer cases to consider!"

When I first joined the parole board, we did not have a psychologist to give us evaluations. I went to Governor Pryor and advised him of that need, and soon we had evaluations from a fine psychologist.

Another change happened during my five-year term. When we entered the prisons, there were no metal detectors. I was never uneasy in interviewing inmates, even clemency for death-sentence inmates or life termers, as I treated all of them with courtesy. However, Melvin often worried that the parole board might be taken hostage. He asked repeatedly if metal detectors might be installed. Ultimately they were.

Parole board duty often reinforced my appreciation of a life filled with blessings. There go I but for the grace of God.

18.
Peaks and Valleys

Peaks and deep valleys marked the last of the seventies.

Travel for the National Federation of Press Women became more frequent. Landing during a heavy snowstorm in Denver was tense, as the Frontier plane used up most of the runway. Snowy landings greeted me on two other flights to the Mile-High City.

Melvin often joined me, especially for national newspaper conferences. Leaving a lasting impression was our visit to the U.S. Supreme Court and talk by Chief Justice Warren Burger. We also heard presidential press secretary Jody Powell, cabinet officers Joseph Califano and Bob Bergland, and budget director Bert Lance.

Flights in and out of the nation's capitol also provided feature and column ideas. On one such trip, I was seated by Charles Colson, a convicted Watergate figure. Then paroled, he was traveling with a friend to promote the Colson book, *Born Again*.

At home, ground was broken for the long-awaited Desha County Museum, a project I had worked toward for 20 years. Participating were the site donors, the Charles Dante and the Jerry Tanenbaum families, as well Doc Puryear, Lamar (Curly) Birch, Mike Murphy (first Museum Society president), Berzent Blagg, Mary Jo Tucker, Amy Frank, and myself. A $10,000 grant from Desha County, $7,500 from the American Bicentennial Commission, and civic club and individual donations provided start-up funds.

The Dante family was known for benevolence, and Dumas grieved when Jack S. Dante died in April. He was our stalwart friend who had led the effort to recruit Melvin and me as publishers.

Dumas had a large delegation at the annual Jefferson-Jackson Day Dinner where Vice President Walter F. Mondale addressed Democrats. When I covered this event, I had no knowledge that two weeks later I would be invited to meet with President Jimmy Carter at a White House briefing. Our group of 30 editors gathered at the Old Executive Office Building to hear Vince Clephas, trade negotiator for the president, and Robert Pastor of the National Security Council. In a second session, Esther Peterson, a dynamic 70-year-old, emphasized her push for a Consumer Affairs Agency.

Going to the West Wing, we were seated in the Cabinet Room and I had the attorney general's chair. (I learned that cabinet officers are given their chairs at the completion of their service.)

Press Secretary Jody Powell came in and said, "The boss will be in shortly." When President Carter appeared, we jumped to our feet and applauded. As I later wrote: "Caricatures have focused on the famous Carter smile which has charmed millions of Americans. His outstanding facial feature, in my opinion, lies in his eyes. They are intense and seem to encompass everything. They are a mirror of his moods, crinkling at the corners a bit as he jokes and becoming direct and forceful when he is making a point. Aides said they get bluer and steely when he is angry."

As the president left, an aide handed me a note to accompany her to meet Griffin Smith III of Little Rock, number-two speech writer for the president and a nephew of Mr. and Mrs. Clay Cross of Dumas. Dr. James Schlesinger, presidential assistant for energy, wrapped the afternoon's discussion. What an enlightening day!

If Esther Peterson charged my batteries for what women might accomplish into older years, so did my friend Mrs. Ida Hopkins of Winchester. At 90, full of vim and vigor, she fired off a letter to

Senator Dale Bumpers to complain of public lassitude. The senator was so charmed that he took her to lunch at the Delta Inn. Once asked who would want to live to 90, she retorted, "Anyone who is 89!" I wrote not only of a chance to meet the famous, but told my admiration for Mrs. Hopkins when she died at 93.

June 1977 was exceptional for me. I was elected president of the National Federation of Press Women. "How can a weekly newspaper editor from Dumas, Arkansas, be elected NFPW president?" some wondered.

My support provided the answer. More than 40 family and friends drove to Biloxi, Mississippi, for the event. NFPW colleagues included Mary Louise Wright, Margaret Woolfolk, Blanche Murray, and Betty Magie. My biggest boosters, my husband and children, were joined by extended family Jim and Nancy Conner, and friends Mamie Hale, Betty Prewitt, Jack and Amy Frank, Mayor Billy and Jessie Margaret Free. Friends also erected large congratulations signs over Dumas.

In an exciting time, my dinner partner was astronaut Thomas Mattingly, and I met Turner Catledge, distinguished executive editor of the *New York Times*, and Nichelle Nichols, who played Lt. Uhura on *Star Trek*.

Clarion operations were thriving as Dumas's population rose nearly to 6,000, and business development along Highway 65 included a new Kentucky Fried Chicken with "inside seating for 76."

Invited to see the space shuttle *Enterprise*'s first free flight, Melvin and I flew to California and coped with rush hour traffic in reaching Edwards Air Force Base, Lancaster. At a briefing, I was seated between the NASA administrator Robert French and Japanese Ambassador Togo, and I kept pinching myself to see if it all was real. While NASA usually provided photos for our publication, this time, Melvin was to make the *Clarion*'s own photo of the space shuttle landing himself.

Tents were set up for VIPs including Senator Barry Goldwater and singer John Denver. After visiting the VIP facilities, we chose places along the flight line for best viewing. The shuttle was piggybacked atop a 747, and after the bolts holding the shuttle were blown, the *Enterprise* came closer into view. The crowd murmured, "Where are the gears?" No worry, the wheels came down and a loud cheer arose.

From California, we flew to Reno where I spoke to Nevada Press Women. Counting previous days when I had flown to Chicago to speak at an American Bar Association hearing on "Free Press, Free Trial," I had logged 7,000 air miles in a week.

My family was constant support. For example, my law student son John gave me added confidence when I wrote the statement of my views for presentation to the American Bar Association at the prestigious Palmer House.

Exciting experiences continued.

As I wrote a news story at home, the phone rang with the inquiry, "Would you like to go to the White House Thursday?"

A hoax? No. I recognized the voice of Attorney General Bill Clinton, whom I had met and supported during his campaign. (He was the only candidate who understood the role of the parole board, on which I was serving.)

"Bill, I don't think I can go on such short notice," I replied.

"Oh, but you must," he persuaded, adding we were going to hear President Carter discuss the proposed Panama Canal treaty. The treaty "to give away the canal" meant fighting words to most of my readers, but I held differing views and wanted to hear the discussion.

Arriving at Little Rock Airport for a 7 a.m. flight to DC, I discovered there were 29 going from Arkansas. Governor David Pryor had flown in the day before and would meet us, and together we would join a group from West Virginia headed by their governor, Jay Rockefeller.

At the airport, Attorney General Clinton said, "I have booked a block of seats, but save me a seat by you." I had no idea why, but upon embarking, found he wanted to discuss his political career. I was a sounding board throughout the flight as he talked about the possibilities of running for governor or U.S. Senate. He outlined pros and cons of both races, while I occasionally chimed in with "that's right" or "on the other hand." As this conversation continued, I could see that Bill had not reached a decision. His plans evoked much speculation by others on the trip.

In DC, we boarded a bus for the Hay-Adams Hotel where Governor Pryor had previously ordered bacon and tomato sandwiches and iced tea on a Dutch-treat basis. The meal was not ready.

"How much will that be?" the governor asked.

"$16.25," replied the hotel clerk.

"EACH?" exclaimed the governor, obviously appalled at the then-steep price.

When the hotel affirmed the cost, the governor said, "We aren't eating." He marched us across Lafayette Park to the White House.

After being admitted to the East Wing, we were met by Pat Moran, Senator Bumpers's aide, and joined the West Virginia delegation in the state dining room. Jack Watson, a native of Pine Bluff and presidential assistant, presided. Speakers included Zbigniew Brzezinski, National Security Council director; Ambassador Sol Linowitz; and General Welborn Dolvin.

A coffee break was held, and we hungry Arkansans descended on the offerings with considerable enthusiasm—noticing the gold-banded china service but pouncing on the array of pastries.

The briefing resumed with Charles Duncan, assistant secretary of defense, and General George Brown, chairman of the Joint Chiefs of Staff, outlining the administration's position. We also met Secretary of the Army Clifford Alexander and Senator Majority Leader Robert Byrd of West Virginia.

The briefing "stopper," of course, was the president, who showed a complete command of the treaty and urged its passage. President Carter remained for 30 minutes to visit with all who came. The other Arkansans were Fred Wulfekuhler, Francis Bland, Ned Moseley, L. C.

Carter, Ed Bethune, J. E. Dunlap, Charles Sanders, Janet Nelson, Hank Haines, Louis Ramsay, Lt. Gov. Joe Purcell, Bill Wilson, Steve Clark, Don Harrell, Hugh Patterson, Bishop James, Rev. James Argue, Dr. Dale Cowling, Dr. W. O. Vaught, Clayton Little, Bob Lamb, Bill Becker, George Stancil, Herb Branscum, Cora McHenry, and Harry McDermott. As we left, I chatted with a Press Woman friend, Sarah McClendon, fiery White House reporter for many a decade.

Ultimately, I endorsed the Panama Canal Treaty, much to the dismay of most of our readers

My Press Women travels allowed me to meet many interesting writers. One I especially enjoyed was Marjorie Holmes, whose inspirational books had then sold more than four million copies. She credited a professor who told her, "You can do anything you want to do." I had received the same advice from my mother. I also met Dr. Cory SerVaas, editor of the resurrected *Saturday Evening Post*, my favorite magazine in earlier years.

I also persisted on projects. I worked on fund-raising for the museum, going to the Chamber of Commerce's industrial committee to seek $6,000 for a roof. I joined others asking support from the Women's Service League and Optimist Club. In Dumas, we often had to use "the piecemeal approach." Without a major bond issue, civic goals were achieved bit by bit through the generosity of Dumas people.

In our small downtown, fire could be a disastrous intruder. A Sunday morning blaze became a conflagration that wiped out Gill Tire Store and heavily damaged Value Mart. Firemen valiantly saved the nearby Wolff Brothers, established here in 1925, and United Cost Plus, successor of the Dante's Store. For a long time the building slab was a grim reminder—until plans were made for a small downtown park. Our son Steve, who then had his own photography business, made notable photos of the fire and wrote the main story. D. W. Gill, who established his business in 1943, and son Danny were to relocate and continue the downtown business.

Between news events at home, I took to the skies, but not without problems. On a flight to an NFPW meeting in Texas, our pilot couldn't retract the wheels, and we returned to the Little Rock airport for a bouncy landing. Mechanics worked on the plane and assured passengers. We took off again, and the gear remained stuck. So it was back to Little Rock for a second bumpy landing. That was enough, so I asked to be booked on another airline. Finally, I was aloft and in San Antonio in time to hear Liz Carpenter, former White House press secretary.

Often I wrote editorials longhand while flying. I pushed for a building for the growing Delta Arts & Crafts Fair, better sidewalks and pedestrian crossings, funds for beautification, a traffic light at Highway 65 and Bowles, mosquito control, and a railroad overpass. Most of these have been realized, except the still-needed overpass.

As National Press Women president, I joined a group of 53 in going on a week's Caribbean cruise. Melvin and Steve accompanied me, and John came home on a break to help with the newspaper. Steve was our young police reporter, and a major news event, robbery of the Citizens Bank at Tillar, occurred while we were away. John delighted in reporting in Steve's absence. At 1 a.m. while aboard ship, we received a cable message.

"What on earth has happened at home?" we wondered. The cable read: "Tillar bank robbed. Too bad Steve." John gleefully had scooped Steve.

We delighted in seeing Jamaica, Grand Cayman, and the Mayan ruins at Tulum, Yucatan, and Cozumel. We came home to wintry reality—with eight snows before spring. Steve's colorful photo coverage of a Jamaican carrying a fruit basket on her head later turned to youngsters on sleds. My travelogues always drew many comments from readers, who said, "When I can't be there, I travel through your eyes."

Most of our editorial subjects were local, but we tackled major issues such as need for a comprehensive energy policy. We read three daily papers and national news magazines for background information. We received strong letters to the editor, such as one from Clifton L. Meador, who analyzed agricultural problems in a responsible way. (In the 1980s, he would become an able agricultural aide to Governor Clinton.)

Winter provided a little time for re-grouping, as I did not have to travel. However, politics heated up with the major U.S. Senate race, and Attorney General Bill Clinton having announced for governor. Desha County circuit clerk J. T. Henley asked for my support of Clinton for governor, as I had supported him in the attorney general's race.

In early March, when I flew to Boise for a Press Women's meeting, I found Idahoans much like Arkansans—warm, open, and without pretension. State meetings of Press Women always were interesting because they afforded visits with the well-known, including the indomitable Helen Thomas of the White House press corps speaking in Jackson, Mississippi, and Cecily Brownstone, Associated Press food editor featured in Shreveport, Louisiana.

Washington Press Women invited me to speak in Olympia, and the gathering numbered more than 400. As cordial as the members were and as pleasant as the sightseeing, including the governor's mansion and Evergreen College, was, my biggest treat was the governor's suite with a sauna the size of a small swimming pool. Were it not for duty, I might have soaked up the visit.

After flying 40,000 miles the first year of my NFPW presidency, I was able to race through the busiest of airports. I was always asked where Dumas is located, but not in Durham, North Carolina, where the ticket agent recognized my accent and said he grew up in Greenville, Mississippi.

One weekend took me through hectic O'Hare Airport in Chicago on to Minneapolis, Minnesota, where Diane and Bill Hand met me and were my hosts in St. Cloud. Bill took me to the airport for my next trip and gallantly joined in my sprint to the gate. Bill panted, "You sure do have to be in good shape to do this job!" I then was, but apprehension about the weather never left me. On the trip to Oklahoma City, our 727 had to circle a huge black tornado, which my seatmate from Scotland called a "hammerhead." The ground looked wonderful that day.

I may have been up in the air, but Melvin and our staff were keeping the *Clarion* humming in the interim. There were looming health problems, however. In May, Melvin faced prostate surgery, with the surgeon telling us that he removed a tumor thought to be benign. Three days later, I overheard another doctor remark, "I have to give Mr. Schexnayder his report." I felt chilled through and through, as I knew he meant cancer.

Ensuing was a real ordeal for Melvin as he had to endure 39 radiation treatments. Our daughter Sarah had finished her junior year at LSU and gave up her summer job to drive Melvin to Little Rock and back home—a 170-mile round trip—each day. He received treatments at Central Arkansas Radiation Therapy Institute and was miserably nauseated and burned by radiation, but CARTI saved his life.

During this crisis, I directed the newspaper staff and kept things at home going. We all tried to keep Melvin's spirits up when he felt that he could not undergo another treatment. We simply coped day by day.

In the midst of a family crisis, long hours at the *Clarion*, and NFPW travel, I was embroiled in the issue of whether the Desha County Courthouse should be moved from Arkansas City to McGehee. My sharp editorial questioning made me the butt of vicious letters in the *McGehee Times*, with one writer suggesting that the county would benefit from three high-priced funerals including mine. Upon coming home from a meeting, I found Steve in tears. "We must laugh, son," I told him, adding my mother's often-quoted biblical advice, "This, too, shall pass." My editorials had been sharply critical of the people's being told there would be no cost to moving the courthouse, but I also pleaded for people to work together on economic development since Desha County's population loss for the decade was projected as the second highest in the state.

As rancor was building in Desha County, I fulfilled my duties as NFPW president and embarked on a trip to Alaska to meet with members there. I greatly missed Melvin, who was unable to make the trip, but there were many highlights in that 10-day venture. As guests of "Alyeska," Press Women were flown to the North Slope to see the beginning of the great pipeline. As a country girl from Tillar, I thought, how great to dip my hands in the Arctic Ocean! We later flew over the Columbia Glacier and landed in Valdez, where we toured operations at the end of the pipeline.

I came to appreciate Alaskan pioneers, embodied in Mary Carey, an NFPW member, who hosted our group in Talkeetna. Memorable was a potluck supper at the Fairview Hotel, where plywood converted billiard tables for a buffet featuring moose loaf, fiddlehead fern salad, and other local fare. Talkeetna citizens brought their dogs to the feast and fed themselves while sharing tidbits with their dogs at their feet. In an evening of conviviality, locals toasted me as NFPW president, visiting Press Women, and Alaskan Press Women. Repetition of this process left quite a few tipsy.

Leaving Alaska amidst a brilliant display of northern lights, we flew to Seattle and thence to Billings, Montana, for our organization's fall board meeting. I was so happy to have Melvin meet me there.

When the University of Arkansas at Little Rock's communication department honored me as Journalist of the Year, Melvin was there for me, as always. I was so gratified; without his love and support, I never could have accomplished very much. Even though he was recovering from radiation, he went to the *Clarion* office every day, with his only break being an afternoon nap.

Editorially, I continued hammering against the move of the Desha County courthouse. November brought the pivotal vote, and the proposal failed by eight votes. As I was writing the story after the election,

R. B. Stimson, a Dumas planter, appeared at my office door. "You beat them [proponents of the move]. You really beat them," he declared, smiling as he left. I smiled back and thought the majority had again prevailed. I wrote: "Once again in a hotly-contested election in Desha County, all kinds of ugly charges are being made. But the truth is that the voting machine printouts are there for public inspection, and the voting machines count the ballots as they are cast. The fact remains that we are governed by the majority, whether by 8 votes, 80 or 800."

Throughout that hectic fall, I constantly worried about Mother's declining health, and I went to the nursing home every day I was home. After a trip to Rapid City, South Dakota, and a visit to Mount Rushmore, Melvin and I returned to find Mother in poor condition. We moved her to the hospital, where she died November 22 as our family gathered for the Thanksgiving holidays. I am forever thankful for her. A mainstay throughout my life, she inspired and encouraged me, expanded my opportunities, and provided vital support in her *Clarion* role. Gentle steel. Mother was always gracious but could be unbending if demanded.

I canceled plans to join the Press Women's trip to China to cope with grief, family illness, and political turmoil.

Despite the challenges, the *Clarion* operations were thriving to match the progress in Dumas. Merle Peterson and Clifton Meador announced plans for the Belmont addition, and the City of Dumas received a half-million-dollar grant for public housing.

January 1979 brought a devastating ice storm. Dumas was blacked out except for two sub-divisions with underground utilities. C&L Electric Cooperative called it the "most devastating storm ever." We had two space heaters at home, and in coat and fur hat, I wrote by candlelight. The *Clarion* was closed for two days. Having no electricity was a first-class pain; our younger generation concurred.

Press Women travels took me to Burlington and Montpelier, Vermont, to organize an affiliate and glimpse New England in the snow, and later to Benton Harbor, Michigan, to speak and visit with a friend, *Detroit Free Press* editor Joe Stroud. Other experiences included a touch of Florida in Clearwater, a beach visit while in San Diego, a conversation with Sen. Nancy Kassebaum of Kansas while in DC, and appointment as an admiral in the non-existent Okoboji Navy while meeting with Iowa Press Women.

National Newspaper Association travel found me visiting the embassy of the People's Republic of China where two women in Mao-style gray pajamas welcomed me. I conversed through an interpreter and only as conversation ended did I learn I was visiting with the ambassador's wife and her interpreter. I mined my travels for columns and features.

However, I did not have to go afar for news. One Saturday morning, we witnessed an altercation and shooting that left a man dead in front of the police station across the street.

My travel was suspended for the high school graduation at which Steve shared top academic honors with Adrienne Hudson, Bud Roberts, and Cindy Daniel. We were equally proud later that May when Sarah graduated from our alma mater, LSU.

Concluding my Press Women presidency at an Indianapolis convention with my family attending, I had the joys of meeting NBC's Jane Pauley and riding the Indy racetrack. Press Women collected funds to present an electric typewriter as an appreciation gift, but I was never to achieve the rhythm I had on my old L. C. Smith manual.

After being the greatest chicken about flying, I had logged 110,000 air miles while leading NFPW, once giving up my seat to a seeing-eye dog and another time serving as a surrogate grandmother to hold a toddler and another baby for a stressed mother.

These memory-rich two years ended just in time for multiple preparations for Sarah's wedding to Mason Holden at First United Methodist Church in Dumas on August 11. They planned to live in Shreveport, Louisiana, where Mason was in medical school.

Returning to everyday reality, I faced long hours in preparing a special edition for Dumas's approaching 75th anniversary to be observed in late July. Women's Service League led the celebration with re-creation of old town Dumas at the high school and a founders' pageant. Citizens who lived here at incorporation in 1904 were honored and included C. W. Meador, Bowles Meador, Marie Berry, Vivian Anderson, Emma Hudson, Ida Bishop, Darlin Ross, Cornelia Lee, Joe Lee McKennon, Ida Caesar, Anita Caesar, and Nathan Battles Fitzgerald. Mayor Billy Free and Mike Murphy, president, also led the opening of the new Desha County Museum. A Community Theatre was organized as an outgrowth of the 75th pageant.

The empty nest feeling hit hardest in September as Steve departed for his freshman year at the University of Arkansas in Fayetteville, also leaving a major hole in our office staff. Since I had been elected to the Arkansas Press Association board, I was busy with those new responsibilities. As the first woman headed toward its presidency, I determined to work diligently and not let my gender be regarded as a cause for failure.

Travel was still calling with a press meeting in Santa Fe and a visit to White Sands Missile Range. I then reached my goal of visiting all 50 states. Another trip took Melvin and me to Orlando, Florida, where we heard presidential candidates George H. W. Bush, Larry Pressler, Harold Stassen, Bob Dole, and John Connally. Readers came to expect my travels duly reported in the *Clarion*.

19.
New Opportunities

The eighties brought new opportunities. Elected to the Winthrop Rockefeller Foundation Board, I was exposed to perceptive minds who sought social change through innovative projects. Enriching both my outlook and my education, fellow board members were outstanding in their fields and included Ray Marshall, secretary of labor in the Carter administration, as well as Win Paul Rockefeller, later to become lieutenant governor.

Among lasting achievements initiated during those visionary years was seeking South Shore Bank of Chicago for guidance on a community development bank in Arkansas.

Previously, I had been selected among the seven Arkansans to meet with the National Endowment for the Humanities in Washington to discuss the formation of an Arkansas Endowment. Our group of academicians and one newspaper editor was led by brilliant law professor Robert Leflar. I joked, with truth, that I was public interpreter to translate the scholarly discussions into plain English.

My prime focus, however, remained at home. The growing energy crisis saw the first gasohol brought into the county. Newsprint costs and availability demanded a slightly narrower and longer paper, still broadsheet. The cost of a carload brought to our plant had jumped from $4,500 to $7,500 in two years, but advertising was still strong. At a barbecue in Selma, U.S. senator David Pryor decried the energy crisis and said that getting action through the federal government was "like nailing Jell-O to a wall."

In a plea for tolerance following the school district's failure to promote a black coach, I wrote a column ending: "I hope you will remember that which I was always taught. Color does not make a person inferior. Behavior does."

Wal-Mart announced plans to build a store in Dumas, and Riceland Foods was constructing an export terminal on the Arkansas River at Pendleton. Among the bright young people attracted to Dumas was Michael Jones, joining Merchants & Farmers Bank as a trust officer and becoming a civic leader.

When journalistic opportunity arose, I answered. A notable response found me sitting in Independence Hall, Philadelphia, by candlelight as a delegate to the national First Amendment Congress.

Recently elected as the first woman board member of the Dumas Chamber of Commerce, I was appointed chair of a committee to begin an annual festival. I proposed that we call the festival "Ding Dong Days," and some thought I was a real ding-dong. In fact, the festival was named for the song, "I'm a Ding Dong Daddy from Dumas," a Tin Pan Alley ditty considered to be racy when it was written by Phil Baxter in the late 1920s. The people of Dumas, Arkansas, swear that he wrote the song when he heard a train conductor call, "All out for Dumas," as the Baxter band, then based in Pine Bluff, was traveling through. The people of Dumas, Texas, disagree, saying Baxter grew up in those parts.

For the coming festival, our Chamber committee was bolstered by sterling volunteers Paul Wilson, M. E. McDonald, Pat Clark, and a group from R. A. Pickens & Son Company, all of whom took over the job of clearing the overgrown grove of Memorial Park, then owned by the Lions Club. For that first festival, we could use only one-third of the park, and two more years were required to clear overgrowth from the inviting native hardwood grove. In the process, as a swarm of bees attacked, I outran Paul Wilson to the safety of his truck.

With private donations, we built a stage through the help of Pat Clark and the Optimist Club, and later, restrooms through work of

Jaycees. I well remember the excitement of one Jaycee who came to me and reported, "The Pickens Company just gave us a commode!" For the first Ding Dong Days, a successor to the city's 75th anniversary, co-chairman Fritz Hudson and I donned early 1900s costumes since the July celebration fell on the anniversary week of Dumas's 1904 incorporation. Spouses Joy Hudson and my Melvin joined as support crew.

Another outgrowth of the 75th birthday was the Dumas Community Theatre, which agreed to stage "The Music Man" with Rev. Bob Presley, First Baptist's music minister, in the lead. He was a cousin of Elvis and possessed a marvelous voice.

Hot air balloon races also were scheduled with direction by Dumas native Wayne Woods, a Little Rock ad executive. Balloonist Gene Pfeifer won a new automobile in a contest to snatch keys from a pole as he swooped over the soybean field next to the park. Lloyds of London, insuring the prize while thinking of the improbability of a winner, took a while to pay off—but did! A dance contest was among many events at the Fun Day, and our son Steve teamed with City Clerk Mary Howard for first in the Charleston. Enhancing culture, the Arkansas State Symphony performed in our high school auditorium.

Civic projects always were in mind. Mother and I tried for 25 years to acquire the log house, once the residence of my great-grandfather, Sam Terry, on Oakwood Bayou four miles east of Dumas. For a long time, the owners wanted a new barn in exchange, unaffordable for us. Imagine my delight when Mrs. Jesse Kennedy called one day to say we could have the log house if we were willing to move it—by the next week! She added that the land on which it was located was to be planted in soybeans. We were able to accomplish the quick move because of the dedication of my former Tillar High School classmate, Lamar (Curly) Birch. He numbered the 18-inch hand-hewn cypress logs in dismantling the structure, and the county road crew helped to move them. One night, some logs were stolen for mantel-boards, and we had to post a guard on site. Replacement cypress came from the Tillar Slough and a year of air drying was required before the house could be re-assembled at our museum.

Although I had completed my two-year Press Women presidency, speaking opportunities abounded. One invitation took me to Plymouth, Massachusetts, for a visit with Rosemary and Ed Carroll and my first chance to see a "Noreaster" storm. A call to address Alabama Press Women took us on a 560-mile drive to Eufaula.

In March, Melvin and I joined Arkansans to attend the National Newspaper Association government conference. At a White House reception, we were photographed with President Ronald Reagan and First Lady Nancy Reagan. We also were greeted by Vice President George H. W. Bush. At the Congressional Club reception, we were joined by Senator David Pryor, Congressman and Mrs. Ed Bethune, and Mrs. John Paul Hammerschmidt, wife of the long-term congressman. The Republican Hammerschmidts always reached out to our mostly Democratic group.

Photo pages, national or local, were a *Clarion* goal. They sold extra copies and drew special interest, whatever the subject—Watson Fish Fry or the White House, agricultural plane fly-in or high school productions. As for feature ideas, we had assistance from readers who phoned in tips, such as a new solar heating project or a sailboat on the Arkansas River en route to the Yucatan.

On occasion, we covered the national news, with our own stories if not presence. One such time was the shooting of President Reagan less than three weeks after we had seen him at the White House. We had met presidential press secretary James Brady, who was badly wounded in the assassination attempt. I observed: "Brady's day ended in tragedy and left us with a sense of melancholy."

The highlight of 1981 for us came April 24 when our first grandchild, Charles, was born to Deanna and John Schexnayder in Baton

Rouge. Few emotions rival cradling a new grandchild. Family joy was mixed with Dumas commitment and challenge.

Our museum had outgrown its original building. How would we finance a new metal building for agricultural artifacts? As cultural chairman with the Chamber leading the way, I suggested business and individual contributions of $25 monthly for three years. Smith Steel constructed the building at cost as a demonstration project.

Years of toil were sometimes applauded. Melvin, Merle Peterson, Mayor Billy Free, and Jack Frank were recognized for 25 years of service on the Dumas Industrial Foundation and its good record of job creation. Meanwhile, economic factors were encouraging as Dumas's population reached 6,091. The *Clarion* began a series on the industrial development here, noting that citizens had given $375,000 to spur industrial growth.

Every year seemed to foster some controversy into which the *Clarion* was thrust. Summer brought a request for additional housing, apartment units at Pecan Grove and Meadowview. Longtime residents objected, saying such units would devalue their property. Others objected, adding, "You don't know who is going to be living there." Both the *Clarion* and the Chamber of Commerce endorsed the housing units. Rarely did I speak at City Council meetings, but I couldn't sit back, noting additional housing was needed and declaring, "I can't believe any city would turn its back on the elderly, the single parent or the poor." Some of my best friends were on the other side, but Mayor Billy Free and I remained solidly in support of the housing.

Another controversy arose when Desha County proposed a sales tax to be shared with the cities. Revenue sharing had ended, and funds were needed to fill the void. Thus it was the Dumas City Council that voted to place the Pecan Grove housing issue on the same October 20 ballot with the sales tax issue. The *Clarion* endorsed both issues, but the Quorum Court rescinded plans for the sales tax election, while the housing referendum was still scheduled.

In our *Clarion* tradition to post returns on election night, Melvin went with flashlight to read the returns posted outside closed voting precincts. While official returns would be much slower in coming, he returned with the results from two precincts.

We were losing the housing issue. Mayor Free grumped, "I am not going to run for re-election if the people of Dumas don't appreciate progress."

I was even more dispirited, declaring, "I just think we will sell the *Clarion* if the people here don't care more than this election shows."

Some minutes later, Melvin returned grinning and said: "You two ought to see the returns from this box." Ward IV had voted three to one in favor of the housing ordinance, giving a 41-vote margin for the new housing. Suddenly, the mayor brightened and immediately reconsidered leaving office. And I wouldn't have sold the paper for any amount!

After winning that fight, Billy Free asked me to introduce him as he was inducted into the Hall of Distinction at his alma mater, Arkansas Tech University. I was able to regale the crowd with tales of some of the battles the mayor and I had fought, sometimes separately but mostly as allies.

My friend Ross Pendergraft, vice president of Donrey Media, also was among the inductees. Ross and I served on our Arkansas Press board, and he had staunchly backed my service as its first woman. When I overheard grumbling about a woman board member, Ross Pendergraft and Frank Robins declared their solid support. Friends helped me to break barriers.

Melvin and I joined the National Federation of Press Women's summer tour to London, my first to Europe. We were inspired when visiting 12 Downing Street to meet with the communications minister and later seeing Parliament in session. As the royal wedding of Prince Charles and Princess Diana was approaching, I interviewed Prince Charles's tailor. Domiciled at Sherlock Holmes Hotel on Baker Street, our tour group particularly enjoyed afternoon gatherings in the lobby—high tea for the women, lager for the men.

My role as the first woman president of the Arkansas Press Association was demanding. We needed "a place of our own." I appointed Cone Magie, Cabot publisher, as chairman of the headquarters search committee. He found a suitable location in the Vestal House, 1701 Broadway in Little Rock's Quapaw Quarter, and we voted on the issue at the June meeting. I was astounded that no real opposition surfaced. Our funding efforts included doubling APA dues over a period of five years.

George Measer of Buffalo, New York, National Newspaper Association president, came to the next APA convention to announce my appointment as the first woman on the NNA board. My children responded with red roses for "QMC." (In notes imploring them to do chores or remember appointments, I had laughingly signed QMC for Queen Mother Charlotte.)

These new responsibilities widened our travel schedule to include board meetings in Washington DC, Phoenix, and San Antonio. Some male board members objected to dissolution of the all-men's club. After several drinks one evening, one told me, "I don't think women ought to be on OUR board." I just smiled as an NNA staffer tried to shut him up. For years, I had faced down those who thought women could not do the job thrust upon them. My mother had proven otherwise. Naysayers abound. An old Chinese proverb says it best: "If you stop every time a dog barks, your path will never end."

I thought of a Dumas project which had long faced problems. After clearing alligators and Native American artifacts as possible environmental hurdles, the new airport for Dumas was nearing reality. The facility became even more exciting for us when the Yellow Bird Express flew in a page ad from New York.

Editorially, I tackled national issues, including the new economics: "The administration continues to advocate that tax incentives given to the wealthy will lead to more jobs in the private sector. Any extra funds coming to the wealthy will go into the money market at high interest rates at no work and risk…and the small business person will be pinched to provide inventories. Call it supply side economics if you wish. We call it the Big Pinch."

When we went to the NNA Government Affairs Conference, Senator Dale Bumpers sent gallery passes for Arkansans. We thus saw all 100 senators assembled to consider the expulsion of Senator Harrison (Pete) Williams of Pennsylvania in the Abscam matter. Senator Daniel Inouye of Hawaii tipped off Harrison's intention to avoid an expulsion vote by indicating that Harrison would resign, which he did in an impassioned speech often quoting the Bible.

We later went to the White House reception where President and Mrs. Reagan welcomed the NNA delegates. He looked vibrant, fully recovered from the attempted assassination the previous year. Our coverage of the event included an article on the opposing economic views in Washington, bringing another dimension to the *Clarion* coverage.

Expanding beyond normal coverage, we also reported the opening of the St. Charles Bridge over the White River, thus creating a more direct route to Memphis. Cultural events also provided widely read copy, including the Hometown Opry emceed by Bob Presley, the Arkansas Symphony pops concert, and *Bye, Bye, Birdie* brought here by the Southeast Arkansas Arts Center.

A great interview opportunity came when famed French author Marguerite Yourcenar accompanied Jerry Wilson, a talented Dumas native, on a visit here. The first woman voted into the Francaise Academie since its establishment in the 17th century, she was charming in discussing her writing. I appreciated her philosophy outlined in her book on Roman emperor Hadrian: "Do the best one can. Do it over again. Then still improve, even if ever so slightly, those retouches."

Politics also dominated coverage. Bill Clinton, accompanied by his wife Hillary, came to Dumas to campaign for governor and regain office after Republican Frank White upset him. Dumas offered a warm welcome by Mayor Free and Mitchellville mayor Emily Bowens. Mayor Free never missed a beat; he equally welcomed Republican Governor Frank White when he campaigned later.

Highly contested elections, both on a local and state basis, were a boon to weekly newspapers. The May primary, in which Desha County judge Bonnie Zook and Sheriff Ben Williams won re-election, also resulted in Bill Clinton and Joe Purcell headed for the run-off primary. Advertising flowed.

To expand our coverage, we often used young people from the high school for special assignments. David Porter III contributed summer coverage. We also counted on friends. Edwin Maxson, our first intern at the *Clarion*, had retired from the Air Force and then achieved a master's in journalism. Returning for several weeks as our summer staffer, he tackled our computers with the same verve he had had as an Air Force pilot when he was shot down three times and returned to fly again.

Melvin, Steve, and I flew to San Francisco for the convention of the National Federation of Press Women, touring the Napa Valley and traveling Highway 1 to view the striking coastal scenery. En route to San Diego, we visited the William Randolph Hearst estate at San Simeon, the Danish village of Solvang, and San Juan Capistrano mission.

During our absence, Citizens Bank of Tillar was closed by the Federal Deposit Insurance Corporation. Citizens was our bank while we lived in Tillar, and its demise was a real blow to the people who still banked there, although FDIC would back deposits to some extent.

Back home, I tackled chairmanship of the summer festival for a third year. Dumas Community Theatre produced *Camelot* as a feature. The U.S. Navy Stage Band from Memphis performed, and hot air balloon races brightened our sky. We also joined in the tri-centennial commemoration of explorer La Salle's visit to this area.

Assistant Editor Lynn Smith left for a teaching job in Fort Smith, and Melvin and I again were relegated to news and advertising. Soon we had good news. Terry Hawkins, a *Clarion* mainstay from 1974 to 1981, returned in October and became associate editor.

The fall election brought hot races. The *Clarion* did not endorse candidates, a practice which I likened unto a kiss of death. However, we always published a detailed explanation of ballot issues and took editorial stands on each. Mayor Free won 1051 to 900 over challenger A. L. Morgan, and Bill Clinton polled 54 percent to regain the governorship.

Publishing a weekly newspaper kept us in the political scene, locally and occasionally nationally. At a board meeting in Georgetown in DC, I attended a reception for Rep. Lindy Boggs of Louisiana. Mr. Speaker Tip O'Neill stopped to talk to us. When I told him I was "a dyed-in-the wool Democrat," he said, "Bless you," and leaned over and kissed me on the cheek. It was the only time I have been so saluted for being a Yellow Dog Democrat.

In December came a great story lasting weeks. During high water, a string of 30 barges broke loose on the Arkansas River, with some crashing into Dam 2 near Pendleton. The accident, threatening the navigation system, happened on a Saturday night. With insufficient photo equipment for the darkness, Melvin and I waited until early Sunday to reach the site. Water was already spilling over the lowlands. Unaware of the rising waters, some people were still in their trailer homes. Their cars and trucks already were in water, and we saw a motorboat going from trailer to trailer.

Rushing pell-mell and carrying all kinds of debris, the river was an angry torrent. Barges had sunk near the north end of Pendleton Bridge. Others barges were aground on sand bars or sinking in the distance. River workers warned that the road to Dam 2 was already under water. Driving the road to the low water dam embankment, we discovered water rushing over the road and decided against trying to ford it in a small car. Later, Gene Weser and Gerald Shepherd stopped and took us to the dam in a four-wheel drive. We forded the water, stopping to photograph a bewildered armadillo in water rushing over the roadbed. A rat had climbed into bushes in an attempt to escape, and a mink was swimming alongside the road.

Upon reaching the dam, we were able to count six barges jammed into gates, and there were more beneath. After getting still photos no one else had, we beat a retreat. We learned the river had risen three inches an hour since midnight, and the crest had not been reached. By afternoon, the Pendleton Bridge was closed and water covered area roads. We came perilously close to losing the navigation system that day since several gates on the dam could not be closed. In a continuing saga, barges had to be cut loose, a huge scour hole had to be filled, and other repairs were necessary.

If that were not enough, our good friends Patsy and Jay Jackson of Clinton were in a December flood that nearly took their lives as it ruined their newspaper plant. Like others in the newspaper fraternity, we drove to Clinton to help, taking a car load of office supplies for their headquarters, then located in their home. Melvin assisted in salvaging wet equipment, while I wrote stories for their newspaper, the *Van Buren County Democrat*. For several months, we produced their commercial printing in our shop as an accommodation.

Our own river story continued as a towboat sank in the salvage operations. Damages to the dam were set at $4.6 million and salvage operations at $4.8 million. Memorable photos were made of filling the scour hole and removal of barges, and features focused on skilled workers there.

Family excitement built as Deanna and John were expecting a second child, whom I hoped would arrive on my Christmas birthday. Their son, Edward Terry, was born December 26, and we again rushed to Baton Rouge.

In January 1983, I represented the Arkansas Press Association in testimony before the legislature's city and county government committee. I had no inkling that someday I would serve on the same committee.

The travel bug bit seriously, and we talked Bob and Christene Fisher, newspaper friends from Clarksville, into a 21-day bus trip touring Europe. We chose August, later learning that was not wise, since many of Europe's holidays occur then. However, unforgettable was the sparkle and ambience of strikingly beautiful Paris which also afforded unusual sightseeing. A woman attendant at the Eiffel Tower insisted on giving Melvin and Bob a restroom tour as it was being used!

Language was no barrier. Melvin quickly regained the French fluency he had as a youngster in Abbeville, Louisiana, schools. On the Champs-Elysees, we visited the Hotel de Crillon where Melvin and buddies had enjoyed a rest leave during World War II. It had become elegant and beyond reach of our travel dollar. Open-air restaurants were fun, and French pastries the best. I smiled and said "please," "good morning," and "thank you" in the languages of various countries, managing so well in Italy that one maitre d' presented me with a large bowl of fruit.

Being serenaded in a Venice gondola on our 37th wedding anniversary was surely the highlight for Melvin and me, but we also enjoyed seeing places in Germany where he had served in World War II. While going through the Catacombs in Rome, I stumbled on a dimly lighted last step and heard a pop in my ankle. That evening at Tivoli, we had the best wine of the trip, $2 per bottle, but the bubbly evening did not prevent my ankle from swelling dreadfully. I hobbled through the tour remainder, and upon return, I found I had a fractured foot.

Back to publishing, we focused on governmental news, with Mayor Free urging a sales tax to finance street maintenance and other needs. We joined State Representative Bain Poole in supporting an additional penny sales tax for state educational improvements led by Arkansas first lady Hillary Clinton.

Mayor Free negotiated a $1,300 grant for plantings along the rail-road tracks, economically necessary but visibly uninviting. Elaine Wolff, civic worker and businesswoman, and I collected matching monies, and joining Elaine in landscaping were Deloris Peterson, Matsy Shea, and Paul Wilson. Later, Annie Mae Matthews, Nell Freeman, and members of the Highway Garden Club worked on beautification.

I was the incoming, and first woman, president of the Dumas Chamber of Commerce when Sunbeam announced, in December 1983, plans to close the Dumas plant. Once employing 600, the facto-ry then had 385 workers. Dumas was the electric mixer capital of the world at the Sunbeam apex. Mayor Free was gracious at the closing announcement and thanked Sunbeam for its contribution to the economy over 17 years, even though he was sorely disappointed that the company was moving operations offshore.

Earlier at a Chamber meeting, I had warned there might be seri-ous economic problems ahead. Later, veteran alderman T. C. Pickett asked how I knew. I was not prescient; I had learned that Sunbeam warehouses were overflowing and their products were not moving. However, I hadn't been prepared for the shattering announcement.

Ahead was even greater tribulation. Sadness descended on our town in 1984 with the loss of Billy Free, our progressive mayor for 27 years. He died January 16 following a heart attack. Billy, as mayor, and I, as editor, often disagreed, but never to the point of being disagree-able. Ours was a friendship through a time when Dumas was growing, and he was the responsible leader with vision we needed.

His death left our town adrift. With plants like Sunbeam, Dumas had experienced a 34.6 percent growth in the 1970s. Dumas was down but certainly not out. Economic challenges had always weighed heav-ily on our cheerful mayor, who always sought the best. He was a voice, not only for Dumas, but he also served on the state Board of Pollution Control, as president of the Arkansas Municipal League, and in numerous leadership positions. An election to replace the mayor was called for April, and his widow, Jessie Margaret Free, defeated opponents George Cossey and Paul Mah.

Along with ink in the blood, I had a tincture of politics. However, if Mayor Free had still been leading Dumas, I likely would not have considered entering politics. If an open seat had not appeared, I would not have ventured.

On February 21, State Representative Bain Poole of McGehee called. "I am not going to run for re-election," he announced. "I am planning to run for county judge since Judge Bonnie Zook is retiring."

"What would you think if I ran for state representative?" I queried.

He may have been shocked, but he never missed a beat. "I'd support you," he declared.

When Melvin and I went home to lunch, we discussed the situation. He said, "You've been wanting to run for office for a long time. Why don't you now?"

That cinched it. If Melvin, always my best supporter, thought it was okay, why not take the plunge? By 3 p.m., I had written my announcement for office and sent it to surrounding newspapers, whose staffs expressed shock but nevertheless published it.

In three weeks, Democrats held a caucus to select presidential delegates, and I tested the waters there to determine if I had any support for legislative office. Two young men, Lary Zeno of Jefferson and Eddie Cox of Watson, also had expressed interest in the race.

National political candidates sent representatives, including David Glenn, son of Sen. John Glenn, and supporters of Rev. Jesse Jackson. At the Democratic caucus, there was positive response to my candidacy. I had worked in the Democratic Party in Desha County for three decades, and had helped with advertising and speeches for many campaigns. Thus, it was possible for me to sew up early support.

At the Democratic primary deadline, I was unopposed for State Representative, District 85. I knew many Desha County leaders, but I campaigned vigorously to meet the electorate in Arkansas and Phillips counties. My Press Woman friend, Mary Louise Wright of DeWitt, drove for me in Arkansas County, where the district included progressive farms operated by energetic families.

Near the Menard Indian Mounds, we came upon a dogtrot farm house with chickens running in the yard and across the porch. I called to the residents, and a large woman came out to hear my pitch for election. After a while, she observed, "You'uns is the only politician we seen out here."

For campaigning in Phillips County, I enlisted my friend Michael Jones and his aunts, Mary Katherine Crisp and Jamie Tucker. Bankers Poindexter and Mary Louise Fiser introduced me around Elaine. I came to enjoy the annual Elaine Christmas celebration and parade, attended by as many as 10,000 in this town of fewer than 3,000.

In Desha County, I campaigned at the Watson Fish Fry, Railroad Days in McGehee, and Ding Dong Days in Dumas. I was greatly aided by Jim Poole, brother of Archie Mae Bealer who was like a member of our family while she cared for my mother and my children. I never had a paid campaign staff, and Michael Jones served as my treasurer. Additional volunteers included Jack Frank, Kathryn Stimson, Fritz and Joy Hudson, Frances Newton, Nell Freeman, John Williams, David Walt, Lee Willie Dale, Patti Jones and daughters Anne and Katherine Britt, James and Mary Wilkerson, Brian Moore, Ernest Bradshaw, Rev. Harould Scott, and Jess Walt.

Then considered a "must" was to visit the county courthouses and city halls and solicit officeholders' support. Filing was extremely time-consuming for the first six years as I had to visit Democratic central committees in Arkansas City, DeWitt, and Helena. A full day was required to file in District 85. No Republicans filed, and being unopposed in the Democratic primary was tantamount to election.

During the summer, a letter from Bolivar County Chamber of Commerce in Cleveland, Mississippi, asked if I would be interested

in working toward a highway-rail bridge across the Mississippi
River. I immediately called to the Chamber executive, Buddy
Foster, and said, "Yes!"

That spark led us to organize the Arkansas-Mississippi Great
River Bridge Association at a McGehee meeting, and thus begin a
long pursuit of the bridge. It also was the beginning of a long friendship with distinguished Cleveland engineer Charles Dean, who
became our spokesman on lobbying trips to Washington. We also
formed a Highway 65 Association to push for a four-lane highway.

Our family was expanding, and we were excited when our first
granddaughter, Lauren, was born to Sarah and Mason Holden in
Shreveport, Louisiana, on December 7. Her arrival made Pearl Harbor
Day 1984 remembered for great happiness.

20.
Donning an Added Hat

In 1985, at age 61, I was sworn into the Arkansas House of Representatives. I had never thought it possible to be elected to any office. As a newspaperwoman, I knew most members of the House would have great distrust of me.

There seemed to be some wariness among men legislators since our freshman class of 17 included four women, thus doubling the number of women in the House. I found solid support from my fellow newcomers, Nancy Balton of Blytheville, Myra Jones of Little Rock, and Wanda Northcutt of Stuttgart. Because I was older, I was referred to as "the den mother of the freshman class."

During my first weeks there, my goal was legislation authorizing Arkansas to enter into a compact with Mississippi for a Great River Bridge linking Desha County and Bolivar County, Mississippi.

During much of the fall, I worked with the Arkansas Legislative Council to draft legislation patterned after the compact for the Natchez, Mississippi, bridge.

Some senior members of the House of Representatives watched the legislation with detached amusement, as it was an ambitious bill for a freshman. I was totally focused, however. I worked the Transportation Committee for support before it reached the agenda, and I consulted with the Arkansas Highway and Transportation Department at length. Commissioner Patsy Thomasson made the only suggestion, as she wanted the Compact Authority to meet on call.

I pre-filed the bill, thus having it on the early calendar. It's always smart to have serious legislation debut early before one has time to develop opposition resulting from voting against another member's legislation.

The House has a tradition of hassling new members with questions, and Rep. John Ward of North Little Rock was appointed to this task. He said, "Representative Schexnayder, this bridge would benefit only southeast Arkansas and not the rest of the state, don't you think?"

I replied, "Mr. Ward, whatever benefits southeast Arkansas benefits all of the state."

Later, he told me, "It was a good bill. That's the only question I could think to ask."

In tradition, on a first bill, members voted red and just before the tally, turn their votes to green. I was not worried. My first bill passed the House 92-0, advancing to the Senate to be handled by Sen. Jack Gibson and pass 32-0.

Governor Bill Clinton signed the compact into law February 9, 1985. The Bridge Compact was my most far-reaching legislation of a political career to span 14 years.

Several weeks after the legislation was signed, Rep. Geno Mazzanti approached me and asked if I wanted to appeal it. His constituents in Chicot County didn't like it. "No," I said. "It is now law."

My seatmates were John Parkerson of Hot Springs, who was to become closely allied with me in thought, and Tim Hutchinson, a conservative Republican later to become a U.S. senator. I often sought to tell Tim of the plight of the Arkansas Delta. Once when he opposed WIC (federal nutrition aid to women and children), I asked if he had ever been in a public health clinic in the Delta. When he said no, I advised, "Just sit down." Despite my frank remarks and his often disagreeing replies, we maintained pleasant relations.

My first term's work included co-signing on Governor Clinton's education and economic development packages, giving me valuable experience before many committees.

During the session, Dean Tom Bruce of the University of Arkansas College of Medicine asked to meet with me. He wondered if I could pass legislation for a mixed drink sales tax to fund a UAMS research chair in alcohol and drug abuse prevention.

"I can try," I replied and soon enlisted politically savvy Rep. Wanda Northcutt of Stuttgart. "Sin tax" bills are brought before the Rules Committee, which then met in a small ante-room just off the House gallery. Dimly lighted and filled with cigarette curls, it was the epitome of a smoke-filled political parley. There were no seats for bill sponsors. We just leaned up against the wall until it was time to speak. I thought there was little hope to get the bill out of committee, but the Arkansas Medical Society brought its lobbying talents to bear and the legislation eked out of committee. After family physicians contacted them, not many representatives were inclined to vote against the tax on mixed drinks. The bill passed the House 82-3 and the Senate with a good majority.

After making his comeback by defeating Frank White, Bill Clinton was a popular governor. We had passed an ambitious rural road program, which he was threatening to veto. Rep. Robin Wynne of Fordyce, another freshman, and I were summoned to meet with the governor on the subject of the veto.

"Would you vote to override his veto?" we were asked. I answered that a rural road program was popular with my district, and I had personally polled mayors to get their sentiments. "I don't think it is a smart thing to veto the legislation, as it is popular with the rural people, and Arkansas is a rural state," I told the governor.

Later as we were descended the steps from the governor's office, Robin asked me, "How can you talk so boldly to the governor?" I laughed, and answered, "Because I am old enough to be his mother." Governor Clinton vetoed the roads program, and the House overrode the veto 67-29, probably a smart move for both. The governor proved he was against a tax increase, and the House voiced the support for rural roads.

Rep. Nap Murphy of Hamburg, the House's version of Colonel Sanders in a white suit and black bowtie, became angered at an unsigned letter in his county newspaper calling him a "traitor." Rep. Murphy introduced a bill to fine editors who published unsigned letters to the editor. As an editor, I took up the challenge, bringing a copy of the U.S. Constitution's First Amendment and declaring the bill patently unconstitutional. I was well-armed with materials allowing me to filibuster; however, I just wanted to make my point and sit down. Nap's bill to fine editors received 10 aye's and 58 no's. Most of the aye's came from members of the committee he chaired. They told me they "dared not vote against the chair."

For the session, Melvin and I had rented a room at the Coachman's Inn where many other legislators were domiciled. With $7,200 annually as legislative salary, I depended on our business income. Our Coachman's stay was pleasant, particularly since its accommodating restaurant offered home cooking at reasonable prices.

During three months in Little Rock, we came home every Friday afternoon to begin catching up at the *Clarion* office. I worked there all day Saturday and after church Sunday. Sarah Mauney assisted editor Terry Hawkins during the session. Melvin came home on Wednesdays to check the books and make the payroll, a very tiring experience since he returned to Little Rock the same day.

Following the session, Melvin and I went to Fayetteville since I was to be recognized for establishing the UAMS chair in alcoholism and drug abuse prevention. We met Art Linkletter there. In his 70s, he was as charming as he was the many times I had seen him on TV.

Melvin and I later joined Bob and Christene Fisher of Clarksville for the National Federation of Press Women's meeting in Chicago. What a thrill to join the July 4th crowd of 750,000 for magnificent fireworks at Grant Park!

At our tiny Dumas festival, we enjoyed a political highlight. The Desha County Museum float featured "The Old Guard Rest Home," the creation of talented cartoonist George Fisher. Riding the float were former office holders Sheriff Marlin Hawkins of Morrilton, state senator Guy (Mutt) Jones, Governor Orval Faubus, and Supreme Court justice Jim Johnson.

Mirroring economic change, Union Pacific cut jobs in McGehee, where railroad employment once exceeded 500. ALCO Discount Store closed in Dumas, and West Department Store shut down in McGehee. However, we always operated on hope.

The *Clarion* production, utilizing our two units of a Cottrell v-15 A press, settled into three sections a week and more with special promotions. We planned feature stories on section fronts; had departmentalized news for agriculture, education, sports, and family; and continued our full editorial page. With a six-column, 14-em-wide format, we featured as many large photos as we could. Most advertising appeared in the *Clarion* pages during a period well before circulars were to take over grocery and discount store advertising. Melvin's siege with cancer had diminished his stamina, so I took over more publishing responsibilities. Professional meetings remained a priority, and we attended the 100th anniversary of the National Newspaper Association in Minneapolis.

We had joyous family news as David, the third son of John and Deanna, was born September 19 in Austin, Texas, where John was enrolled in the University of Texas to work on a joint degree in law and public policy, and Deanna was associated with the University's LBJ School.

In October, we joined our traveling companions, Bob and Christene Fisher, for a pleasant two weeks in England, Scotland, and Wales. They were most helpful, as Melvin had cataract surgery six weeks before the trip. Returning home, we were distressed to learn that our baby granddaughter Lauren Holden had been very ill with meningitis. We rushed to Shreveport, and I tried to give my daughter Sarah and Grandmother Joan Holden a break. The Good Lord saw Lauren through the ordeal. As busy as we were, family was top priority.

At home, Dumas School enrollment, which had peaked at 2,563 in 1974, had fallen to 2,378 by 1985. Later, "white flight" was to exacerbate the problem.

Dumas Industrial Foundation, under the leadership of Fred Williams, planned a speculative building to attract industry, a move resulting in the Binkley, Inc., plant. Merle and Deloris Peterson, who had served as volunteer directors for the Chamber, resigned after giving great service to the industrial push, and Gary Weaver was named executive.

One day, Loral Adcock called me into his office at Merchants & Farmers Bank and said, "We're thinking of a new bank on Highway 65 and would give the Chamber a room for an office there. Or you all could have the old bank building and fix it up."

"I don't know what the others will think, but I vote for the old bank building," I replied. When Gary Weaver became director, the Chamber office later moved into the municipal building. Ultimately, Merchants & Farmers Bank management decided to renovate its downtown facility and donate the historic building at Waterman and Main to the Chamber. Gary Weaver was a godsend. He not only supervised the renovation, but he did much work in preserving the 1913 building.

Another good piece of news was that the U.S. Senate had passed the Great River Bridge Compact on December 3. Still pushing the bridge project and going to the NNA board meeting in Washington DC in December, we savored the Christmas lighting and theatre, seeing Rex Harrison and Claudette Colbert in the comedy *Aren't We All?*

In 1986, when we joined in marking the 150 years of Arkansas's statehood, a special-issue stamp was unveiled. Among the 2,000 in Little Rock's Robinson Auditorium for the occasion was Winchester postmaster Jesse Peacock. A state friend nudged Melvin and said, "Who is that?" Melvin replied, "The postmaster of Winchester." "Oh," said the state friend, "I thought it was someone important." No one enjoyed that story more than the postmaster of Winchester.

The shocking loss of the space shuttle *Challenger* that January kept us glued to television sets. I remembered meeting Astronaut Deke Slayton at the first free flight of the space shuttle at Edwards Air Force Base in California in 1977. In his talk, he stressed that there were three minutes or less to prevent a disaster.

Then came more wrenching news. Across Waterman Street from the *Clarion* building was our first business location, then occupied by Leon Harvey's home and auto supply store. On March 31, Harvey's store caught fire. Many memories surfaced as we watched flames consume it.

Even more distressing was the next evening when we heard multiple sirens and went to Highway 65 south to cover a wreck. In one of the saddest experiences I had in the newspaper business, I learned that an 18-wheeler loaded with steel had run over and demolished a car. Bodies were strewn over a nearby field. Parking a quarter mile away and walking in the dark, I asked a policeman, "Who is it?" He replied, "Miss Madge and her family." Madge Moore Youree, 74, retired superintendent of Arkansas City Schools, had resided in my Tillar home as a young teacher and was as close as a sister to me. Madge, her son John Youree, his wife, and their two small children were the victims of that awful highway carnage. After learning that all but the baby were dead and she was so critical she would not survive, I grieved and wrote. Tears flowed most of the night.

Another loss occurred two weeks later in the death of C. W. (Rock) Meador, whose familiar face and strong personality made him a town institution for more than 90 years. His public service included 18 years on the Dumas School Board, 15 years on the City Council, and 50 years on the Methodist Church board.

In May, Melvin and I had the unusual opportunity to join an adult exchange program between Arkansas and South Australia, both celebrating their sesquicentennials. We joined 39 Arkansans for the trip, organized by Arkansas Parks & Tourism. On arrival in Sydney after a 15-hour flight from Los Angeles, we had a short nap before attending the performance of the hit musical *Cats*. Glorious music is all I remember of the show; none of us could stay awake.

The rest was delightfully eye-opening. Flying to Adelaide, where we were assigned to spend four days as guests in homes, and we met hosts Keith and Carmel Frost, who became friends for life. He was a retired printing company executive, and together they showed us how Aussies live. Sightseeing in their vintage Mercedes, we cuddled koala bears and marveled at numerous kangaroos and native species at a wildlife park. (Fifteen years later, in 2000, they came to Dumas to renew the friendship. We were lucky to get tickets for a Democratic fundraiser in Little Rock, where they met President Bill Clinton and Vice President Al Gore.)

Before ending our "Down Under" tour, my legislative ally Wanda Northcutt of Stuttgart, fellow newspaper publishers Cone and Betty Magie of Cabot, and Bob and Christene Fisher of Clarksville joined Melvin and me in touring New Zealand for several days. Arkansas's Democratic primary was held shortly after our return, and, without opposition, Wanda and I were re-elected to the House.

Always on the move, Melvin and I took Jesus Poyatus, a Spanish exchange student at Dumas High School, to the "Hands Across America" program. As 300,000 stretched across our state, we lined up near Lonoke. First Methodist Church of Dumas sent a busload to join the line near Malvern. More than five million Americans participated, raising funds for the hungry and homeless.

Soon our guests during Arkansas's Sesquicentennial Celebration in Little Rock were Martin and Kathy Baily, an Adelaide couple whom we had met. Harold Jones lent his silver Mercedes, and Michael Jones chauffeured the Bailys and the Schexnayders in the parade. Desha County's float was a colorful replica of the *Kate Adams* steamboat, built by Girl Scout Troop 210 of Dumas, parents, and friends. Desha County native Michael Rice, a talented pianist and composer, opened the fanfare at War Memorial Stadium with composition, "Arkansas Forever."

For our own summer festival, I wrote a historical pageant focusing on Desha County. Thirty-five donned costumes for the event at Memorial Park. Gary Weaver was such a good sport that he wore de Soto garb with long stockings, saying, "Anything for Ding Dong Days!" My role was that of U.S. senator Hattie Caraway, and Loral (Popeye) Adcock, as her campaign manager Huey Long, was a crowd favorite.

Arrival of 1987 brought new family joys. On February 27, we welcomed a new family member, Emily Claire, born to Sarah and Mason Holden in Baton Rouge, where Mason was in medical practice with his father.

Steve and fiancée Rebecca Eldridge of DeWitt planned their wedding following his graduation from UA School of Medicine. Becky was serving her internship in pediatrics, and he planned a career in pediatrics and internal medicine. Both would serve on the Arkansas Children's Hospital staff.

When Steve received the Faculty Key in the honors convocation, Melvin and I looked at one another proudly and whispered congratulations. Even though friends thought we, as older parents, might not live to see him educated, we beamed at his accomplishment. Life was so full!

Our family gathered to celebrate Steve and Becky's May 23 nuptials at Quapaw Quarter's United Methodist Church and reception at picturesque Villa Marre in Little Rock. It was an extra effort for Sarah and Mason, whose little ones were just getting over chicken pox.

Mixing family, journalism, and politics seemed natural.

21.
Hot Water

While maintaining family responsibilities and supervising the *Clarion* operations, I was serving in the House during an 82-day session in 1987 called "unproductive and vacillating." It was hardly that to me.

Wanda Northcutt and I successfully "re-upped" the tax on mixed drinks for the UAMS Chair in Alcohol Abuse Prevention. After highway tax records had been closed as a provision in a new weight-distance tax on heavy trucks, I led a battle to reopen the records commensurate with the Tax Procedures Act requiring all revenue records to be open to the public. "Never give up" was my thought as I lost the amendment in a floor vote. With the help of parliamentary-savvy friends and the support of Governor Clinton later, I maneuvered the amendment out of committee on a voice vote, and it passed the House without dissent.

I also joined House Speaker Ernest Cunningham of Helena, who had befriended me, in a fight to open industrial recruitment records of the Arkansas Industrial Development Commission. Late one afternoon, the speaker said, "Mrs. Schexnayder, will you take the chair?" I was so astonished that I could hardly rise from my desk and ascend steps to the speaker's podium. What a nice surprise and honor!

However, it was my penchant for saying what I think and getting involved that drove me into hot water in the legislature, much as it had in the newspaper business. If there was an issue involving the media, I was in the thick of it, and controversy sometimes stuck to me like glue as in a 1988 special session.

I became the target for two Little Rock columnists, John Robert Starr and Meredith Oakley. The flap began when leadership of the House became irritated at reporters—who stood in the back of the Chamber and observed and talked—and the governor's men (lobbying for his agenda), who worked the floor. There was reason for the irritation at all the confusion. Most of the House members, aside from committee chairs, had no offices except for the desks and small filing cabinets on the House floor. Even though I carried all important papers in a bulging briefcase, I had papers disappear from my desk, as had other members.

A row of desks for eight reporters was placed between the speaker's podium and the "well," where we went to address the House. Major media had regularly assigned reporters, and one place was for visiting press. Other reporters stood wherever convenient to witness the proceedings, and photographers roamed. In this scenario, the House leadership called for removal of the press and governor's men from the House floor into gallery space.

During the debate, I rose to say that I thought a compromise was possible, controlling floor use but still allowing the press access in the reserved area. I mentioned the Society of Professional Journalists, of which I was a member, but said I was speaking for myself. I was immediately accused of speaking for all the media.

That evening, I happened to be seated by Speaker Cunningham at a legislators' dinner and quietly said to him, "Mr. Speaker, I don't think you want to be remembered as the speaker who banned the press from the House floor." He discussed options.

Attacks on me began the next morning in the *Arkansas Democrat*, where John Robert Starr and Meredith Oakley wrote political columns. Starr said he would run me out of the legislature. Oakley proclaimed, "Schexnayder sells out to the good ole boys." It would have been difficult to sell out to the good old boys since I was never included in their parleys.

When I arrived at the State Capitol, some House members came to me and said, "You ARE going to take a time of personal privilege and defend yourself, aren't you?" "No," I replied. "Critics can read the *House Journal*. I didn't speak for anyone but myself."

When the session convened, Speaker Cunningham asked for personal privilege and came to the well to defend me. He said, "The reason the press is still on the floor of the House today is because of Charlotte Schexnayder," adding that I had fought the original proposal to bar all reporters.

Compromise occurred after the speaker named a committee to work with media. (I was not included.) The number of governor's lobbyists was limited. Reporters were allowed only in the reserved section and photographers in a designated area, with others relegated to a new press area in the gallery. Years later, I happened to see John Robert Starr at the Excelsior Hotel. "Well, John Robert, I see you have retired, and I am still in the legislature." It was the first time I had seen him speechless.

After the legislative hot seat, I took two days' leave to join Judge Bain Poole, Ann Cash, and Michael Jones as the first delegation to Washington in support of the Great River Bridge. We met with Senators Dale Bumpers and David Pryor of Arkansas, John Stennis and Thad Cochran of Mississippi, as well as Congressmen Beryl Anthony of Arkansas, and Trent Lott, Jamie Whitten, and Mike Espy of Mississippi. My continuous causes in the Arkansas Legislature included promoting the bridge effort and rural development.

I also led the request for funding for Yellow Bend Port. While in the Northwest during the summer, I was summoned to Washington. Senator David Pryor asked that I join Sam Bowman of McGehee, chairman of Yellow Bend Port Authority, flying in from his vacation in Georgia. Senator Pryor called us to meet Under Secretary of the Army Bob Dawson. After hearing the senator's and our pleas for funding, the under secretary admonished, "We will never build Yellow Bend

Port." Senator Pryor's eyes grew steely and his voice icy as he crossed his arms over his chest and declared, "Oh, but we will!" From that moment, I never doubted. The first federal funding of $1 million was possible because of persistent Senators Bumpers and Pryor. On the state level, McGehee mayor Rosalie Gould and I frequented the governor's office with the goal of getting $1 million in state funding.

Not all of my legislative efforts required big money. My simple legislative resolution urging the Arkansas Highway Department to set up an "Adopt a Highway" program was beginning to take off.

The National Newspaper Association convention drew us westward. With Bob and Christene Fisher, we flew to San Francisco for sightseeing before driving through the Napa Valley and along the coast to Portland, Oregon. Our trip through the magnificent redwoods proved a highlight. In Crescent City we met Cone and Betty Magie of Cabot to attend the newspaper convention in Portland and tour Mt. Hood and the volcano-ravaged Mount St. Helens area.

Terry Hawkins left the *Clarion* for other journalistic pursuits, and Randal Seyler became associate editor. Major stories, such as a murder, mostly were a team effort.

One of the most chilling to report was the stabbing death of Mrs. Laverne Sanderlin at her downtown fabric business. A parolee from Cummins Prison, Larry Dean Robertson, had been left in Dumas to wander streets overnight while waiting for the next day's bus. The next morning, he went into the fabric store of Mrs. Sanderlin and allegedly stabbed her with scissors from her business, just two blocks from the *Clarion* office.

Robertson was at large in the middle of the city, and every door was locked for a 21-hour period. Seyler and Melvin monitored the police investigation and manhunt, feeding details while I wrote and re-wrote the story as it developed from Tuesday until late Wednesday morning when the murderer was caught in a downtown garbage bin.

Law enforcement officers performed magnificently to avert more loss of life. Police Chief Richard Bonds, Sheriff Ben Williams, and State Police Lt. David Rosegrant had led the search to capture Robertson. We scooped the dailies, always a journalistic coup for me, but the tragedy hung heavily over all of us.

Summer found us touring again. We went to the 50th high school reunion of Melvin's 1937 class in Franklin, Louisiana, and two weeks later, flew to Williamsburg, Virginia, to join in the 50th anniversary of the National Federation of Press Women. Back home, we joined in the Tillar reunion, which brought 510 to reminisce about days at the school, no longer in use. That number was double the Tillar population.

Of that experience, I wrote: "The floor creaks as might be expected for a building erected in 1917. The stairs seem steeper than I remembered. The classroom has been re-arranged with the desks facing south rather than east. And I wonder who remembers the cloakroom by the classroom, or how the stage was located just across the hall. The old walnut desk the teacher used is gone. But her spirit is still there, and I felt it as I visited the classroom where she taught English and literature, and served as a journalism teacher for much of her 23-year career....It is natural that I would remember, but even more gratifying that many others who came for the Tillar High School reunion on Friday would recall my mother, Bertha Terry Tillar, for her contributions to their lives."

Even with this penchant for nostalgia, I balanced legislative and newspaper duties, then spending about 60 percent of my time on the *Clarion*. Often these coincided, as when I covered the organization of the Arkansas-Mississippi Compact Authority for the Great River Bridge. Mayor Rosalie Gould and Ann Cash of McGehee, Judge Bain Poole, Mayor Bill Hopmann, Merle Peterson, and I went to Washington to promote study monies for the bridge. I was a state representative who carried a camera and a reporter's notebook.

While 1988 was an "off-year," during biennial sessions, there were countless meetings to attend. An experience to record and remember was covering presidential-hopeful Michael Dukakis's visit to Little Rock.

There were always possibilities for called sessions of the legislature, sometimes on short notice. One came in January 1988.

Governor Clinton named me to a task force focusing on writing public ethics legislation. When I stepped into the hall to consult with a constituent, I was named chair of the committee writing the public disclosure section. Cohorts were Ark Monroe, highly respected Little Rock attorney; Bobbie Hill, president of the League of Women Voters; and Jim Sherrill, a popular county judge. We 19 members of the Public Ethics Commission did not receive a dime, and we worked diligently in bill drafting.

An intense process, it was far more difficult later. Seventy-three amendments were offered in special session, many with intent to kill. Sen. Charlie Cole Chaffin and I were lead sponsors with Sen. Jay Bradford and Rep. Bynum Gibson as co-sponsors. I advised the governor that I needed an orator, and Bynum, my seatmate by my second term, certainly qualified. In fact, if there were a controversy, Bynum and I gravitated there. He would pause at my desk and exclaim, "We are in the darndest fight," of which I knew not. But we soon were.

Ethics bill sponsors gathered in the governor's office at 7:30 a.m. to map strategy, and often after a day of committee meetings, negotiations, and no lunch, we returned to Clinton's office until 7 p.m. The governor worked the phones three to four hours in evening while attempting to sway support. I admired his resolve and stamina.

House Bill 1032 was amended 19 times, but thanks to Speaker Ernest Cunningham, we brought the bill to a committee vote on the session's ninth day. After 20 hours of committee consideration, the bill received a "do-pass." Bynum and I figured we had 55 to 58 votes (safe margin with minimum 51 needed), but sensed a great change in mood. The bill zipped through the House 93-4, throwing the ethics responsibility on the Senate. Alas, that was its demise, as we did not get four votes needed to pass out of Senate committee.

The governor was slowed but not stopped. An initiated act was to follow. As 600 attended a capitol rally opening the petition drive, the governor was the first to sign as he propped the petition on my shoulder. Arkansans passed the public ethics code in November 1988, and in following sessions, I was involved in amendments to strengthen it.

Mixing responsibilities, I was trying to make progress with the *Clarion* as well. To create interest in additional agricultural markets, we began using soybean ink. Although more expensive, it had a pleasant scent, quite a change from the chemical-based inks. Stressing printing quality, we discarded copies not up to our standards and stopped the press when necessary to assure better ink distribution on the ink-water process. Our paper was still 25 cents a copy. The *Clarion* added a new computer system, tying the news and advertising departments together and resulting in added confusion in the short run.

Dumas continued to excel in recruitment, bringing the Binkley Company to the three-year-old speculative building erected by the Industrial Foundation. Binkley manufactured slides used on truck trailers to change the location of rear wheels in order to distribute the cargo weight. The plant initially employed 50.

Focus on the impoverished Delta continued as three young governors, Clinton of Arkansas, Ray Mabus of Mississippi, and Buddy Roemer of Louisiana, met on a barge in the Mississippi River between Rosedale and Watson to ink a pact of cooperation. Another notable story came in the groundbreaking for the Yellow Bend slack-water harbor on the Mississippi, with Senators Bumpers and Pryor and Governor Clinton joining local proponents in the celebration.

When the National Federation of Press Women held its annual conference in Little Rock, programming included a National Center for Toxicological Research tour, a barge dinner trip on the Arkansas

River, and a barbecue on Petit Jean Mountain. Governor Bill and First Lady Hillary Clinton were hits as speakers. Just a week later, we were standing on the rim of the Grand Canyon, a grandiose experience made possible when we joined the National Newspaper board meeting in Flagstaff, Arizona.

At home, the focus was on Ding Dong Days, with entertainment by the Navy band "High Tide"; the Community Theatre's staging of *South Pacific*, starring Hardy Peacock and Cindy Grimes; and a celebration of the 150th birthday of Desha County.

The festival brought an unusual reunion. In 1943, the 372nd Engineers of the U.S. Army had bivouacked in a field near Dumas as they sand-bagged the levee to fight flood waters. Herman Hoffman of Michigan City, Michigan, remembered Dumas Business Women and church women then opening the American Legion hut to provide weekend hospitality for the men. Re-contacting Dumas, he and his buddies were invited to be festival guests. As the Corps of Engineers was seeking to build alliances, I was delegated to raise funds for a catfish supper on a Corps barge. Some 350 boarded the *Shorty Baird* tug and barges for the "evening cruise" on the Arkansas River with the Engineers stressing the river's potential.

Amid summer celebrations came reality. Melvin faced major surgery to rebuild his left shoulder, which had numerous dislocations following a World War II injury. That extremely painful surgery was followed by a second urological operation. Between nursing duties, I met *Clarion* deadlines.

My next challenge came at the National Newspaper Association convention in San Antonio, where there was an effort to "ditch" me as the first woman on the board, bypassing me in the officer chain. I knew some on the nominating committee disdained a woman officer. However, Adam Kelly of West Virginia and Frank Garred of Washington State staunchly backed me, and Adam enjoyed calling me "Darned Old Democrat." Dennis Schick,

Arkansas Press Association executive, and our state group weighed in for me. Thus, I was nominated as treasurer-elect, the first woman to hold an NNA office in its 104-year history. Colleagues are invaluable in smashing any glass ceiling.

Reaching age 65 on Christmas Day, I wrote that I had lived on two biblical principles instilled in me by my mother. Paraphrasing them, they are: "To whom much is given, much is required," and "Everything works to the good of those who love the Lord." These were quotes so often heard during my younger life.

22.
Not in Our Backyard

Battle-tested, I faced a significant fight in the 1989 assembly. At a Desha Quorum Court meeting a month earlier, state senator Jack Gibson of Jerome appeared on behalf of a group, Keeg Arkansas, proposing to buy a Desha County landfill as a dumping ground for East Coast garbage. The waste would be shipped from the East Coast through the Mississippi River port Senator Gibson owned and was developing.

Monetary enticement was not enough to create a huge landfill for East Coast garbage. I thought the fertile Delta should not become a giant dump, but the senator was adamant. "There is no way you can keep it out," Senator Gibson told the Quorum Court meeting I attended. "This is interstate commerce." Sitting on the front row in the Desha County courtroom in Arkansas City, I watched anxiously as the Quorum Court deferred action.

Before the legislature was in session, I had staked the *Clarion* position in an editorial entitled "Speak Out." I wrote, "It is imperative that the people be heard. The 'carrot' being offered to the county in terms of large sums of money to accept garbage from the East Coast is an enticement for some; however, the ramifications of huge piles of waste being stored in this county raise monumental questions as to the preservation of our high quality water supply and clean air."

Knowing of my solid opposition, my legislative ally Bynum Gibson of Dermott (a cousin to Senator Jack) called to join the fight. Truly that was a courageous stance for Bynum. Partners in the legislative battle, Bynum was the fiery spokesman and I was the floor worker for votes to prevent the Keeg Arkansas move.

Bynum and I introduced House Bill 1055 requiring a public referendum if a quorum court approves an agreement on solid waste disposal with a private firm. Representatives Wanda Northcutt, James Jordan, Lacy Landers, and Ode Maddox signed as co-sponsors, and the measure passed the House 94-0. However, we knew there would be trouble in the Senate committee.

At the *Clarion*, Randal Seyler, assistant editor, began investigation into the background of Keeg Arkansas. He subsequently found that the company forming Keeg Arkansas had major environmental violations in Georgia, its headquarters. Then came the revelation that Arkansas's Geological Commission had paid for tests on the site in Desha and Chicot counties two days before Keeg Arkansas approached the Quorum Court.

For the session, I had used seniority to move to new committees—Education (at the request of Governor Clinton) and City, County and Local Affairs (where I thought I might have some input on the garbage issue).

In our next move, Bynum and I filed legislation creating a two-year moratorium on importing out-of-state garbage and establishing a task force, appointed by the governor, to study the problem. The old tactic: if we couldn't get it through the Senate, we would sidetrack the issue enough to defeat it. Our bill passed the House 93-0, and a public hearing was scheduled in a Senate committee chaired by Sen. Knox Nelson, ruling ally of Jack Gibson.

Power of the people surfaced. Hundreds of calls against East Coast garbage jammed lines into the governor's office. Thousands signed petitions against the trash importation. And even more stirring was the caravan bringing 250 people in 50 cars from southeast Arkansas to the Senate hearing. Of course, there was no space for all citizens in the committee room, but they were in the halls of the

Capitol! Organizing the caravan were Frances Newton and Jimmie Appleberry of Dumas, and Mayor Rosalie Gould, Vivion Tullos, and Tootsie Hoffman of McGehee. An opposition group entitled SOIL (Save Our Innocent Land) enrolled hundreds. It was a grand example of public outrage reaching the legislature, and although the legislation for a moratorium did not immediately pass the Senate Committee, the will of the people was evident and the rush to bring in East Coast garbage had met its match.

In an effort to keep the project alive, Keeg Arkansas shifted focus to another site. Our House bill had stalled in Senate committee for three weeks when Keeg Arkansas withdrew its environmental application for a landfill. Momentum led to the formation of a commission to study and recommend landfill regulations for the state. Talented lawyer-legislator Bynum Gibson chaired its work.

In the contentious session, it was not the garbage issue which most threatened me. Representative Northcutt and I sought to make the mixed drink sales tax permanent to provide funding for construction of a research center at the University of Arkansas for Medical Sciences. Strongly opposed were owners of restaurants and bars, principally in the Little Rock area.

In the successful struggle to move the bill out of the rules committee onto the House floor, I was accosted. Upon leaving the committee room following the vote, I was accompanied by UAMS dean Dr. Dodd Wilson. As I passed a group of opponents in the halls, one declared vehemently at my back, "You'll never forget this day!" I turned around and went back to face the group. "Who said that?" I demanded. Not one word in reply. Angrily, I replied, "Don't you ever threaten me! I will not be threatened!" Still no reply.

The House grapevine was at work. After climbing stairs to the third floor, I entered the House Chamber. Sitting at the back was Rep. Lacy Landers. "Hey, do you need a bodyguard?" he asked. "No!" I declared. "I can take care of myself." He replied, "I kind of figured you could."

Although major issues kept me busy, sometimes it was the smaller roles in the legislature that were rewarding. I recommended brilliant Jo Carol Gill, young Dumas attorney, for an appointed circuit judge position. She was the youngest to serve in that position when Governor Clinton named her.

When the legislature was not in session, events still drew me to Little Rock. When a Soviet women's exchange group visited, I wore two hats, discussing both politics and journalism. I was a state representative who carried a notebook and camera. Later, going to cherry-blossom-brilliant Washington in behalf of the Great River Bridge provided an opportunity to see the consultant Blaze Carrier of Howard, Needles, Tammen, & Bergendoff unveil a perspective of the bridge said to have a benefit/cost ratio of 1.57 to 1.

When returning to the *Clarion*, the mantra was "Promote." Special sections helped to pick up revenues for both our weekly and Delta Advertiser shopper, lagging when I was away.

In Dumas, all was not well. On March 1, 1989, Dollar General Corporation announced plans to close a 330,000-square-foot warehouse and thus eliminate 160 jobs. Dumas had to cope with another economic blow. Several months later, through the efforts of the Chamber of Commerce and Merle Peterson, Dumas was able to locate a U.S. Cotton Classing Office on Highway 65. Belden also announced expansion of its automotive harness operation. Moreover, we were able to obtain a $504,000 grant toward a new industrial park.

Involved on many fronts, I assisted Jane Pickens Lambi in her school enrichment project of "Replace a Recess," sought sponsorships for a Corps of Engineers' Evening on the Arkansas River, and participated in the hearings of the Lower Mississippi Delta Commission.

Invited to address the Maine Media Women, I was joined by Melvin, along with Bob and Christene Fisher, for the flight to Portland. Also it provided a springboard for a Maritime Provinces trip. Melvin was excited to visit Nova Scotia, as his mother's ancestors were Acadians ousted there and re-located to Louisiana. At St. Anne's Museum, we found his mother's maiden name of Meaux. Sightseeing included seeing the fishing fleets at Digby as they were "shocking" or shucking the scallop shells into the bay.

The summer brought us a fine staffer, Marla Helms, whose husband Roger worked for the Department of Corrections at Cummins. A reporter, she also planned section pages ahead, much to my approval.

Extra personnel gave us the opportunity to fill a busy schedule. I went to the governor's office to inquire if a special session might be forthcoming, and was assured it was not. Melvin and I headed for the Press Women's conference in Idaho and its pre-convention tour to Glacier National Park, including a snowstorm at the park's peak, and a visit to Fort Steele, Canada, where a letterpress printing exhibit evoked memories. Upon reaching Glacier lodge, I had notification from the governor calling a session to address budget shortfalls.

En route to Coeur d'Alene Airport, I developed severe food poisoning. Melvin assisted me on and off planes in a first-class flight costing $1,100 each—painful physically and economically. Pale as a ghost, I reached the legislative session and hadn't attended a single Press Women's session! "Why didn't you stop me from going?" I asked Betsey Wright, the governor's chief of staff. "We didn't know for certain when the session would be," she replied.

My summer revolved around preparations for Dumas's annual festival. *All the Way Home*, an original musical by Miles Fish, proved a hit.

Civic projects were mixed with my newspaper responsibilities. The City of Dumas agreed to donate the land for a new library, the site of the old icehouse where luscious melons once brought steady customers. Betty Vickers and Lorene Clayton led fundraising here. A match was needed from the state, so I asked the State Library Board for a $150,000 grant, relating needs of the impoverished Delta. Senator Stephen Luelf of Mountain Home spoke on behalf of his area, and he later said he told the Library Board, "Give the money to her. The Delta needs it much worse."

Another far-reaching step in Dumas's continuing progress was the passage of a hamburger tax, assessed on restaurants and motels, as financing for a community center. Passage came after the City Council deadlocked. T. C. Pickett, James Jackson, Bill Morris, and Linda Rankin voted for the tax. Voting no were Clay Oldner, Lewis Ray Baker, Henry Reding, and Roy Dalton. In perhaps his most courageous vote, Mayor Bill Hopmann affirmatively broke the tie.

Forming the new civic center commission were Tim Yarnell, chairman; David Rainey, Maxine Stubbs, Loral Adcock, Herman Vickers, Will Cox, Martha Clark, Jimmy Locke, Charles Higdon, Sarah Taylor, and William (Doc) Puryear. The new auditorium was designed to attract regional and state meetings, as well as to provide facilities for the Delta Arts & Crafts Fair, other exhibitions, weddings, civic meetings, and even funerals. I had long been its editorial advocate.

A milestone in school improvement came when Dumas district voters approved a 6.2 mill tax hike supporting a $1.6 million bond issue for Reed campus and other school facilities. In a concerted effort, Superintendent Don McHan pushed updating of all facilities.

On the recreational front, my long quest for a dam on the Arkansas River's old channel was successful. The project, thus creating an ox bow lake at Morgan Bendway, received congressional support through the persistence of Senator Bumpers and senatorial aide Carmie Henry.

Travel beckoned. Three weeks before the fall of the Berlin Wall, we embarked on a tour of the Soviet Union without an inkling of the wall's historic demolition. Joining the National Press Women's two-week tour, we found it our most revealing trip. At Helsinki, Finland, we changed to Russian aircraft, and we immediately identified KGB secret agents scanning the crowd, adding to our apprehension.

Because of so few lights when we landed in Moscow, we could hardly believe it to be a major city. With no rubles to pay airport attendants, we resorted to giving a Dallas Cowboys' souvenir cigarette lighter to the sky-hop, who gleefully handled our luggage. Into the city, we found that autos ran on parking lights, relatively few streetlights burned, and little lighted advertising was on buildings.

At our hotel Kosmos, built in 1979 for the Olympics, workmanship had left gaps—tiles did not meet and cracks were evident. We always felt the rooms were "bugged." Most disconcerting was the system of women hall monitors picking up our passports in exchange for our room keys when we left the hotel. No chance to venture on our own.

Russians then were wild about the dollar. At the first hotel breakfast, waiters whispered "rubles for dollars," certainly illegal. The ruble was pegged at 1.65 to the dollar, but the black market would give 10 rubles for a dollar. In the museums, at tour bus stops, and even on streets, we were stopped by those willing to trade rubles for dollars. Three nice sets of nested dolls were offered for $5, and hand-painted black lacquer boxes for $10 to $25. In a major "department store" where the abacus was used instead of adding machine or calculator, a traditional black fur hat was only $10.

However, it was the people who most surprised us. Tour guides openly questioned their government. People on the streets were gracious and outgoing. On a streetcar, two women rose and insisted that standing Melvin and Bob Fisher take their seats. When we tried to pay streetcar fare, we were waved off and other riders paid for us. We walked Red Square when the lights dimmed sharply at 9 p.m. and felt no alarm. The Russian people were friendly at every encounter.

Our tour guide for the entire trip controlled our plane and train tickets. When we flew to Tbilisi, we found the capital of Georgia in ferment. Protesters with freedom signs were massing in the streets, and Melvin and Bob walked among them for photographs. Invited in a group to visit an elementary school, we were treated like celebrities and given hand-carved wooden toys made by the children. We were free to write what we wished, but teachers pleaded for us not to disclose that first graders were being taught freedom slogans.

On a street, a young man asked if we were American. Saying "yes," we asked if he were Russian. "No," he declared. "I am Georgian."

Most amazing was the woman I sat by on a bus. She said, "I have brother in Baltimore." I thought she knew English—but it was only those words. By sign language and a map, I showed her Arkansas and Baltimore. Then she tugged on my arm and pulled me to get off at the next stop.

"Where are we going?' asked Melvin, Bob, and Christene.

"I don't know, but we are going," I replied. I figured there was safety in numbers.

We followed the woman down the street, up an alley to a set of steps, and then into an apartment building. She motioned to the elevator, and took us to her apartment, giving us a chance to see how a Moscow citizen lived. She pulled out a tablecloth and began to set the table for a meal.

I shook my head, "No," as we had to return to our hotel and board a train for Sochi. She pleaded; we shook our heads. Then she motioned for us to wait, as she presented gifts. First, a bottle of vodka to each couple. Second, handmade candles. Third, a bowl of large persimmons dumped into newspaper.

"What are you giving her?" my companions asked. I had only a small handheld calculator. It sufficed.

As we left Tbilisi by train, we expected a half-day journey, but it turned into 23 interesting hours. The Fishers shared a compartment with us. On a seat just outside the compartment was a young woman and her son Giorgi, age five. She noticed I was wearing a Georgian pin (given to me by schoolchildren), and she promptly produced a small Georgian flag for me. I took off an Arkansas pin I was wearing and gave it to Giorgi. I fished around in luggage for cheese crackers which Giorgi promptly sampled.

The boy and mother left but came back with pear and lemon sodas and four candy bars for us. We returned the favor with some dinosaur stickers for Giorgi, who crawled into the compartment with us. An hour or so later, they left the train and gave me an address. We kept in touch, but I lost track of them after they moved to Greece.

In Sochi, we visited a daily newspaper office. Comparing professions, I found it most revealing. Sergei Beliov, deputy editor of an 80,000-circulation daily, said his staff numbered 68, including "27 creative people." They published four pages daily for five days, with about 25 percent advertising. He said five percent of the news came from Tass, official news agency for Russia, and the rest was local. By comparison, with 10 fulltime and two part-time employees on average, we published 20 to 24 pages weekly.

Printing by letterpress (a process which our newspaper had abandoned 21 years previously), the Russians said, "We are sorry to admit our technology is very old." I saw reporters writing stories in longhand and a few typewriters. There was a teletype such as frequently found in U.S. newspapers 40 years earlier. The Russians found it difficult to believe we had laser printers and computers.

Galia Mityagi, deputy woman editor, said the Sochi newspaper had one woman on staff five years ago and "now has five." Asked how long was the workweek, she added, "Who counts?" Later, it was said to average 42 hours.

Sochi then received 200,000 foreign visitors annually, she commented. Forty-seven were warmly greeted members of the NFPW tour. Entertainment included a famed Russian circus.

Our final stop was Leningrad, which later returned to its old name of St. Petersburg. Known as the Venice of the North, the city had magnificent palaces of Peter the Great that were truly memorable. With 1,000 rooms and 117 staircases, the winter palace overlooks the

Neva River, but we could not take our eyes from its interior splendor and the art of Italian, Spanish, Dutch, German, and French masters.

During a 900-day siege in World War II, Leningrad withstood every German thrust, but one-third of the buildings were destroyed. Forty-four years after the war's end in Europe, we became the first American group of Americans to talk face-to-face with Leningrad Journalist Union members.

Sweeping changes were coming. Acknowledged one Russian journalist, "So far there is no special law providing rights of journalists…but in the process of restructuring Perestroika, this needs to be specified." American press freedom, how grand!

Back to the U.S. and our own deadlines, we focused on the Elaine Christmas Parade, considered so politically important that Congressman Bill Alexander and his bride were there nine hours after their nuptials at Washington's National Cathedral. We wouldn't have dared to miss it, either.

23.
Into the Nineties

The nineties are most remembered, and enjoyed, because of additional grandchildren, those born to Becky and Steve in Little Rock: beginning with Allison Kate April 20, 1990, followed by Daniel Stephen, April 19, 1994; Anne Charlotte, April 22, 1996; and Amy Grace, August 2, 1999. Visiting grandchildren became a priority and continuing pleasure in our dual lifestyle.

Mostly focusing on our newspaper business, we joined in efforts to update downtown Dumas. Vacant aging storefronts, cracked uneven sidewalks, and straggling weeds along railroad tracks demanded attention if downtown Dumas was to survive.

However, town stores bustled. At Meador Pharmacy, farmers helped owner Bill Canada open at 5 a.m. for coffee, a lunch crowd gathered for tuna fish and pimento cheese sandwiches, and afternoon brought a social hour for coffee, sodas, and ice cream. At Wolff Bros. on another anchor corner, Haskell Wolff surveyed store operations from his elevated office and called to friends, "Come tell what's going on." D. W. and Eleanor Gill and son Danny made a first step in Main Street renovation by remodeling buildings adjacent to their furniture store.

Bob Smallwood and son Robbie pumped gas, aired tires, and cleaned windshields at the Exxon station. George Hunnicutt and customers swapped stories as he snipped hair. E. C. Freeman greeted customers with shared reminiscence at his appliance store. Betty Jane Oldner and son Clay staged a Labor Day sale becoming a festival of its own. Bill and Margaret Cagle and son Junior ran their appliance service, but next door, long-gone Bud's Big Dip (favorite for its soft ice cream) became a bail bond office. And Berry's Hardware seemed in continual expansion.

Steel rose for the new ARKAT mill to produce fish feed in the new Dumas Industrial Park. Kelly Farmer, whose father Edgar Farmer pioneered in the production of farm-raised catfish, led the mill development.

Dumas Chamber of Commerce promoted an "Edcenter" offering workforce training and education. Our group joined Lanny Halsell, state director of Vocational Education Commission, on a chartered plane to visit the Golden Triangle in North Carolina—far above our capabilities but an inspiration for a center in Brookhaven Shopping Center.

Anxiety reigned when the Arkansas River rose to its highest level in 47 years, flooding a dozen mobile homes at Pendleton. However, the levee system built following the disastrous 1927 flood held, preventing another catastrophe.

Following a federal court order creating eight black-majority House districts and two Senate districts in the Delta, Desha County was divided into multiple legislative districts. The new House District (80) in which I was incumbent encompassed the northern tip of Desha County, the eastern half of Lincoln County, and eastern Jefferson County. Dumas was the largest town, a key to my remaining in office.

Politics brought us to the annual Gillett Coon Supper, and Governor Clinton led the 1,100 attendance. Did I care for the taste of coon? No! However, like other politicos there, I gamely took a few bites and focused on ham.

As the 78th Assembly convened, I had many new constituents to meet. A priority for Rep. Wanda Northcutt and me was rural development. Like many phases of incremental legislation, an initial study evolved into bills for a Rural Development Commission and an Office of Rural Advocacy over a period of four years.

My toughest job, coming at the beginning of the session, was chairing a committee determining those to be seated in two contested elections. How I ended up in this position, I have never understood. An unlikely choice for parliamentary ability, I hoped I could be fair in a disputatious process, taking a week to examine election records and hear testimony.

In this busy session, I joined my friend Bynum Gibson in a large legislative package on expanding the moratorium on out-of-state garbage. I also sponsored a state loan program for small business in rural areas, a local option on a sales tax for airports and river ports, and legislation to reopen tax records previously closed. Colleagues often assumed that I, as a newspaper publisher, would fight for FOI (Freedom of Information), and to the best of my ability, I always did. I also was involved in efforts to increase funding for education and in passage of a four-lane highway program in which Highway 65 was to have been the first priority.

When I took a leave for the government conference, the NNA asked me to introduce General Colin Powell. I was advised to meet him outside the Hyatt Regency Hotel and to walk slowly through the hotel lobby so people could see him. He double-timed, and I did, too. I found General Powell to be engaging and highly intelligent, and I was nervous when I introduced him. He was cordial, saying that we both were breaking barriers, he as the first African American to become chairman of the Joint Chiefs of Staff and I as the first woman in line for the NNA presidency.

I never could have done double duty without Melvin's help. He often drove for me and kept a sharp eye on legislation, pointing out potential traps as he watched proceedings from the gallery or committee rooms. At the *Clarion*, he monitored the bottom line. He never complained that I had so many "irons in the fire."

In my NNA role, I shared head table seating with Henry Kissinger. I wondered how I would converse with this brilliant former secretary of state known over the world. He was congenial and outgoing. He asked if I had been to China; I said no but I had traveled in

254 SALTY OLD EDITOR: AN ADVENTURE IN INK

Russia and talked to people there. "Tell me more," he said. "I've always had to go as a VIP and never get to talk to the people." Dr. Kissinger also told of a woman who greeted him by saying: "I hear you are a fascinating man. Fascinate me!" I managed to avoid that gaffe.

At the same conference, President George H. W. Bush addressed attendees at the Old Executive Office Building. As I stood on the front row, President Bush turned to shake hands with me. One of the president's remarks struck a chord with me. "The United States cannot remain a world-class economy without world-class goals, including higher educational standards," he said. He was poised and articulate, reflecting his extensive background in government.

Through my NNA office, Melvin and I were invited to the inauguration of the president of Taiwan, Dr. Lee Teng-hui. Assembling in San Francisco on Mother's Day, our group included Bruce and Jo Brown of Oconomowoc, Wisconsin; John and Elaine Andrist of Crosby, North Dakota; Tom and Carol Bradlee of Elkton, Maryland; and Dave and Lois Simonson of Washington DC. We traveled business class on China Airlines, a plus for the 13½-hour flight. Crossing the International Dateline, we arrived in Taipei early Monday evening.

In this city of three million people appeared to be one million motor scooters or cycles. No order or reason was seen in the traffic patterns with five vehicles often in three lanes. Explained our van driver, "You just find a place and go there." When stuck in a jam for 80 minutes, our driver just waited patiently for it to untangle.

Neither the traffic nor the gala inauguration was most impressive for this journalist, among 150 from all over the world. Unforgettable was our visit to Hsiyuan Elementary School. As we stepped from press vans, 3,400 students on three tiers of balconies sang and clapped a magnitudinous welcome. The school's Little League team lined up as greeters. Accompanied by recorded music, students sang and clapped for 15 minutes before assembling for a program emphasizing music, mathematics, acrobatics, and precision routines.

Third-, fourth-, fifth-, and sixth-grade orchestras performed. At the end, the children were just as eager to touch our hands as we were to respond. We exited through the school's honor guard as all students assembled to clap and sing goodbye.

At the pomp-filled inaugural, we talked with two fellow Arkansans, Congressman John Paul Hammerschmidt and Speaker B. G. Hendrix of the State House of Representatives. Dr. Lee, the Taiwanese president, received a Ruffles and Flourishes welcome by a white-uniformed band and 21-gun salute from miniature cannon.

During our week there, we visited newspapers, where I was photographed and interviewed, with the story appearing in Chinese. I hoped it was favorable. Policy briefings, as well as visits to the harbors and science-based industrial parks, the Grand Hotel, and other sites kept us busy.

I was badly in need of a hair appointment, and Melvin volunteered to accompany me. Our hotel directions first led us to a massage parlor, from which we made a quick exit before we continued down an alley to a beauty shop. With hand signals, I explained my need for a shampoo and set. My graying blond locks were quite different from theirs, and the operators took turns in rolling my hair. During the shampoo, the operators administered sharp slaps on the head to stimulate the scalp—long remembered!

From Taipei, we added a three-day side trip to Hong Kong, a shoppers' paradise. My collage of memories includes having dinner while watching the most colorful harbor I'd seen, taking a costly cab ride to Victoria Peak to join the train descent through tiers of the city, riding the Star Ferry to Kowloon, seeing hundreds of sampans, and savoring a three-dollar cup of coffee at the famed Regent Hotel.

Our group hired a silver Mercedes van and driver to travel to Sham Chun at the border with mainland China. Our driver was a cheerful gambler who had studied in the United States. A stop at Lok Ma Chau, a walled city near the border, provided a glimpse of China of yesteryear, and elderly women in pajama-style garments hounded us to buy postcards. Four women posed for us for $2 each in Hong Kong dollars (27 cents each).

Upon our return to Hong Kong, we had a message from George and Joan Measer of Buffalo, New York, longtime newspaper friends, and we met them for a short visit at the Regent Hotel.

Our return home brought us to cruel reality. The son of friends was charged in the shooting death of a young woman, and our newspaper had to cover the story, which spanned from the event through the trial in which he was acquitted. It is never easy to cover stories that happen to friends, but we did and that was the most difficult year in my half-century in the newspaper business.

Beverly Burks, an energetic and capable graduate from Rhodes College, had joined our staff after Randal Seyler resigned, and she had the difficult job of reporting the murder trial as she began her newspaper career. I thought she did an outstanding job and was fair. She must have been accurate because the defense attorney said he used her summation in preparing final statements leading to acquittal. I later promoted Beverly to managing editor.

Always seeking feature stories, I tried for years to interview two World War II heroes about their experiences. Urban Hopmann made the brutal Bataan Death March, was transported to Japan, and survived because of a friendly native slipping him the occasional raw fish or egg. William Warren (Bill) Gooch, a B-24 crew member, survived the bombing of the Ploesti, Romania, oil fields and a crash landing only to be taken prisoner. Moved to 13 different camps, he was saved by the kindness of British POWs who carried him when he couldn't walk and cared for him. In taking notes on these two ordeals, my tears flowed as often as theirs.

For our 44th wedding anniversary, we were joined by Bob and Christene Fisher for a flight to Anchorage, Alaska, followed by a boat trip to Portage Glacier and sighting of beluga whales at Turnagain

Arm. Boarding a dome train for Denali National Park, we viewed Willow, Wasilla, and Talkeetna before reaching Mount McKinley, or Denali, hiding in fog.

Boarding a bus at 4 a.m. for our 50-mile trip into Denali Park, we were given snack bags (reindeer salami among the treats) and admonished to eat on the bus because of bears. Our cameras recorded Dall sheep, moose, caribou, and at a distance, two bears chasing another. Many other highlights followed, including a sternwheeler ride at Fairbanks; watching Mary Shields work her dog team; stopping at North Pole, Alaska; and traveling in the Yukon territory.

Overnight at Beaver Creek, we admired a wildlife museum at the motel. At 2 a.m., we were awakened with, "The lights!" Hastily donning outer garments, we dashed outside to view brilliant northern lights. We ended the journey with visits to Juneau, Skagway, and Sitka while sailing the inside passage to Vancouver.

Regrouping at home, we headed for Kansas City and the Newspaper Association convention where I was elected vice president (president-elect). How could I possibly manage to serve in the State Legislature and NNA? Fate would allow me to serve as NNA president on the "off year" when the legislature was not in session.

Co-mingling tasks and juggling hats seemed normal.

A tornado smashed some windows and felled trees in downtown Dumas in early April 1991, but no one was injured. The steel top was blown from the 90-year-old water tank, a landmark, and ultimately it was razed.

Through this period I was busy with a 128-page photo history of the area, called *Images of the Past*, to be published in October. Melvin and I personally underwrote the book.

In July, we joined Bob and Christene Fisher of Clarksville for a two-week bus tour of Northern Europe. After two days in London, we sailed to the Netherlands to begin the tour which also included Germany to Denmark, Norway, and Sweden. In Hamburg, Germany, we visited Heinrich Toepfer and his wife in their elegant home, and he took us on a tour. The Toepfer family owns a farm in Arkansas City.

Labor Day 1991 brought a historic meeting when Governor Bill Clinton met with 100 supporters at the Delta Inn in Dumas. He had promised to fulfill the governor's position before running for national office. Would we Democrats forgive him if he didn't complete his term and ran for the Democratic presidential nomination? Our local group was among the first to urge him to "go for it." Even in this truly Clinton Country, hardly any envisioned that he would become president so soon.

24.
A New Honor

On September 27, 1991, I was elected by the National Newspaper Association as the first woman president in its 106-year history. Forty of my family and loyal friends formed my cheering section in Little Rock. During my 10-year board tenure, reaching the top leadership often seemed improbable. Some men board members thought I lacked the strength for tough decisions, although I had many opportunities to prove it on a weekly newspaper.

Solidly backed and promoted by the Arkansas Press Association, the convention proved a real draw. During the nine years APA executive Dennis Schick and I worked to bring the NNA convention to our state, we were sometimes told that Little Rock had no appeal and attendance would be light. How wrong were the naysayers! More than 850 delegates came, including many who drove from mid-America.

Two presidential hopefuls, Gov. Bill Clinton and Texas billionaire Ross Perot, were featured. Caroline Kennedy and Ellen Alderman came to promote their book, *In Our Defense*, focusing on cases enhancing the Bill of Rights. Anthony Lewis of the *New York Times* spoke and autographed his book, *Make No Law*.

Melvin and I drove to the airport to meet Ross Perot as he arrived in his private jet. He asked to borrow my watch to time his speech, "a stem-winder" of its own. He was an engaging dinner partner and quite unpretentious.

Governor Clinton did not announce for president, although convention delegates crowded around him, figuring correctly that the governor would seek the Democratic nomination. I considered it a fine honor to be photographed with a future president and the daughter of a famous president.

Little Rock Air Force Base, home to C-130s, staged an impressive display, including flyovers to land cargo and troops. Betty and Cone Magie of Cabot, Melvin, and I hosted a board dinner at Marlsgate Plantation, an event dazzling even the most sophisticated.

The NNA presidency meant Melvin and I would be invited to state conventions and national meetings. Twice before taking office, I addressed congressional committees, discussing postal matters and telecommunications as they affected the newspaper industry.

Of the greatest help in that extremely busy year was the November return of Terry Hawkins, who had worked with us twice previously. Terry knew our operations and understood southeast Arkansas. I named him assistant publisher. Beverly Burks continued to handle news, and Anita Clemons moved over to help with advertising.

Terry was indispensable. I was a delegate to the First Amendment Congress in Richmond, Virginia, as well as attending the Audit Bureau of Circulation convention in Los Angeles, the Southern Newspaper Publishers Convention in Boca Raton, Florida, with Secretary of Defense Dick Cheney as keynoter, and the NNA winter board meeting in Washington.

After a holiday break, we resumed travel in January with a trip to Stevens Point, Wisconsin, for the Wisconsin Press meeting and an overnight visit with our NNA friends, Bruce and Jo Brown in Oconomowoc. Then it was to Jackson, Mississippi, to debate communications policy at the Mississippi Press Association, and two weeks later, to the Minnesota Press Association's convention in Minneapolis. A special treat was a trip to the California Newspaper Publishers Convention at Del Coronado, San Diego, to review arrangements for the next convention.

I managed to fulfill legislative responsibilities during the week, meeting with the Corps of Engineers in efforts to get a lake at Morgan Point on the old Arkansas River channel, taking part in the startup of the Rural Development Commission, introducing Edgar (Chip) Farmer of Dumas as he was inducted into the Arkansas Agriculture Hall of Fame, and announcing for re-election in March.

My legislative role was evolving. Rep. Buddy Turner of Pine Bluff retired after 30 years in the House, and as his alternate, I was named to the Legislative Council. Also, I was able to rent his apartment in the Capitol Hill building. While the space included only a bedroom, kitchen, hall, and bath, it was comfortable and more accessible, especially for Melvin to come and go to the Capitol as he wished. Later I chose Joint Budget Committee over the Council, as I thought service there would be more effective in obtaining projects for my district.

At the request of state library leaders, I joined Sen. Jay Bradford of Pine Bluff and Rep. Bobby Wood of Jonesboro in chairing the drive to pass a proposed amendment authorizing expanded millage and library bonds when approved by voters. Library causes and ethics initiatives always gladdened my heart.

Leave was granted for me to attend the NNA governmental conference in March. President George H. W. Bush invited the delegates to the White House, and I was standing at the back of the East Room as he began his remarks and suddenly said, "Where's Charlotte?" I was astonished to be called to the podium to stand with popular First Lady Barbara Bush during the president's talk. I tried to be most dignified, but mostly, I smiled and smiled, while marveling at the recognition.

Sometimes we mixed journalism and political visits. Heading for the Nebraska Press Association where NNA friends Jack and Betty Tarr guided us over Lincoln, we toured the Nebraska capitol and its unicameral legislature where Senator Haberman introduced me from the floor. After combining a visit with son John and family and a journalism seminar in Austin, we flew to Sioux Falls for the South Dakota Press Association and a visit to the colorful Corn Palace in Mitchell.

Through my NNA year, I battled the organization's financial problems coming to a head when NNA lost a suit over a broken lease. For years, the board often dismissed the possibility that NNA could lose the suit, but it did (more than $300,000 judgment) shortly after I began my tenure as president. The result was that I directed our executive to cut positions and make other adjustments.

NNA executive David Simonson announced retirement, and we began to search for a new director. The board selected Tonda Rush, a counsel with the association of large dailies. I first met Tonda when she was an award-winning news reporter in Kansas and found her so bright that I urged her to continue her education. She wisely completed a law degree before heading for Washington.

Among many invitations during my year as NNA president was the Current Strategy Seminar at the Navy War College. When I wasn't attending sessions stretching my mind, Melvin and I managed to visit to Hammersmith Farm, the home of Jacqueline Kennedy Onassis's mother and stepfather. Glitter remained in the Kennedy memorabilia there. From Rhode Island we flew to Jackson Hole, Wyoming, for the meeting of the Wyoming Press Association and another chance to see the majestic Teton Mountains.

In Portland, Melvin and I visited the Oregon Press Association. An Oregon newspaperman asked Melvin if he knew Bill Clinton. "Yes," replied Melvin, adding "and he is going to be the next president." "I hope not!" replied the Oregonian.

While I was traveling to meet with news people afar, Little Rock was becoming a media capital of its own. With Bill Clinton frontrunner for the Democratic presidential nomination, even I was sought for occasional comment. It was a heady time. My visiting grandsons, Charles, Edward, and David Schexnayder, joined us to see the Clinton campaign organization at full steam in the former *Arkansas Gazette* building. Two friends, Merle Peterson of Dumas and Dorothy Moore of Arkansas City, volunteered in the prevailing mix of exhaustion, excitement, and euphoria. No surprise that Governor Clinton would be nominated.

After the Democratic team of Bill Clinton and Al Gore, accompanied by wives Hillary and Tipper, completed a seven-state bus trip, the Clintons were welcomed home at their headquarters. When emcee Skip Rutherford needed a break, national committeewoman Lottie Shackleford led a group of us in waving campaign signs to the music. For me, political participation topped by-standing.

When Melvin and I went to Miami for the Southern Legislative Conference, Candidate Clinton was a principal speaker and received two standing ovations. After seeing him charm the crowd, I had a strong sense he was going to win in November. We departed Miami just in time, for the following week Hurricane Andrew struck with a vengeance and left standing water in the hotel lobby where we had been.

I hosted a legislative sub-committee, Jobs for Arkansans, on a tour of Dumas industries, including ARKAT, Belden, and Binkley, before taking to the skies again. My final state trip as NNA president took us to St. Louis for the Missouri Press convention.

In San Diego for the NNA convention ending my presidency, we arranged for our children, their spouses, and our grandchildren to join us. Highlights were a tour of the USS *New Orleans* helicopter-launching ship; dinner at the San Diego Yacht Club; and visits to fabulous San Diego Zoo and Old Town San Diego. During my California trips, I also met two prominent woman politicians, later U.S. senators: Barbara Boxer and Dianne Feinstein.

At convention's end, Melvin and I joined Bob and Christene Fisher to fly to Singapore. Northwest Airlines had advertised an inaugural flight from Los Angeles and return, including five nights in a five-star hotel, for $1,000. After the NNA presidency, I truly needed rest and relaxation.

While reading in the Narita Airport, Tokyo, I saw a young man pass by me several times. He finally stopped and said, "Is your name Schexnayder?"

"Yes," I replied.

"I'm Bob Martin," he continued. "I haven't seen you in a long time, but I thought I recognized you." What were the odds of meeting Bob, a Dumas native, in a Tokyo airport? Millions to one, I supposed. We all enjoyed a nice visit with Bob, a quality engineer traveling for Compaq Computers.

Our destination of Singapore was a lush garden city with the cleanest streets I have ever seen. We learned that everything in Singapore comes in fours. Four principal populations, Chinese, Malaysian, Indian, and Eurasian, and four principal languages, English, Chinese, Malay, and some dialects of India.

A bus tour took us to the Buddha Temple of a Thousand Lights, Changi Prison where Japanese held Allied prisoners in World War II, Singapore Air Force Base, and a crocodile farm. On our own, we were quite safe in walking through the city or taking cabs, but in the strict Singapore rule, we often felt as though someone was looking over our shoulders. We went to the famous Raffles Hotel for a Singapore Sling, far too strong a drink for me, and we visited the modern harbor.

Our return stopover in Kona, Hawaii, provided a delightful rest and tour of Kilauea Volcano, black sand beaches, Parker Ranch, and the Japanese gardens at Hilo.

At home, excited expectation rose as Governor Clinton led presidential polls, with President George H. W. Bush second, and Ross Perot third. On election afternoon, Melvin and I savored the celebration at Little Rock's Excelsior Hotel. We later joined the throng at the Old State House where the Clintons and Gores were to speak. In the most festive crowd I've seen, we cheered every time another state came into the Clinton column posted on a huge TV downtown. Since 4,000 media people were covering the event, we watched our footsteps in the jumble of cables. What a special time in history!

Two days later, President-elect Clinton came to our House of Representatives "quiet room" to visit his strong supporters. I wouldn't have missed the chance! Overnight, the capitol had changed, with Secret Service stationed throughout the building. Joviality prevailed among the Clinton staff and the visitors seeking a glimpse of the triumphant candidate. After the bashing during the campaign when our state was called "the lowest of the low," Arkansans basked in the Clinton victory.

In October, we had booked lodging for the inaugural at the Ritz Carlton, where many of the Arkansas delegation planned to stay. This was a risk because the $300-a-day room had to be guaranteed for five days and would not be credited back to us if Governor Clinton lost. Our children thought us to be overly optimistic. I gambled, and all's well that ends well. Later, wearing my saxophone pin as a Friend of Bill, I was told by a Capitol bookstore clerk, "Arkansas is in!"

25.
Inaugural Time

An Arkansas inaugural preceded the national ceremony. Jim Guy Tucker, lieutenant governor and acting governor during the Clinton campaign, was sworn in Saturday afternoon, December 12. Melvin and I had a late start for Little Rock and were hustling along Highway 65 north of Grady when a state trooper pulled us over. He sat and studied the license plate designating my seniority position in the House. Finally, he came to our car, and leaning across driver Melvin, proffered his hand to me, saying: "I just wanted to shake hands with Representative Schexnayder."

We reached the capitol in time for the ceremonies also involving the president-elect and photographing a keepsake page for the *Clarion*.

In 1993, we had a first for the *Clarion*: a special section in tribute to the Arkansan elected to the presidency, William Jefferson Clinton. Another first: we had an official invitation to the Clinton Inauguration. It was pinch-me time for Arkansans.

Amid the sheer exuberance of Arkansans at the inaugural, we couldn't go a block without seeing someone we knew. Our own celebratory bunch included son John and wife Deanna, daughter Sarah, our editor Terry Hawkins, and his sister Lyn Friscia.

The Arkansas touch was prominent at our hotel, the Ritz-Carlton. Our bellhop was from Pine Bluff, and we wondered if they imported him. Although the Mayflower was the official Arkansas hotel, we Friends of Bill had the royal treatment. Delicacies, such as festive cake and a white chocolate capitol dome surrounded by straw-berries, were delivered daily to our door.

Our official tickets did not arrive before we left Dumas. (Later, we found that 60,000 responses to the inauguration invitations were hung up in mail wrongly delivered to north Arkansas.) Since I was a member of the Electoral College, we ultimately succeeded in being heard, particularly after I engaged a young man with a clipboard.

We joined a throng of more than a half-million on the Mall for the opening entertainment. Shoulder to shoulder, we couldn't budge and decided to retreat to safer distance to enjoy the experience. On Monday, we stood 1½ hours in 34-degree weather to get tickets for the Arkansans' open house slated for Thursday at the White House. Joining in that line were Rosa Go and children, and David and Maxine Stubbs and children of Dumas.

For the inaugural tickets, I went to the capitol to show an ID confirming presidential elector status. We next attended a magnificent brunch given by International Paper Co., and received commemora-tive red mufflers from the Arkansas Democratic Party. Governors Jim Guy Tucker of Arkansas and Ned McWherter of Tennessee then hosted a reception at the Freedom Forum.

We dared not miss the Arkansas State Society's Gala at the Grand Hyatt, and found that 10,000 wanted to attend but only 3,500 could. Lines were on every stopped escalator for three floors. We greeted Craig Smith, a Clinton gubernatorial aide who opened the first national campaign office. "I'm calling it an adventure," he told us. We also chatted with Sam Wolff, a native of Dumas, and wife Marcia.

On Tuesday, Mark Sheehan of the National Newspaper Association invited Melvin and me to accompany him to hear James Carville, brilliant political strategist for Clinton, at the National Press Club. Celebrities abounded there, and later at the MTV "Rock the Vote" reception at our hotel. We gathered in the lobby for daughter

Sarah to clue us in on the arrivals of Christopher Reeve, Henry Winkler, Kim Basinger, Quincy Jones, and others.

"Get there early" seemed pertinent advice. On Inaugural Day, we left the hotel at 6:45 a.m. for a Capitol Hill brunch given by Don Tyson honoring Senators David Pryor and Dale Bumpers. We joined David Walt, Erica Walt, and Julie Beth Walt of Dumas to walk to the capitol grounds where we found seats five rows from the congressional delegation.

When William Jefferson Clinton was sworn in, all the walking and waiting were worth the effort. The woman next to me grasped my hand, and exclaimed, "Can you believe this?" as the band played "Hail to the Chief." The president, noted for his hour-long talks, limited the inaugural speech to 14 minutes. The crowd stretched as far back as I could see, and Democratic euphoria prevailed.

After Dr. Billy Graham's benediction, we retreated slowly with the crowd. Reaching parade route seats by the Treasury Building, we found Louie and Carolyn Schaufele of Little Rock next to us. When the new president and first lady walked the last few blocks of the parade, Hillary Clinton saw us and waved, giving Melvin a memorable photo opportunity for the *Clarion*.

With barely time to soak icy feet and revive ourselves with coffee, we donned formal attire for the Arkansas Inaugural Ball. The presidential couple danced to "It Had to be You," as 12,000 tried to get a glimpse, and the president reached for a saxophone to play "Your Mama Won't Dance."

This mama could not dance. My aching feet sent us hotel-bound just after midnight. After all, we had to wait in line for the next day's White House reception and hugs from the president and first lady.

Our state legislature had recessed for the inaugural. Upon return, we were involved in a long and grueling session, dealing with fee increases to meet revenue needs, workers' compensation insurance, prison reforms, and educational issues.

Exciting for me was completion of the Bio-Medical Research Building financed by the mixed drink tax that Rep. Wanda Northcutt and I had passed. I again worked on ethics legislation, and also testified for a hydropower plant at Dam 2 on the Arkansas River near Dumas. My legislative friend Bynum Gibson had been named to head the State Democratic Party, meaning that he would continue a strong role in policy making.

In Dumas, things were not so gala. A storm of protest erupted over a plan to use the Dollar General's former warehouse (330,000 square feet) as a minimum-security facility for the Department of Correction. "Not in My Back Yard" attitudes killed the offer of additional jobs. While working in the session, I received the brunt of controversy on the weekends.

As we entered our 40th year as *Clarion* publishers, I wrote: "As with life, the ups and downs of a newspaper test one's mettle, resolve and desire to serve." I alluded to guiding a newspaper while serving in the legislature. As always, we found the bottom line sagging when we were absent. I had always tried to sell small ads in multiples because they were the "bread and butter" for the newspaper, but my time was limited and often drawn to side issues.

For the National Newspaper Association's government conference in March, I sought to arrange a White House reception. With no response, I called Craig Smith, political operative at the White House, and said, "Can you tell me why the White House is rejecting the hometown press that largely supported Clinton in his election? I don't think that it is politically smart."

"I didn't know that. Let me call you back," he replied. My hotel room phone rang 45 minutes later, and he said, "You're in. Wait for the official call."

When we arrived at the White House, two Arkansans were leaving and saying, "We're escaping from the coming snow storm." They were wise, for we were to be snowbound that weekend.

The president arranged a private reception for 28 Arkansans in the Diplomatic Reception Room before the association reception in the East Room. The president sandwiched us in between a day on an aircraft carrier and a speech, but he appeared in no hurry as he greeted us individually.

The blizzard of 1993 trapped us in the Capitol Hilton for three days. When we finally reached the airport for standby, the airline gave Melvin and me the last seats on the plane. Approaching Little Rock, we circled and circled over nearby towns. When a stewardess answered three bells and raced down the aisle with an emergency manual, we were chilled. We learned the wheels wouldn't come down but the co-pilot had hand-cranked them into position. More than a few prayers ensued, and immense gratitude came as we landed safely surrounded by emergency vehicles. We headed for the state capitol, where I handled two small bills and thanked the Good Lord.

In the nineties, laptop computers began to show up over the House floor. I had used a laptop since I had arrived for Capitol duty, and in the mid-1980s, House members would come by my desk to ask what I was doing. It was a very simple laptop which connected into the *Clarion* computer system. It would be 1995 before implementation of a computer system began for the entire House and 1997 when laptops were used on every desk. An immense time and paper saver!

The Clinton presence in DC opened many doors. On a later trip, his former gubernatorial chief of staff, Betsey Wright, hosted a luncheon at the Ann Wexler consulting firm she had joined. Mack McLarty, White House chief of staff, also greeted us, and his assistant, Mark Middleton, took us on a tour of the West Wing.

If our focus seemed to be on Washington, we also sandwiched in a trip to Huntington Beach, California, for the 100th birthday celebration of my mother's first cousin, Marguerite Dent Ireland. When we asked the secret of her longevity, she replied, "I was raised on LARD!"

The International Newspaper Marketing Association invited us to their meeting in Toronto, but we had a hard time getting into the country. Previously, we had only to show a driver's license to enter Canada, but a customs official refused our ID's and voters' cards. "Okay," I said. "We'll advise the newspaper convention and return home." He relented, and we had a pleasant visit including viewing the Hockey Hall of Fame and a Blue Jays–Baltimore Orioles game.

At home, the economic climate needed a boost. It came in the form of a hydro-electric plant at Dam 2 on the Arkansas River. As state representative, I testified for the Arkansas Electric Cooperatives' project before the Public Service Commission.

In June, Melvin and I flew to Vancouver, Canada, and had no trouble entering. We attended the NNA board meeting as guests of the British Columbia and Yukon Community newspapers. Just two weeks later we were in Kansas City, Missouri, where Marj Carpenter presented me with the president's award from the National Federation of Press Women—an original sculpture of a reporter's hands and note-book. NFPW was my extended support system.

Newspaper meetings were mixed in with legislative responsibili-ties. Proponents for Interstate 69, an international highway from Canada to Mexico with the prospects of traversing Desha County, came on the scene. When I attended the first advocacy meeting in Helena, Senator David Pryor called I-69 the most promising project on which he had worked. Several hundred people later came here for an I-69 meeting at the First United Methodist Church.

Terry Hawkins, our talented assistant publisher, had an ominous bruise on his arm and no way to explain it. The diagnosis was possible leukemia, and when confirmed, Terry began the fight for his life. Our staff was very supportive.

Melvin and I continued scheduling trips, including the NNA con-vention in Cincinnati and a National Federation of Press Women con-ference in DC at which Mark Gearan, White House communications director, spoke. Our conferees were invited to see the Oval Office, Cabinet Room, Roosevelt Room, press room, and the Rose Garden. The Oval Office had undergone a striking change as Kaki Hockersmith of Little Rock used red, royal blue, white, and gold in redecorating. After meeting many Arkansans there, a Press Woman asked, "Is anybody home?" I replied, "Not if they have a chance to be in DC."

In the quickest fund-raising with which I had been associated, sufficient funds were donated in three weeks to build a Desha County Veterans Memorial on the museum grounds. Charles Holloway and Raymond Riggins headed the effort. Hershell Gober, deputy secretary for veterans' affairs, and Senator Dale Bumpers dedicated the memorial in late November.

At home or afar, our experiences were stimulating. Appointed to the U.S. Chamber's Small Business Panel, I heard Ira Magaziner, architect of health care reform which ultimately came to naught, and Kirk Campbell, advocate for the North American Free Trade Agreement which became reality.

For a break, we joined travel companions Bob and Christene Fisher for a cruise aboard the *Song of Norway*, a small but gleaming ship, through the Caribbean, visiting St. John, St. Thomas, Curacao, and Costa Rica, and traversing the Panama Canal before ending in Acapulco. The Panama Canal was truly the marvel I had always imagined, and Melvin and I observed its operations during most of the day-long passage.

Three weeks later while in Washington for a legislative conference, Melvin and I were invited to a White House reception following the lighting of the nation's Christmas tree. We admired the brilliant décor and met Treasury Secretary Lloyd Bentsen and actress Sandy Duncan. The Clintons, true to their friends, made their years very special for us.

Hardly missing an opportunity, we joined the Arkansas Press Association's tour to Cancun and an especial archeological treat of seeing the Mayan ruins at Chichen-Itza.

When a terrible ice storm struck the first week of February, Dumas's only lights were at the hospital and the National Guard Armory using generators. Closing three days, we hired a backhoe to break up sidewalk ice; otherwise it was a skating rink.

The Armory offered shelter and a soup kitchen. Constantly trying to solve problems, such as electricity to the homes of invalids, I also worked in the Armory kitchen. Our home had no electricity for five days, but we used an extension cord to connect to a neighboring home. "Hallelujah!" was our response to "Lights on!"

During the spring, I campaigned to retain my House seat, the first time I had an opponent. Edward Spears of Wabbaseka had filed against me. Campaigning at Tamo with my cards in hand, I stopped at a large house. Melvin was driving, and as I walked along the driveway, I noticed a sizable black dog advancing. "Open the back door of the car," I commanded Melvin. "What?" he said from the car's safety. "OPEN THE BACK DOOR!" I shouted. As I dived into the back seat, the dog snatched my candidate card with his teeth. Dogs were the bane of candidates, but I was never bitten. Most of the time, campaigning was pleasant, as I enjoyed meeting people. At Moscow (Jefferson County, not Russia), an elderly woman looked at me intently. "Are you a Democrat?" she inquired. "Yellow Dog kind," I replied. "I'll vote for you," she assured.

Taking time out for the NNA conference in DC, we were greeted at a reception hosted by the president and first lady. I observed they appeared happy, despite the Whitewater bashing, and just as determined as ever. Both Senator Bob Dole and President Clinton spoke during the conference, lining up for the national race in the fall.

Ding Dong Days festival was moved to an April weekend, with much cooler weather but lesser crowds than in simmering July. Dumas celebrated its 90th birthday with the Arts Council staging *Murder in the Magnolias*, a concert by the Army National Guard Band, and the usual Fun Day and barbecue.

Extensive meetings were held between Desha County and Chicot County citizens to draft an Enterprise Community application. Meetings were my only break from door-to-door, or farm-to-farm, campaigning for the coming May election. I won with 61 percent of the vote and received 77 percent in my home county of Desha.

Bonds were sold, assuring the long Dumas quest for a civic auditorium. I had worked toward this project so long that I was an ex-officio member of the auditorium commission.

Summer was bustling. Meeting Heloise II, daughter of the original Heloise, was an enjoyable feature the Press Women's conference in Las Vegas. She ascribes to a Southern Belle Primer of "always do your homework, be the best you can, and have a sense of humor." That perfectly described Mama.

Summers also were set aside for grandchildren's visits. I always cooked their favorites, pitched baseball for them, and simply enjoyed them. A great delight for them was picking veggies from Melvin's prolific garden, as he had the greenest of thumbs.

I found career pleasure in interviews, particularly with "Aunt Mary" Thompson, an African American citizen who had reached her 112th birthday and was living alone in a Dumas apartment. An ardent Democrat who loved television, she had such a lively mind for a woman who would live to be 119.

We enjoyed every opportunity creating features, columns, and photos for the *Clarion*. Melvin and I attended the Southern Legislature Conference in Norfolk, Virginia, and the NNA convention and NNA Convention at Disney World in Orlando. A side trip provided an insight into the shuttle program at NASA Kennedy Space Center, Cape Canaveral.

When I was later inducted into the Hall of Distinction at Louisiana State University, the honor came 50 years after my graduation. Matsy Shea and her late husband, Tommy, both LSU graduates, nominated me. For the Baton Rouge ceremony, we were joined by our family and Matsy Shea. Melvin and I left Baton Rouge for White Sulphur Springs, West Virginia, to attend the Southern Legislative Conference. We were hardly home from the posh Greenbrier before going to a Mississippi River conference in New Orleans.

Dumas began the new year with a new mayor. Clay Oldner was sworn in, having defeated Lewis Ray Baker. Construction of the hydropower plant on the Arkansas River had spurred construction in Dumas with the building of a new Subway sandwich shop, expansion of the Days Inn, and construction of Carlton Apartments.

On Melvin's 78th birthday, our family celebrated in Dumas. Grandchildren joining in were Daniel, 9 months, who couldn't get enough cake; Charles with changing voice of a teen; Edward of sly wit; Lauren of artistic talent; David of happy disposition; Emily so adept at coping; and Allie, our general organizer. The Texas grandchildren listened to the weather bulletins and wished, "Let It Snow!" The elements complied; they stayed overnight to play in the snow.

In another New Year's event, Melvin and I joined 2,498 others for a reception hosted by President Clinton at Little Rock's Excelsior Hotel. The Clintons shook hands for four and a half hours and personally greeted everyone.

Re-elected District 80 representative while continuing as *Clarion* publisher, I faced as much as 14-hour days, quite a task for someone in her 70s.

Speaker Bobby Hogue appointed me one of four assistant speakers. Named to the powerful Rules committee, I also served on Joint Budget, beginning work at 7:30 a.m. daily; Revenue and Tax; State Agencies; and Governmental Affairs committees. Much of the assembly was devoted to an educational funding formula. Governor Jim Guy Tucker's efforts at constitutional reform were in the spotlight but ended on the table.

Midway in the session, Bynum Gibson, Arkansas Democratic Party chairman, contacted me. "I have a bill I want you to sponsor and it must be secret until you file it," he said. State Republicans had filed a lawsuit, declaring party-financed primary elections unconstitutional and seeking state funding. Bynum's proffered bill called for state-financed primary elections. For Democrats, primary financing was heaped on candidates. Republicans, fewer in number, found it more difficult and thought change would balance the system, which ultimately happened.

Causing a stir among both parties, the bill passed by comfortable margin. After the session, I was named among the 10 Best Legislators, an honor previously accorded to Bynum. My fervent hope was that I would not land in the 10 Worst list, also chosen by the *Arkansas Democrat-Gazette*.

Focusing on the depressed Delta, Bynum and I also worked with State Senator Kevin Smith to form the Arkansas Delta Council. "Writing off the Delta" was popular, but how could we abandon the people who love it? I savor the earthy aroma of freshly disked fields in spring, brown grass crust transformed to variegated shades of green, white cotton carpet, golden to rust grains of autumn, cypress sloughs with turtles sunning on logs, towering corn turning to crisp beige, and humming harvests.

Daughters (and sons) of the Delta hardly ever miss the catfish dinner benefits, pit barbecues, and chicken suppers where supporters enlist others for causes like Main Street and libraries. Auctions attract determined bidders vying for supremacy over a favorite T-shirt boasting a hole, and church congregations sing old-time "I'll Fly Away" straight from the heart. We have our spats and our prejudices, but when someone faces grief, there isn't room in the kitchen for all the food that friends and neighbors bring. Writing off the Delta isn't an option. It is too precious.

26.
Overnight in the Lincoln Bedroom

An invitation of a lifetime: "Would you like to spend the night at the White House?"

Carolyn Huber extended the invitation from the president and first lady. Our newspaper friends, Cone and Betty Magie, were also invited when we planned to attend the NNA government conference.

The White House sent a car to our hotel, and Carolyn, hostess for Arkansans, greeted us at the diplomatic reception room. "You will be staying in the Lincoln Bedroom," she said to Melvin and me, "and the Magies will be in the Queen's Bedroom across the hall." Our names were later published among White House guests during the Clinton administration, with the implication that we all paid major political bucks. Not so for us and the Magies. We were simply long-time Clinton friends

So much to absorb and admire, and I wanted to preserve it in memory. The Lincoln Bedroom, where the Emancipation Proclamation was signed, commanded a sense of reverence. But we chuckled when the Magies invited us to see their quarters, saying, "We bet we have something you don't have. Come see our bathroom." There, a commode was enshrined with a wicker chair, making it the queen's throne.

Although we had toured downstairs, seeing President Clinton's upstairs office was a first as we admired his books and desk collection. The cheerful upstairs reception rooms were particularly inviting, but less formal than downstairs where we again viewed our favorite, the library, where we seemed to hear the fireside chats of President Franklin D. Roosevelt seen in newsreels during our youth. After studying historic and distinctive furnishings in the diplomatic reception room, we also admired the china collection in other rooms. Stepping onto the south balcony, we sensed the history of all who had lived with this sweeping view. Continually soaking up the grand atmosphere, we had freedom to inspect the grounds as we walked the new jogging track, inspected the children's playground, and appreciated the carefully landscaped grounds and delightful gardens.

Invited to dinner in the Solarium, we were even more awe-struck to be in the family quarters. As we were finishing our meal, President Clinton arrived and another place was set. "I looked out of my office and saw you walking on the grounds earlier," he commented. As he ate, our spirited conversation ranged from Arkansas to international topics. An hour later, the first lady came to visit. She had returned the previous day from a three-day trip to Denmark. Recording the evening, I had treasured photos.

Immersed in a dream, I later made it real by phoning our children: "This is your mother calling from the Lincoln Bedroom." I didn't dare sleep, as I watched to see if ghosts were on the prowl. Midnight came before I had finished reading all of the historical documents and studying furnishings. When I dared stretch out on that massive seven-foot Lincoln bed, I finally dozed. I awakened at about 3 a.m., listened for a while, but the only sounds were Washington sirens.

Selecting from a menu presented earlier, we returned for breakfast in the Solarium. Later, we stopped for photos with the president in the West Wing, and toured the kitchen, flower shop, and press room. A White House car took us to our noon appointment to the National Press Club, where we heard Republican presidential aspirants Bob Dole, Arlen Specter, Phil Gramm, and Richard Lugar.

When we returned that afternoon to the White House for an NNA gala reception in the East Room, we still were agog. How astonishing and gratifying that small-town newspaper people were accorded those opportunities!

How does one transition from a White House high to handle the legislative reality? Switching hats had become my forte.

Returning to daily reality, I described just one morning in my State Capitol log: "I presided over the amendment calendar in the House chamber, raced to the fourth floor to get a fax on Freedom of Information from Bill Rutherford of Cabot. After Joint Budget Committee, I helped draft a freedom of information amendment clarifying the State Health Department statistics bill. By then, I had to call Grady Schools to discuss the funding formula, and Terry at the *Clarion* office where I learned he was heading to Little Rock for a bone marrow test. At Revenue and Tax Committee, I handled the Pollution Control and Ecology bill on permits, and it turned out to be a rather beleaguered experience."

While I was toiling in Little Rock, spring brought some notable news in Dumas. Dumas School District was freed of the desegregation suit brought by Gould and Grady Schools. Superintendent Don McHan and Board President David Walt applauded Judge Stephen Reasoner's dismissal of the suit because Dumas and other area districts had followed the rules in desegregation.

Ground was broken for the new Community Center. Dumas Cotton Gin LLC, led by Charles Dante, embarked on an $8 million facility. Dumas State Bank, founded by Merle Peterson and others, was bought by Simmons Bank and renamed Simmons First of Dumas.

The '95 Ding Dong Days included a Union Pacific train ride from Dumas to Pickens and Winchester. Royal Bros. Circus also was part of the celebration. County Judge Mark McElroy starred in *God's Favorite* at the Community Theatre.

Our valuable staff member, Terry Hawkins, won the sweepstakes in Arkansas Press Women contests which allowed men entrants, but the award was made in absentia. Fighting leukemia, he underwent a bone marrow transplant (with brother Phil as donor) at the University of Arkansas for Medical Sciences in Little Rock.

A weekly can't afford specialists, and we all helped to fill Terry's position. Lisa Faircloth of North Carolina joined us as a reporter. Ad manager Glenda Ward became a photographer when necessary, and talented Jim Bailey provided photos when he was home from Fayetteville.

Senator David Pryor, who had surprised the state by announcing his retirement effective in 1996, joined President Bill Clinton in staging the White House Conference on Aging. The senator named me as a delegate. After getting the *Clarion* on the press, Melvin and I flew to DC. I joined in the conference, enjoying opportunities such as meeting Health, Education and Welfare Secretary Donna Shalala and hearing Vice President Al Gore and First Lady Hillary Clinton. We Arkansans went to the White House grounds to visit President Clinton before he left in a helicopter.

When President and Mrs. Clinton, and Vice President and Mrs. Gore, came to Little Rock in June, we were able to photograph them for a page in the *Clarion*. Never turning down a photo-op with a friend, we greeted the presidential party in Pine Bluff the following morning.

During the summer, I attended a legislative seminar in Keystone, Colorado, and Melvin and I had our first trip to the Colorado Mountains in a decade. Several weeks later, we returned to the West. As a member of the citizen committee advising the Pine Bluff Arsenal's efforts to destroy its World War II stockpile of weapons, I toured the Tooele Depot near Salt Lake City. I thought the process to destroy outdated weapons was very detailed and apparently successful.

A September invitation arrived for an Arkansas picnic at the White House. On the south lawn, the president and first lady greeted the majority of 1,500 guests. Sue and Clifton Meador, Kathryn and Hardy Peacock, Loetta Williams, Charlotte Parker, and Mayor Clay and Sherry Oldner were among those we photographed at the gala event, which featured an army band. Most memorable was the perfect ending with a crescent moon glimmering over the lighted Washington Monument, Jefferson Memorial, and golden glow of the south portico. Only in America, I thought, could we have these opportunities.

During a run-run fall, we flew to St. Paul for the National Newspaper Association, where I visited with Garrison Keillor, the *Prairie Home Companion* radio show storyteller, and came home for the new building celebration at Dumas Motor Co., owned by our first printer's devil, Fred Williams, and wife Loetta.

With the highs were the lows of losing my Tillar friend, Betty Davidson Prewitt Mowrey, who also had written the Tillar news for the *Clarion*, and Mrs. Ruby Price Clayton, our longtime Jefferson reporter. Our correspondents were passing from the weekly newspaper scene, and with them, their colorful dispatches. Later when my best friend and valued neighbor Amy Frank died, I knew I would never replace but would always be grateful for her kindness and caring for us.

The new Community Center opened in time for the 21st Delta Arts & Crafts Fair in November, and the Dumas economy also was stimulated by construction of the Arkansas Electric Cooperatives' hydropower plant at Dam 2. The project had brought personnel from Europe. For a while, Dumas sounded like an international city with French, German, and Spanish mixing into Delta drawl.

Semi-regulars on the Washington scene, Melvin and I were joined by son John and grandsons Charles and Edward for the NNA government conference. John and boys toured, while Melvin and I listened to House Speaker Newt Gingrich as well as the president. Then we had a White House visit and family photo with the president.

President Clinton asked if I would consider running for Congress from Arkansas's Fourth District, adding, "I would support you." Thanking him for the flattering request, I replied, "I am too old." A White House photographer caught the moment with the president pulling on my right hand and Melvin tugging on the left. Congressman Steny Hoyer and Senator David Pryor also called to sway me, but judgment told me a final term in the Arkansas House was a better decision for both Melvin and me.

My state career had allowed me to focus on local, state, and national scenes as I continued as *Clarion* publisher. I participated in a wide scope of events, such as our Chamber of Commerce's first Merchants Fair drawing 2,200 to the Community Center.

Re-joining our *Clarion* crew after a stint in Monticello, Beverly Burks made it much easier for me to run for re-election. Still working a full schedule at the *Clarion*, I campaigned in the afternoons and on Saturdays. My opponent was Edward Spears of Altheimer—for a second time—as I covered much of my district.

Fritz Hudson drove for me as I canvassed farms of Lincoln County, where there seemed to be two to five dogs per home. From the driver's seat, Fritz instructed, "That one looks friendly. Go to him first." Sometimes I managed to thread my way through the pack to the door, but I never could tell which dog was friendly.

Constituents, however, were very friendly and supportive. In all my 14 years on the campaign trail, I only ran into two rude people— a woman in a service station in Grady and a man working on an old car in West Dumas.

Enriching my campaigning were kind friends who volunteered as drivers and canvassers—thoughtfulness never to be forgotten. Ever-loyal Melvin was my willing driver as his time allowed. In Dumas, Jim Poole walked one side of a street to hand out cards for me while I walked the other.

In the midst of my re-election run, Melvin and I joined Desha County and Bolivar County groups lobbying congressional offices in Washington in behalf of the Great River Bridge. Federal Highway director Rodney Slater hosted us in his office, and we had great reception at offices of Senators Pryor and Bumpers.

The trip did not deter my election bid. I carried the vote in all three counties I represented, portions of Desha, Lincoln, and Jefferson, and won by 63 percent in a black majority district.

Soon I was witness to high drama in the State Capitol. Governor Jim Guy Tucker was reported to be resigning after his jury conviction in the financial dealings brought about by the Whitewater federal investigation. Lieutenant Governor Mike Huckabee decided to abandon his U.S. Senate bid in order to become governor.

The legislature was called into special session for the transition, and I was appointed to the committee to escort Lt. Gov. Huckabee to the House floor. At 1:55 p.m. on that Monday in July, Governor Tucker issued a statement saying that he would not resign, and instead, would take a leave of absence until the court heard an August appeal on his conviction. Legislative leaders asked Tucker to resign, and Attorney General Winston Bryant announced he was preparing papers to remove Tucker from office. In the House of Representatives came calls for impeachment.

We "escorts" went as appointed to the lieutenant governor's office in the Capitol, stood and waited—only to learn that the impasse had not been resolved. Telephone lines were busy as friends and Democratic Party leaders tried to influence Governor Tucker to resign. At the lieutenant governor's office, where we waited through the process, there was great uncertainty and extensive conferencing.

At 5:15 p.m., Lt. Gov. Huckabee went on television to read an ultimatum which he, Speaker of the House Bobby Hogue, and Senate President Pro Tem Stanley Russ had prepared, urging Tucker to resign by 9 a.m. Tuesday or face impeachment proceedings. Tucker finally handed in his resignation before the end of the 6 p.m. newscasts, and we escorted Huckabee to the House to take office. Many of us felt that Governor Tucker was a "political fall guy" for business dealings unrelated to the Whitewater investigation.

The summer was busy with trips and honors. Always a team, Melvin and I were cited for courage in journalism and presented the Eugene Cervi Award from the International Society of Weekly Newspaper Editors in a session at Boston University. We later joined Bob Fisher of Clarksville and Dean Walls of DeValls Bluff in receiving the 50-Year Achievement Award from the Arkansas Press Association.

27.
Golden Is Our Celebration

As August 18, 1996, approached, Melvin and I planned a proper celebration. Instead of golden décor for our 50th anniversary, our florist friend William Gamble decreed red, white, and blue for the Dumas Community Center. George Anderson, *Pine Bluff News* publisher, was drummer for a jazz band which we booked for the occasion. Our immediate family, including three-month-old Anne Charlotte in a baby swing, joined us. Melvin's sister Mabel Darcey and husband Gilbert (best man at our wedding) came with other Louisiana relatives, as did several hundred friends.

On a trip to Europe for our 37th wedding anniversary, we had purchased a cuckoo clock, and its performances delighted our grandchildren. When it fell silent and failed to perform a decade later, we couldn't find anyone to repair it even though it still ticked. On our golden anniversary week, we returned home one afternoon to find the clock sounding and performing joyously.

As I wrote in my column, "We are frequently asked how we have achieved 50 years of marriage, including working together in the newspaper business for more than 48 years. The answer is: through the Grace of God plus a lot of hard work and commitment."

We left for Chicago several days later, as I was an Arkansas delegate to the National Democratic Convention, an event I had always desired to attend. Melvin had a guest pass enabling him to sit in President Clinton's box and an occasional floor pass to sit with me.

With my straw hat declaring "Proud to be an Arkansas Democrat," I was interviewed by various news organizations and was seen on TV at odd hours. Comedy Central even asked me, "Did you ever date the president?" "Heavens alive, no," I said. "I am old enough to be his mother!"

While many delegates arrived late on the convention floor, I joined the staunchest of Democrats, Levi Phillips of Berryville, leaving on the first bus to the United Center, where the 4,300 delegates convened. Delegates no longer paraded in the aisles as in yesteryear, but we waved signs, cheered energetically, and enjoyed camaraderie with Arkansans and other states, including Al Gore's Tennessee. When proceedings slowed, the band struck up the "Macarena" and "YMCA," and even oldies such as I went into action.

Top memories include meeting with the president and first lady, hearing courageous paralyzed Christopher Reeve, and listening to the melodic Kenny G on the sax and majestic Met opera star Jessye Norman. Bynum Gilson, my legislative ally and then chairman of the Arkansas Democratic Party, had the honor of re-nominating President Clinton.

I was amazed at the quest for Arkansas buttons. Hershel Gober, deputy director of Veterans Affairs, gave Melvin a "Veterans for Clinton-Gore" button, for which Melvin was ultimately offered $100. I might have caved in; Melvin came home with the button.

A month later when we joined Merle and Deloris Peterson for a 12-day Mediterranean cruise, we flew to Barcelona. Imagine our surprise at seeing James Hall, our former neighbor in Dumas, returning from a previous cruise. Another home touch came in a Rome walking tour led by Betty Ruth Holmes Carretta, a Dumas native. Other favorite experiences included sailing the Grand Canal in Venice, seeing the charming villages in Provence, and admiring the magnificent art in Florence. One could never get enough of Florence.

If it appears that I always had a bag partially packed, I had.

At home, changes were under way, and they were disturbing. A curfew was initiated to curb the drug scene, which had invaded rural America. Fire destroyed a popular gathering place, the Delta Inn. A man was killed in a drive-by shooting, a rarity in our area.

But we could cheer when President Bill Clinton scored a major win in the Electoral College, and Merle Peterson was named a presidential elector. Kids Voting brought a new experience to Dumas students. A kindergartener explained the presidential candidates thusly: "There's Bill and he's from here. (Clinton) There's the P-man Daddy talks about. (Perot) And there's the banana man. (Dole)"

A public hearing on a location for the Great River Bridge was held. However, six years were to pass before an environmental impact statement was approved for the bridge as the Interstate 69 crossing at the southern alternative route near Arkansas City.

The second inauguration of President Bill Clinton drew 5,000 from Arkansas, including about 40 from our area. Some of the highlights for us were a brunch at the Mayflower Hotel, a festive luncheon at the White House, Arkansas State Society reception at the Grand Hyatt, and Millennium Ball at the Mayflower. We were also fortunate to have prayer breakfast tickets at Metropolitan AME Church. On leaving the service, Vice President Gore stopped to shake hands with Melvin. We had grand seats near the White House for the marvelous inaugural parade. The 1993 inaugural had been wildly exhilarating while the 1997 version was enthusiastic, more relaxed, and better organized.

After the presidential party left the inaugural ball, we, too, decided to depart. A *Washington Post* reporter asked Deloris Peterson, "Why are you leaving so early?" Deloris put it succinctly: "Age." The reporter folded her notebook.

We came home with photos galore, but there was always local news to cover. A meth bust and drug sweep preceded the Dumas vote on a three-story municipal complex to house the paramedics, police department, and jail. Mayor Oldner led the effort to pass a one-cent bond issue, and the affirmative vote exceeded two to one.

In March while we were in legislative session, devastating tornadoes stuck Arkansas, heavily damaging Arkadelphia. President Clinton flew in on Air Force One, and I was invited to meet him at the airport. A week later, the White House invited Wanda Northcutt, Myra Jones, Irma Hunter Brown, and me to greet the first lady as she came for a tour.

Then in legislative session, I described a work day: "During the day it was joint budget time, revenue and tax committee where we passed out the one-half cent sales tax for roads, rules committee at noon, and a session which lasted until 5:15. We were passing budget bills [which had already cleared Joint Budget] two a minute."

Tedious days were sometimes lightened with member levity. One such instance that I recorded was the following:

"To pass his bill, Dennis Young arrived with a T-shirt proclaiming The Natural State. He proceeded to put on a cap with 'Arkansas: The Natural State.'

"The hullabaloo followed when point of order was made on whether men could wear a hat in the House. The speaker ruled he couldn't.

"Jimmie Wilson moved to suspend the rules so Young could wear a cap. We voted to suspend the rules. The speaker told Young he could put his cap on.

"We proceeded with a lively debate on 'The Natural State' vs. the present 'Land of Opportunity.'

"The vote was 63 for, and 'sound the ballot' was called. It held at 52." (Some issues persist. In 2011, the legislature defeated a bill to return the state's motto to "The Land of Opportunity.")

During the 1997 session, a short leave allowed me to join our annual trip to the NNA government conference in Washington. After a White House reception, we were greeted by President Clinton. We also attended *Paper Moon,* and to our delight, the musical director was Desha County native Michael Rice. Bits of his background appear in productions with which he has been associated. In *Paper Moon,* it was Tyro, the parent community from which Dumas was founded. Michael once worked on a presentation called "A Bridge to Rosedale," in which this determined editor was a character.

Determination was a facet of my character I never denied. In the 1997 legislative session, my last, I found persistence rewarded. For seven terms, I sponsored a proposed constitutional amendment changing state tax policy to three-fifths vote on all taxation. In the 1930s, a young business group had successfully led an effort to call for a simple majority, 51 percent, on the sales tax and three-fourths vote on all other taxation. It was much easier to block a tax measure with 26 votes, the result being that many tax efforts were directed to the sales tax, sometimes the only achievable way to finance bond issues and other efforts.

A three-fifths vote on taxation was among the reforms offered in a study by the Winthrop Rockefeller Foundation when I was on that board from 1980 to 1985. I was convinced and pursued the goal.

Few thought the proposed amendment could be passed in the legislature, ultimately to be referred to voters. However, Senator Jim Argue, a prince of a legislative integrity, and I knew it worth the continuing effort. We had become friendly while he served in the House prior to going to the Senate. Business interests, strongly opposing the amendment since they could better control tax policy, tolerated our efforts and let it get out of committee onto the floor.

In my log, I described that busy March 26: "We're heading down the stretch with the House and Senate battling to the finish. The House wants a co-chairman of the Legislative Council and is willing to go to the wire, even at the risk of no budget for the Council staff. Oh, the games we play! All Yes's from Senators, and No's from Representative on Joint Budget.

"The exciting part of the day was my passing HJR 1006 [the three-fifths vote on taxation] through the House with 77 votes. It came out of Joint State Agencies Committee yesterday as one of three constitutional amendments recommended. I have carried this joint resolution for seven terms."

On the final week of the session, Jim Argue and I used parliamentary procedure to avert lobbyist efforts to the Joint Resolution through revision in the Senate. Lo and behold, that proposed amendment on which I had worked for seven terms was to be considered by voters!

In the following election, however, public support for three-fifths vote on taxation was leading by 60 percent until the State Chamber of Commerce and other business interests ploughed $300,000 into a television campaign two weeks before the election and killed it. However, that recommended constitutional amendment remains a proud effort for me.

Another determined effort, made over several years, led me to getting $450,000 to build a new State Police Station in Dumas. The old building, located at Reedville just north of Dumas, had to be razed because its septic system collapsed. The Dumas Industrial Committee helped to provide a new site in the north city limits so the State Police presence could be maintained.

I also was able to pass a bill establishing an Arkansas Women's Commission and was named to serve on it. Later, though, Republican appointees to the commission killed it.

Rep. Dennis Young of Texarkana and I proposed legislation to remove the sales tax on groceries. It went nowhere. Representative Cunningham and I sponsored a bill to raise the cap (from $2,000 to $5,000) on the price of used cars before they become subject to the state sales tax, then 4.5 percent. It passed handily. Win some and often lose more in the legislature!

Growing pleasure from legislation I co-sponsored with Rep. Wanda Northcutt came as a result of the Rural Advocacy Agency we established and its small grant program. It was such a valuable program for rural people seeking funding to match their efforts. Most unusual was the high school class who wrote a grant application for $5,000 to renovate a baseball field. All of the students came to receive the check and were delighted.

In my log, I described the final day of the 1997 session when term limits would take effect:

"The last vote was by far the most difficult of my seven-term service in the House of Representatives.

"Leaders of the House and Senate met with the governor's representatives for 12 hours yesterday to craft a bill for Capital Improvements [legislation to dispense monies to projects]. They agreed on priorities, and it came down to who was going to give out the money.

"I was successful in the final cut—leading the Southeast delegation [of which I was then chairman] to get its fair share. In the first draft we had only $50,000 for Southeast Tech, $250,000 for Plum Bayou Levee District, and $150,000 for Phillips Community College in Stuttgart and DeWitt. We were able to negotiate $3 million for UAPB Stadium, $400,000 for UAM water lines, $600,000 for the Rural Physician Program, $400,000 for Fire Ant Program, and $3 million for the Water Development Fund."

I noted that they also included funds for the Dumas State Police headquarters.

"With this success, I agreed to support the legislative bill over the governor's.

"It was a day of crescendos—a morning when we didn't know how many there would be to override a veto but thought it would be 58. By afternoon, it had solidified, and the legislative bill passed 65-33.

"So much rain fell last night that the dome over the House leaked. Ode Maddox said, 'I hope we have enough money to buy shingles,' pointing to the trash cans catching the drip on his desk. Seatmate Tim Woolridge had an umbrella up.

"Replied the speaker, 'You are fortunate to have running water at your desk!'

"During the many recesses, we amused ourselves with doggerel on the computers.

"The closing ceremonies were relatively brief as we were so worn out.

"Charley Stewart made a brief speech about his 44 years in the House. He started to cry when he saw his wife in the gallery, but regained his composure.

"Tim Massanelli, parliamentarian, had to leave the floor when he started crying about all those leaving.

"I managed to get out without tears and joined Myra Jones and Wanda Northcutt Hartz for a final photo.

"Serving in the House truly has enhanced my life. I leave with the joys of friendship, appreciation of the opportunity to serve, and expanded knowledge. What a grand run!"

Fifty of the House members gathered on the capitol steps for a final photo—terms being limited to six years on the House side and two terms plus a possible two-year draw in the Senate. I considered that imbalance to give the Senate more power than it previously had. However, age told me I was ready for retirement.

The Poultry Federation held a "Roostering Out" party for those of us saying goodbye, and George Wimberley brought his pet rooster.

I would never end my interest in state government and policy. I enjoyed the many dedicated people with whom I served, some of whom became friends for life. I even smiled upon hearing one Dumas voter call me "Ole Tax and Spend Democrat."

28.
A 30-Dash to Our Career

Returning to the newspaper, I enjoyed reporting achievements and recognition of those who have meant much to the area. We covered the installation of Vernon Scott, Tillar & Company manager for many years, in the Arkansas Agricultural Hall of Fame. Vernon was a bright light and innovator in agriculture, and led in educational and civic activities as well.

While Dumas long has been a caring community, we began in the nineties to see major efforts to preserve the historical downtown area. Romona Weatherford, Chamber executive, and Mayor Oldner led the effort to have Dumas included in the Arkansas Main Street program.

Capping the last half of the decade downtown were the $4.5 million Dumas Municipal Complex and the $650,000 Family Life Center erected by First Baptist Church. Spurring preservation was our Main Street Arkansas program and thus, the ability to gain federal and state funds matching local contributions for street, lighting, and landscaping improvements. Long had I advocated downtown preservation because I had seen dying Delta cities with boarded-up downtowns. To help with Dumas's match, I "sold" antique light poles with memorial/honorary plaques for $1,000 each, thus raising $60,000.

A project on which I had worked for 15 years came to fruition in May 1997 when Governor Mike Huckabee and Corps of Engineers district engineer Scott Morris signed an agreement to restore Morgan Point Bendway Lake. The old channel of the Arkansas River, cut off by the building of Dam 2, thus would be renewed.

When Mayor Billy Free and I had pushed for the project in the 1980s, we thought the cost to be $500,000. By 1997, it was $3.8 million. (At one point, we waited four years for congressional language which would allow in-kind contributions from Arkansas Game & Fish Commission and Desha County. During that time, affected congressional committees weren't speaking!)

A study in behalf of the proposed Interstate 69 first recommended a crossing of the Mississippi River at Rosedale, but that hope was not to be. However, all of the preliminary work on the Great River Bridge made the crossing from Desha County to Bolivar County as the favored site for I-69.

Announcement of the site was made by the State Highway director Dan Flowers, chairman of the I-69 Steering Committee, at a meeting in Dumas, resulting in an uproar from Pine Bluff citizens. They had been certain that Congressman Jay Dickey would get his "Dickey Split"—a route coming through Helena to Pine Bluff and another south through Drew County.

In June, seventeen from Desha County went to Washington to lobby for I-69 and met with Senators Trent Lott and Thad Cochran of Mississippi, and Dale Bumpers and Tim Hutchinson of Arkansas. This was our last trip with Charles Dean, Cleveland, Mississippi, engineer who had the vision for the Great River Bridge. His death from cancer in 1998 robbed us of our most valuable spokesman.

The Dumas economy was spurred by construction of the Arkansas Electric Cooperatives Corporation hydropower plant at Dam 2, and a by-product was a suit by Arkansas County vs. Desha County for the taxes on the plant. The facility later was ruled in Desha County, which kept the revenues.

Building continued with a $500,000 migrant center erected in the Dumas industrial area, bringing a new opportunity for migrant child care and new payroll for Dumas. Portions of the Dumas High School structure built in 1927 also were razed to make way for a new junior high school.

An area project of significance also began. Costing $186 million, a lock and dam was to be located where the Arkansas and White Rivers flow into the Mississippi. Thus assured was a road to Big Island, previously accessible only by boat, and construction jobs needed by the area.

Always planning travel, Melvin and I went to St. Paul, Minnesota, for the National Federation of Press Women's convention to hear Helen Thomas, dean of the White House Press Corps, and our friend Joe Stroud, editor of the *Detroit Free Press*. A week later, we flew to Jackson Hole, Wyoming, for a meeting of past presidents of the National Newspaper Association. We drove into magnificent Yellowstone National Park, where burned-out forests were regenerating and the Teton Mountains and Old Faithful Geyser were as magnificent as ever.

Family always was foremost, and we were excited over the July 26 wedding of our daughter Sarah (divorced for seven years) to Mark Steen, an architect for computer bases. Our family gathered in Dallas to share their happiness.

When Melvin and I attended the National Conference of State Legislators in Philadelphia in August, we were among 7,500 attendees. Gould native and state senator Gene Roebuck remarked, "This convention center is bigger than the whole town of Gould!" My program favorites were the performance of the Philadelphia Pops Orchestra directed by Peter Nero, a parade by the Mummers and Fralinger String Band, and an insightful side trip into the Amish country near Lancaster.

The National Order of Women Legislators invited me to give a report from Arkansas at their national meeting in Maui, Hawaiian Islands. Because I was a lame duck, I paid my way. Vacationing in one of the most beautiful places on earth, Melvin and I also visited with Admiral Joseph Prueher, commander-in-chief of the Pacific Command; former governor Ann Richards of Texas; and Arkansan James Lee Witt, Federal Emergency Management Agency director.

Among the pleasures were our trips to National Newspaper Association conventions, and in 1997, we enjoyed the culture and cowboys city of Fort Worth. Fun times were dinner at Colonial Country Club, golfing home of Ben Hogan; tours of Kimball Art Museum and Amon Carter Museum; Thistle Hill Victorian Mansion; and, of course, barbecue at Billy Bob's honky-tonk in the Stockyards District.

Taking advantage of our mobility in our seventies, Melvin and I joined Merle and Deloris Peterson of Dumas for a cruise on *Enchantment of the Seas*, so impressive a ship that 2,000 turned out on the dock in Quebec City. Our day tours included Acadia National Park, Cape Breton Island in Nova Scotia, St. John in New Brunswick, and the distinctive French flavor of Quebec City.

At home, I continued my civic roles. Since the 1980s, I had worked on the Serendipity Auction, a fund-raiser for the Desha County Museum and Dumas Business Women, and the 1997 event cleared $10,000. We also went to a Christmas reception at the White House, for which I never declined an invitation.

Throughout the last half of 1997 we had met with a newspaper broker and prospective buyers for the *Clarion*. It was not my wish to sell the newspaper, as I had been warned by press colleagues, "it is like selling a child."

At 75, I worked long and sometimes grueling days. Moreover, Melvin, who had diabetes and other health problems, was worn with pressures of the newspaper business. Our children were successful in other pursuits; they were concerned and thought we should sell. The newspaper market was relatively good.

We kept the negotiations as quiet as possible, not only because we were trying to sell to an individual, but basically, I still did not want to sell the paper. However, the *Clarion* sale represented our retirement income, and if we could manage a good deal, it was important for our financial future.

Such an agonizing decision! We completed the transaction in April 1998, selling the *Clarion* to Wyatt Emmerich of Jackson, Mississippi, for his family-owned newspaper chain. Tears flowed when I had to tell our staff.

In my early newspaper career, we used a —30— to end our stories. Now, we had signed off our career with a 30-dash.

I cried for weeks after the sale. The *Clarion* indeed had felt like a member of the family, as had our staff. But I resolved to make the best of the remaining years of my life. My husband would have less strain and enjoy home life. And we would travel as long as we could—as it happened, into his 82nd year and my 78th year.

Honors coincided with the sale when I was chosen for the Hall of Fame of LSU's Manship School of Mass Communication and received the prestigious Horizon Award for my political service from the Arkansas League of Women Voters.

How could I forever grieve the sale of the *Clarion* when there were memories to last a lifetime!

In January 1999, I wrapped up 14 years in the Arkansas House and later I would undertake many civic tasks, but there was one role I would always love best: editor.

Why did I choose to invest 52 of my most active years in a community newspaper? My fingers on the typewriter, later computers, provided power so I could:

- offer our community a vision and possible ways to achieve it;
- stimulate public thought and advance commerce at the same time (my favorite editorial page was rivaled by the pleasure of designing and selling advertising, some of which is still running);
- listen to those with little hope and the mighty with agendas;
- question why people of good will can't change age-old hatreds;
- offer consolation when one in despair cried at my desk;
- find fun and challenge in every day;

- take the town pulse on a stroll down Main or a bike ride to Highway 65;
- photograph a dead six-foot rattlesnake, when I couldn't stand its sight, or an eight-point buck, when I would rather have seen it alive;
- help the elderly man who had no suit in which to bury his brother;
- tell our community ways to assist families left bereft by fire or tragedy;
- dress in a 1920s Middy Blouse costume for Ding Dong Days, and hear Senator Bumpers observe, "Only you could get away with an outfit like that!"
- record the milestones in family histories;
- set a project course and, through many years, see it to completion;
- smudge my hands in ink, and however exhausted, still feel its magic;
- laud the heroic and chide the self-anointed;
- expose government excess or impropriety;
- express my thoughts in a free country without government repression;
- expand my cubicle at the *Clarion* to a vision of the world, from the White House to Red Square, from Fleet Street to the Arctic Ocean; and
- find contentment among people who believed in Melvin and me as we always believed in Dumas, the Delta, our state, and our nation.

More than often, I stumbled or miserably failed. When I succeeded, my heart soared.

Epilogue

After selling the *Clarion*, there was never any doubt where we would retire: Dumas—in the same home, albeit remodeled six times since 1954.

Where else...

- would friends so graciously accept my flaws and join in my causes?
- could I find a neighbor who clears my driveway of a five-inch snow and builds me a snowman as a surprise?
- would a passing ambulance driver see me in my yard, lower the vehicle window, and call, "Hi, Miss Charlotte!"
- would a visit to the post office bring hugs from other customers, age or race no barrier?
- could I stir the civic pot with energy and pleasure at the same time?

Trust that I share with the warm people of southeast Arkansas has always enriched my life and placed me among its characters. "Call Charlotte," is often said, "She probably knows." And so go the many calls—and these are just a few of the actual queries I've had:

"Who worked in the drive-in in 1964?"

"How do we get rid of beaver dams blocking the bayou and flooding the back of our church?"

"Can you tell me how to locate a woman I believe to be my birth mother?"

"I have been turned down by Social Security Disability. What do I do next?"

A few still believe I am a state legislator, but most think I will simply listen to them as I have all my life. The same still happens to my friend and House of Representatives successor, David Rainey.

If my antique typewriter could speak, it would affirm my family's moniker for me: "Salty Old Editor."

When incensed at some perceived wrong, I would often declare, "I am going to write a hot editorial." I would tone down those editorials in an effort to include opposing views, but mostly, I seldom wavered from convictions.

From typewriter, I moved to electric style, then to Justowriter, Compugraphic, Microtech, and Baseview systems. I am looking forward to the day when some inventor will find a way to attach sensors to the head, catching brain waves and ultimately transmitting them to the computer system. Still it won't be half as much fun as I had.

After an ever-in-motion lifestyle, I think of our retirement years as "sweet." They were sweet because Melvin and I had time together without constant deadlines and payrolls to meet. No political pressure, either. We could visit family, enjoy leisurely meals with spirited conversation, and join in the civic life to which I am addicted. Until Melvin's health deteriorated, our travel included Alaska as well as sailing around the Horn of South America, even circling it twice, visiting Greece, Turkey, and the Ukraine. Sliding along marble streets of Ephesus in the rain, I was imbued with reverence-inspiration because the Apostle Paul once walked there. Seeing Yalta where Roosevelt, Churchill, and Stalin once conferred stirred my historical passion.

Until Melvin's heart attack in 2000, I maintained an office in the Chamber of Commerce building to work on area projects. Thereafter, I have worked from home on diverse projects ranging from Main Street development to a Delta Technology Education Center, from serving as volunteer director of the Delta Area Community Foundation to unpolished grant writer for the Desha County Museum—and for 32 years as a member of the Ding Dong Days Commission.

Do I miss the newspaper business? Immensely. Do I miss capitol politics? Of course. I miss contacts with the people. I still mentally report events I attend and write as needed, and I'll always enjoy politics.

Most of all, I will always miss Melvin, the love of my life, who died September 12, 2007. We were truly blessed to share 61 years together, particularly savoring our three children, their spouses, and nine grandchildren. Becoming great-grandparents magnified our joy. I am particularly grateful that Melvin remained mentally alert, even though his physical discomfort was always ongoing. On the day before he died, he read the daily newspaper—completely—as always. Losing a life partner is a piercing pain transitioning to an ache persisting even through passage of time

In retirement, I have focused on education and economic development as critical to the southeast Arkansas Delta I love. Job creation remains a critical challenge. As Patricia Grimes, a Dumas High graduate, once said: "Young people are the future of Dumas, but if the jobs aren't here, how can we be the future of Dumas?"

Our small towns can survive through innovation and aggressive leadership. Volunteers can be a major component for progress, and I am happy to be among them.

Perhaps I best expressed my career convictions in an acceptance speech when presented the National Press Woman of the Year award in 1970:

> A country editor is a durable lot. And the satisfactions have far exceeded the hard times and pettiness of the people. To be able to report the truth is a special charge in these times, and it is an almost sacred one. Much of the nation's course depends upon how well informed are its people. Perhaps not since the days of the American Revolution and the Civil War has the press been so challenged as we are today. To be able to hear both sides of a controversy and report them fairly and truthfully requires professional skill, great stamina and dedication. To avoid being

swayed to the crowd demands wisdom and determination. This is as much so in a small town as in a great city.

My life has been enriched by great friendships, inky adventures, and political participation. I hope I will be remembered for never, never, ever giving up!

Acknowledgements

In describing my journey, I choose a French phrase my husband enjoyed: "*C'est magnifique!*"

Magnificent have been the places I've toured and the famous people I've happened to meet.

Magnificent has been the support of family and friends. Always foremost was my beloved, devoted life partner Melvin, to whom I owe so much credit. My heart is full with gratitude toward my children and their spouses, John and Deanna, Sarah and Mark, and Steve and Becky, and my grandchildren, Charles, Edward, David, Lauren, Emily, Allie, Daniel, Annie, and Amy.

I am particularly grateful to Skip Rutherford of the Clinton School of Public Service for his continuing encouragement. David Stricklin, Rod Lorenzen, and the staff of the Butler Center for Arkansas Studies have offered fine professional help. My special thanks go to Ali Welky, who was gracious, proficient, and even tolerant of my miscues as she edited my manuscript. I also appreciate the work of skillful designer H. K. Stewart, the technical assistance of Shalaunda Jones and Melanie Berry at our new Delta Technology Education Center, and Terry Hawkins's help with the *Clarion* files. I thank Tom W. Dillard for his interest in my dual career.

Volunteers make small towns hum, and there are so many with whom I have been associated. I fear of omitting some, so as I continue to pursue projects, I think of the support I've had from so many friends and associates and know that progress came as a result of their involvement: How I enjoyed working alongside them!

Others deserving my appreciation are our former *Clarion* staffers as well as colleagues of Arkansas Press Women and Arkansas Press Association.

Thanks to all of you who enhanced my inky adventure.

APA TimeLine
1873 ✳══════✳ 1998
Celebrating 125 years of the Arkansas Press Association

by CRAIG OGILVIE

THE **SCHEXNAYDERS**, MELVIN AND CHARLOTTE, OF THE "DUMAS CLARION" WERE THE FIRST HUSBAND-WIFE COMBINATION TO SERVE AS PRESIDENTS OF THE ARKANSAS PRESS ASSOCIATION. HE WAS ELECTED IN 1962 AND HIS WIFE SERVED IN 1981.

CHARLOTTE WAS THE FIRST WOMAN ELECTED PRESIDENT OF THE APA, AND ALSO THE FIRST FEMALE PRESIDENT OF THE NATIONAL NEWSPAPER ASSOCIATION.

THEY HAVE BEEN A PART OF THE "DUMAS CLARION" FOR OVER 44 YEARS!

CPSIA information can be obtained
at www.ICGtesting.com
Printed in the USA
BVHW081210050820
585471BV00001B/5